Learning Aid

for use with

Basic Marketing

Sixth Canadian Edition

E. Jerome McCarthy
Michigan State University

Stanley J. Shapiro
Simon Fraser University

William D. Perreault, Jr.
The University of North Carolina

IRWIN

Homewood, IL 60430
Boston, MA 02116

© Richard D. Irwin Inc., 1975, 1979, 1983, 1986, 1989, and 1992

Printed in the United States of America.

ISBN 0-256-10347-X

1 2 3 4 5 6 7 8 9 0 MG 9 8 7 6 5 4 3 2

Contents

Introduction

This *Learning Aid* is designed to help you organize and learn all of the material that is presented in *Basic Marketing*, Sixth Canadian Edition. Feedback from marketing instructors--and students--indicates that students who use the *Learning Aid* regularly do tend to learn the material better--and also tend to do better on examinations.

Please note, however, that the *Learning Aid* is intended to be used along with *Basic Marketing*. *It is not a substitute for reading and carefully studying the text!*

How the Learning Aid Is Organized

The *Learning Aid* is divided into 23 chapters--one chapter for each corresponding chapter in *Basic Marketing*. There are also separate chapters for Appendix A: Economics Fundamentals and Appendix C: Marketing Arithmetic.

Each chapter in the *Learning Aid* contains the following five sections:

> A. What this chapter is about
> B. Important terms
> C. True-false questions
> D. Multiple-choice questions
> E. Application exercises

The purpose of each of these sections is explained below. Please note that some sections are designed to be used *before* you read each chapter in *Basic Marketing*.

What This Chapter Is About

This section provides a brief introduction to each chapter in *Basic Marketing*. It should be read *before* you read the text--to help you focus on the important points in each chapter.

Important Terms

This section lists the important new terms introduced in each chapter of *Basic Marketing*--and the page on which each term first appears. (These terms are shown in blue in the text to help you find them.)

You should look over the list of important terms *before* reading each chapter--to help you focus on the key points in the chapter. *After* reading each chapter, you should review the list of important terms to make sure you understand each term. If you have any doubts about what a particular term means, use the indicated page number to find and restudy its definition in the text--or look up the term's definition in the Glossary at the end of the text. Some students even write out the definitions of each important term on 3 x 5 cards--to help them study for exams.

True-False Questions

This section provides a series of *self-testing* true-false questions--to test your understanding of the material presented in *Basic Marketing*. The correct answer for each question is given at the end of the test--along with a page number showing where the correct answer can be found in the text.

After reading each chapter in the text and reviewing the important terms, try to answer all of the true-false questions *before* looking at the correct answers. Then check your answers--and for each question that you answered wrong, review the related text material to find out *why* your answer is wrong. This is an important step! Simply memorizing the correct answers is *not* likely to improve your exam performance!

Multiple-Choice Questions

This section contains a series of *self-testing* multiple-choice questions--to further test your understanding and comprehension of the material presented in *Basic Marketing*. Again, the correct answer for each question is given at the end of the questions--along with a page number showing where the correct answer can be found in the text.

Ideally, you should take the multiple-choice tests only *after* you have read the text, reviewed the important terms, and tried the true-false questions. Again, you should try to answer all of the questions *before* looking at the correct answers--and make sure you review the text material to learn *why* your wrong answers were wrong!

Finally, keep in mind that the self-testing true-false and multiple-choice questions are just a *sample* of what you might expect on an exam. They do not cover every single concept discussed in the text--nor do they cover every possible type of question that might be asked. In other words, *simply answering these self-testing questions is not adequate preparation for exams*. You must also read and study the text!

Application Exercises

This section includes two or more exercises for each of the chapters in *Basic Marketing* (not including the appendices). Each exercise is designed to illustrate and apply some of the more important concepts and analytical approaches introduced in the text.

Although these exercises are designed mainly to be discussed in class and/or assigned as homework--*you can still benefit from doing them even if your instructor does not assign them*. Many students find the "Introductions" to each exercise quite helpful in understanding the related text material. And many of the exercises contain short "caselets" which show how concepts discussed in the text can be applied in the "real world." Doing these exercises will not only improve your understanding of the text material--but will also better prepare you for more advanced marketing and business case courses.

How to Study for Examinations

While no study routine works best for everyone, the following suggestions are based on proven learning principles and should be of benefit to most students. *For every chapter your instructor assigns in Basic Marketing*:

1. Read the *what this chapter is about* section in the *Learning Aid*.

2. Look over the *important terms* section in the *Learning Aid*.

3. Read the learning objectives listed at the beginning of the chapter.

4. Read the chapter from beginning to end without any interruptions--and *without doing any underlining or note-taking*. (Underlining key points while you read interrupts your flow of thought and tends to reduce reading comprehension.)

5. Read the chapter again--this time underlining key points and/or writing notes in the page margins. Look at the exhibits and illustrations, and think about how they relate to the text material.

6. Review the *important terms* section in the *Learning Aid* to make sure you can define each term.

7. Take the self-testing true-false test in the *Learning Aid*--and go back to the text to study any questions you answered wrong

8. Take the self-testing multiple-choice test in the *Learning Aid*--and go back to the text to study any questions you answered wrong.

9. Take detailed classroom lecture notes--and review them *immediately after class* to make sure that they are complete and that you understand everything your instructor said.

10. Do any *application exercises* that your instructor assigns.

11. *Optional:* Do the *application exercises* that were not assigned.

12. Just before the examination--review:
    a. the points you underlined in the text and/or your notes in the page margins.
    b. the *important terms* in the *Learning Aid*.
    c. the self-testing true-false and multiple-choice questions in the *Learning Aid*--especially the questions you answered wrong the first time.
    d. any *application exercises* that were assigned.
    e. your lecture notes. Good luck!

Acknowledgments

All the exercises in this edition of the *Learning Aid* were updated and/or revised, but the continuing influence of the creative abilities of Professor Andrew Brogowicz (of Western Michigan University) will be obvious to previous users. Really good ideas endure!

The *Learning Aid* exercises were revised for the Sixth Canadian Edition by Ann Porter.

E. Jerome McCarthy

Stanley J. Shapiro

William D. Perreault, Jr.

Chapter 1
Marketing's role in society

What This Chapter Is About

Chapter I introduces the concept of marketing. First, we show how marketing relates to production--and why it is important to you and to society. Then the text shows that there are two kinds of marketing--micro-marketing and macro-marketing. The importance of a macro-marketing system in any kind of economic system is emphasized.

The vital role of marketing functions is discussed. It is emphasized that producers, consumers, *and* marketing specialists perform marketing functions. You will learn that responsibility for performing the marketing functions can be shifted and shared in a variety of ways, but that from a macro viewpoint all of the functions must be performed by someone. No function can be completely eliminated.

The main focus of *this chapter* is on macro-marketing--to give you a broad introduction. But the focus of *this text* is on management-oriented micro-marketing--beginning in Chapter 2.

Important Terms

production, p. 5
utility, p. 5
form utility, p. 5
possession utility, p. 6
time utility, p. 6
place utility, p. 6
micro-marketing, p. 8
macro-marketing, p. 10
economic system, p. 10
planned economic system, p. 11
market-directed economic system, p. 12
micro-macro dilemma, p. 13
pure subsistence economy, p. 14
market, p. 14

central market, p. 14
middleman, p. 15
economics of scale, p. 18
universal functions of marketing, p. 19
buying function, p. 19
selling function, pp. 19-20
transporting function, p. 20
storing function, p. 20
standardization and grading, p. 20
financing, p. 20
risk taking, p. 20
marketing information function, p. 20
facilitators, p. 21
innovation, p. 22

True-False Questions

1. According to the text, marketing means "selling" or "advertising."

2. Production is a more important economic activity than marketing.

1

F 3. Actually making goods or performing services is called marketing.

✓ T 4. Marketing provides time, place, and possession utility.

✓ T 5. It is estimated that marketing costs about 50 percent of each consumer's dollar.

✓ T 6. Marketing is both a set of activities performed by organizations and a social process.

✓ T 7. Micro-marketing is the performance of activities which seek to accomplish an organization's objectives by anticipating customer or client needs and directing a flow of need-satisfying goods and services from producer to customer or client.

✓ F 8. Micro-marketing activities should be of no interest to a nonprofit organization.

(F) X T 9. Macro-marketing is a set of activities which direct an economy's flow of goods and services from producers to consumers in a way which effectively matches supply and demand and accomplishes the objectives of society.

✓ T 10. Macro-marketing emphasizes how the whole system works, rather than the activities of individual organizations.

F 11. Only market-directed societies need an economic system.

(T) ✓ F 12. In a market-directed economy, government planners decide what and how much is to be produced and distributed by whom, when, and to whom.

T 13. In a market-directed economy, the prices of consumer goods and services serve roughly as a measure of their social importance.

✓ T 14. Sometimes micro-macro dilemmas arise because what is "good" for some producers and consumers may not be "good" for society as a whole.

✓ F 15. The Canadian economy is entirely market-directed.

✓ T 16. A pure subsistence economy is an economy in which each family unit produces everything it consumes.

✓ F 17. Marketing takes place whenever a person needs something of value.

✓ T 18. The term marketing comes from the word market--which is a group of sellers and buyers who are willing to exchange goods and/or services for something of value.

(F) X T 19. While central markets facilitate exchange, middlemen usually complicate exchange by increasing the total number of transactions required.

(F) X T 20. More effective macro-marketing systems are the result of greater economic development.

✓ T 21. Without an effective macro-marketing system, the less-developed nations may be doomed to a "vicious circle of poverty."

✓ T 22. "Economies of scale" means that as a company produces larger numbers of a particular product, the cost for each of these products goes down.

✓ F 23. "Universal functions of marketing" consist only of buying, selling, transporting, and storing.

F 24. Achieving effective marketing in an advanced economy is simplified by the fact that producers are separated from consumers in only two ways: time and space.

T 25. In a market-directed economy, marketing functions are performed by producers, consumers, and a variety of marketing institutions.

✓ F 26. Marketing facilitators are any firms which provide the marketing functions of buying and selling.

✓ T 27. Responsibility for performing the marketing functions can be shifted and shared in a variety of ways, but no function can be completely eliminated.

✓ F 28. Our market-directed macro-marketing system discourages the development and spread of new ideas and products.

Answers to True-False Questions

1. F, p. 3	11. F, pp. 10-11	21. T, pp. 16-17
2. F, p. 5	12. T, p. 11	22. T, p. 18
3. F, p. 5	13. T, p. 12	23. F, p. 19
4. T, p. 5	14. T, p. 13	24. F, pp. 18-19
5. T, p. 6	15. F, p. 13	25. T, p. 19
6. T, p. 8	16. T, p. 14	26. F, p. 20
7. T, p. 8	17. F, p. 14	27. T, pp. 21-22
8. F, p. 8	18. T, p. 14	28. F, p. 22
9. F, p. 10	19 F, p. 15	
10. T, p. 10	20. F, p. 16	

Chapter 1

Multiple-Choice Questions (Circle the correct response)

1. According to the text:

   a. marketing is much more than selling or advertising.
   b. the cost of marketing is about 25 percent of the consumer's dollar.
   c. production is a more essential economic activity than marketing.
   d. only marketing creates economic utility.
   e. all of the above are true statements.

2. When a "fruit peddler" drives his truck through residential neighborhoods and sells fruits and vegetables grown by farmers, he is creating:

   a. form utility.
   b. time and place utility.
   c. possession utility.
   d. all of the above.
   e. all of the above, *except* a.

3. Tam Furniture Stores recently purchased several rail carloads of dining room tables. The tables were distributed to their retail outlets in Ontario, where they sold rapidly to customers. In this situation, Tam Furniture Stores created:

   a. both place and possession utility
   b. both place and time utility.
   c. place, time, and possession utility.
   d. only place utility.
   e. both form and place utility.

4. The text stresses that:

   a. advertising and selling are not really part of marketing.
   b. marketing is nothing more than a set of business activities performed by individual firms.
   c. marketing techniques have no application for nonprofit organizations.
   d. marketing is a social process and a set of activities performed by organizations.
   e. a good product usually sells itself.

5. *Micro*-marketing:

   a. is concerned with need-satisfying goods, but not with services.
   b. involves an attempt to anticipate customer or client needs.
   c. is primarily concerned with efficient use of resources and fair allocation of output.
   d. includes activities such as accounting, production, and financial management.
   e. is the process of selling and distributing manufactured goods.

6. *Macro*-marketing:

   a. is not concerned with the flow of goods and services from producers to consumers.
   b. seeks to match homogeneous supply capabilities with homogeneous demands for goods and services.
   c. refers to a set of activities performed by both profit and nonprofit organizations.
   d. focuses on the objectives of society.
   e. all of the above are true statements.

7. Which of the following statements about economic decision making is *true*?

   a. In a market-directed system, the micro-level decisions of individual producers and consumers determine the macro-level decisions.
   b. Government planning usually works best when economies become more complex and the variety of goods and services produced is fairly large.
   c. Canada may be considered a pure market-directed economy.
   d. Planned economic systems usually rely on market forces to determine prices.
   e. All of the above are true statements.

8. Which of the following is NOT an example of the micro-macro dilemma?

   a. Having a dog or cat can teach a child responsibility, but add expenses to the family budget.
   b. Some people like to smoke cigarettes, but the smell annoys many others.
   c. Aluminum soft-drink cans are convenient, but expensive to pick up along the highway.
   d. Nuclear power may reduce your fuel bill, but worry others.
   e. Driving fast can be fun, but is hazardous to other people.

9. Marketing cannot occur unless:

   a. an economy is market-directed rather than planned.
   b. producers and consumers can enter into face-to-face negotiations at some physical location.
   c. an economy has a money system.
   d. there are two or more parties who each have something of value they want to exchange for something else.
   e. middlemen are present to facilitate exchange.

10. The development of marketing middlemen:

    a. tends to make the exchange process more complicated, more costly, and harder to carry out.
    b. usually reduces the total number of transactions necessary to carry out exchange.
    c. tends to increase place utility but decrease time utility.
    d. becomes less advantageous as the number of producers and consumers, their distance apart, and the number and variety of products increase.
    e. All of the above are true statements.

11. In advanced economies:

    a. mass production capability is a necessary and sufficient condition for satisfying consumer needs.
    b. exchange is simplified by discrepancies of quantity and assortment.
    c. the creation of time, place, and possession utilities tends to be easy.
    d. both supply and demand tend to be homogeneous in nature.
    e. producers and consumers experience a separation of values.

12. Which of the following is *not* one of the "universal functions of marketing"?

    a. Production
    b. Standardization
    c. Financing
    d. Buying
    e. Transporting

13. Which of the following is a *true* statement?

   a. Since marketing is concerned with many thousands of different products, there is no one set of marketing functions that applies to all products.
   b. Responsibility for performing marketing functions can be shifted and shared, but no function can be completely eliminated.
   c. From a micro viewpoint, every firm must perform all of the marketing functions.
   d. Marketing functions should be performed only by marketing middlemen or facilitators.
   e. Many marketing functions are not necessary in planned economies.

14. A brief review of the many complaints against marketing suggests that:

   a. this criticism is only concerned with the overall role of marketing and the performance of the entire economic system.
   b. marketing costs too much.
   c. this criticism is mainly directed toward the activities of individual firms.
   d. we must define and evaluate marketing at two levels--the macro level and the micro level
   e. such complaints are obviously unjustified.

Answers to Multiple-Choice Questions

1. a, p. 3
2. e, p. 6
3. c, p. 6
4. d, p. 8
5. b, p. 8

6. d, p. 10
7. a, p. 12
8. a, p. 13
9. d, p. 14
10. b, p. 15

11. e, p. 19
12. a, p. 19
13. b, pp. 21-22
14. d, p. 22

Exercise 1-1
What is marketing?

Introduction

Society ignored or even criticized the contributions of marketing until the beginning of the 20th century. At that time, economies once marked by a scarcity of goods began to enjoy an abundance of goods. Marketing skills were needed to solve the distribution problems that resulted. Thus, it was not until the early 1900s that the importance of marketing was realized--and that marketing was accepted as a separate academic subject in schools and colleges.

Even today, many people do not have a very clear understanding of marketing. No one single definition of marketing will satisfy everyone. Many people--including some students and business managers--tend to think of marketing as "selling" or "advertising." Others see marketing as an all-inclusive social process that can solve all the world's problems. Some critics, meanwhile, seem to blame marketing for most of society's ills!

This exercise is intended to help you see more clearly what marketing is all about. One way to learn about marketing is to study the definitions in the text. Another way is to use these definitions. This is the approach you will follow in this exercise.

Assignment

Listed below are some commonly asked questions about marketing. Answer each of these questions in a way which shows your understanding of marketing.

1. Do "marketing" and "selling" mean the same thing?

    No. mktg means includes all the organizations functions to deliver product to consumers (i.e advertising, price, transport, storage, promotion. Selling means the physical act of salesperson selling to consumer product/service

2. What activities does marketing involve besides selling?

    see above

3. Would there be any need for marketing activities if manufacturers would just try to produce better products? Why or why not? *Yes, issue needs other functions not just building a better mousetrap*

4. Marketing is a subject a lot of people think they know a great deal about. Many hold the opinion that "marketing is just common sense." Look at the following statements. Which statements do you think are true? Which are false? Justify your answers.

   a. Advertising is a waste of dollars and is deceptive.

      True/False: *F*

      Justification: *Accurate mktg is key to meeting consumer demand.*

   b. Marketing forces fashion changes.

      True/False: *T*

      Justification: *up-to-date - increases status*

   c. Marketing serves the rich and exploits the poor.

      True/False: *F*

      Justification: *all mediums are available in wide variety of price ranges.*

   d. Advertisements that fail to please are ineffective.

      True/False: *T*

      Justification: *if attention isn't attracted no impulse to purchase on part of consumer*

   e. The most effective way to sell products is through low prices.

      True/False: *F*

      Justification: *education of product is key*

   f. Marketing makes people materialistic.

      True/False: _____

      Justification:

8

g. Middlemen are necessary.

True/False: _T_

Justification: *all fu some firms don't have staff or expertise in all areas - facilitators simply process*

h. Marketing research is a waste of both time and money.

True/False: _F_

Justification: *research helps pinpoint target market*

5. Is marketing useful for non-profit organizations? Explain. *Yes. Services (ie career counseling, religion, selective organizations) need promo as well.*

6. Why do we need middlemen? Don't they just add to the cost of distributing products to consumers? *Yes, but simplify overall process*

7. If marketing activities are so important, why are they found only in market-directed economic systems?

Consumers make a society's production decision when they make choices in the market place (dollar votes)

8. Why is effective marketing needed in an advanced economy? Isn't mass production--with its economies of scale--the real key to meeting consumer needs at the lowest cost? *Multitude of products (range, scale)*

Question for Discussion

Should marketing be viewed as a set of activities performed by business and nonprofit organizations, or alternately as a social process? Why is it important to make this decision?

Exercise 1-2

How markets and marketing middlemen develop to facilitate exchange

Introduction

The functions of exchange--buying and selling--are at the heart of the marketing process. Generally, as economies become more advanced, exchange becomes more complicated. In modern economies, markets and marketing middlemen develop to smooth exchange. How well exchange is carried out affects consumer welfare. This is because goods take on value only when they are in the right place at the right time so that the customer can take possession of them.

The purpose of this exercise is to look at the way exchange works as it moves from its simplest stage to more complex stages. We will focus on three basic forms of exchange: (a) decentralized exchange, (b) centralized exchange, and (c) centralized exchange through marketing middlemen.

To simplify our study, we will look at the way exchange evolves in a small barter economy. A money system would speed trading, but it would not change the basic nature of how and why markets and marketing middlemen develop.

Assignment

The following case about the "Sunrise Republic" shows important aspects of the evolution of exchange. Questions appear at various points throughout the case to test your understanding of the material--and especially the implications for a highly developed economy like ours in Canada. Read the case carefully and answer the questions--*as they appear*--in the space provided.

SUNRISE REPUBLIC

Sunrise Republic is a small, developing nation whose population is mostly self-sufficient family units. Most of the goods used in a household are produced by members of the household. Sometimes, some families manage to produce a small surplus of goods and want to exchange their extra goods with other families who also have extra goods.

Recently, the people of Sunrise Republic began to see that some household needs could be filled better by exchange than by production. For example, one family might be better at making shoes and another at growing vegetables. If both families were to concentrate on producing the goods they can make best and then trade, both may get better quality products in larger quantities. In other words, exchange provides a way of getting the advantages of specialization in production.

Decentralized Exchange

Tinkerville, a small town located within the Sunrise Republic, consists of five widely scattered families. Each family specializes in producing only the kinds of goods that it can make best. So, each family has to exchange its goods directly with four other families to get needed articles.

The network of exchange in Tinkerville is shown in Figure 1-1a. Ten separate transactions are needed to carry out decentralized exchange--with the five families having to seek each other out to complete each transaction.

FIGURE 1-1a
Decentralized Exchange
for Five Families

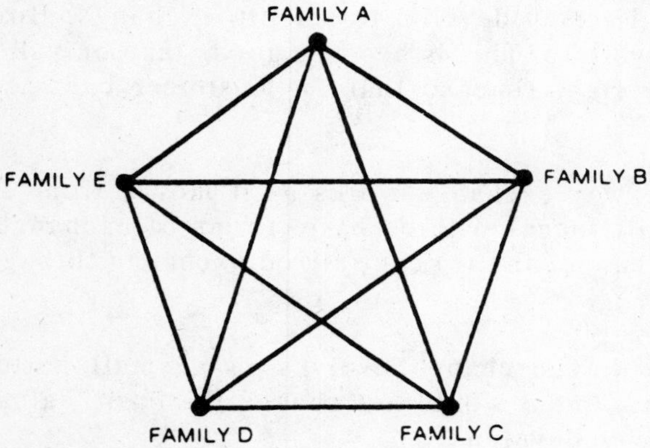

FIGURE 1-1b
Decentralized Exchange
for Ten Families

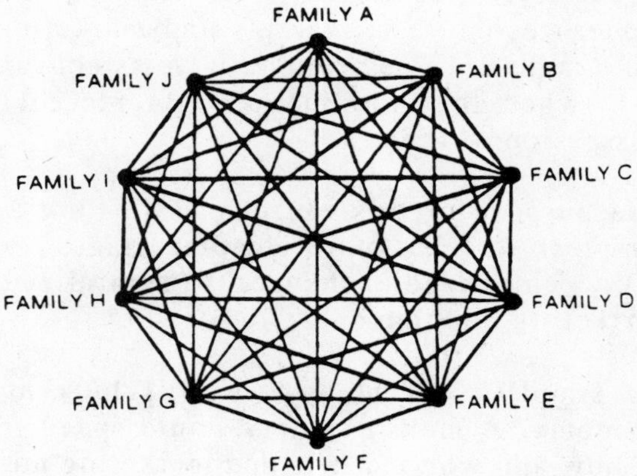

1. Decentralized exchange becomes extremely complex as the population increases in size. For example, Figure 1-1b shows what the network of exchange would look like in Tinkerville if there were ten families instead of five. If you were to count all of the connecting lines, you would find that 45 separate transactions would be required to carry out decentralized exchange among the ten families. (Picture in your mind what the network of decentralized exchange would look like for a city of 1,000,000 people!) Calculate the number of separate transactions that would be required to carry out decentralized exchange if there were: (a) 100 families living in Tinkerville; (b) 500 families. Show your work.

   Hint: The number of transactions (T) necessary to carry out decentralized exchange is:

$$T = \frac{n(n - 1)}{2}$$

   where *n* is the number of producers and each makes only one article. For example, we saw in Figure 1-1a that ten transactions were required when there were five families engaged in decentralized exchange. This fact could also have been determined mathematically using the above formula as follows:

$$T = \frac{5(5 - 1)}{2} = 10$$

   a) 50 families:

$$T = \frac{50 \times (49)}{2} = \frac{2450}{2} = 1{,}225.$$

   b) 500 families:

$$T = \frac{500 \times (499)}{2} = \frac{249{,}500}{2} = 124{,}750$$

Centralized Exchange

The people in Tinkerville soon saw that in spite of the benefits of specialization, the process of decentralized exchange was most inefficient and inconvenient. For one thing, all five traders probably had to travel and seek each other out to complete each transaction. Also, there was no guarantee that each family would be home and would have goods to trade at any given time. Long-distance trips were often wasted when no exchange could take place.

To remedy this situation, the villagers created a *central market* to make exchange easier and allow greater time for production. All agreed to meet together at the marketplace each Saturday at noon to trade goods. Exchange was easier when all five traders met at the same time and place. A total of only five trips were required--one by each family--although ten separate transactions were still needed as shown in Figure 1-2.

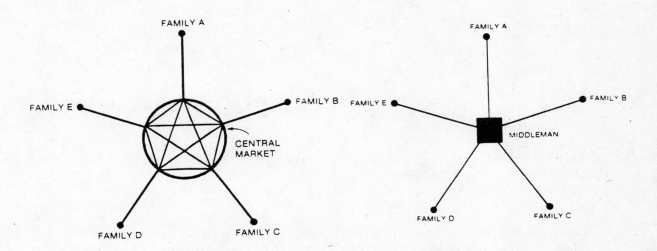

FIGURE 1-2
Centralized Exchange

FIGURE 1-3
Centralized Exchange for a Middleman

Centralized Exchange through Middlemen

The process of exchange was made much easier in Tinkerville by the use of a central market. Soon, however, the operation of the market was taken over by a new resident--called a "middleman." The new villager came to town without any special production skills. Trying to develop some specialty to provide for the needs of his family, he noticed that while the villagers benefited a lot from specialization in production, the exchange process was very complicated. Even with a central market, much time and effort were needed to complete all transactions between families. So, he decided to open up a trading business to serve the local market.

The five producing families of Tinkerville now exchange with the middleman rather than with each other. The families bring all they want to trade to the middleman--trading with him for different goods. The baker, for example, exchanges bread for other items needed by his household. And he does this all in a single transaction--rather than through four separate transactions with the other producers in Tinkerville. The total number of transactions for the entire village is cut in half from ten to five--as each family trades only with the middleman. This is shown in Figure 1-3.

By specializing in trading, the middleman transfers goods from producer to consumer with less effort than would be involved in direct trading. He does this by reducing the number of transactions involved in creating complete assortments of goods for every household. In payment for his services, the middleman keeps a small portion of each producer's output to satisfy the needs of his own family.

2. In our simple example of an economy with five producers, the presence of a marketing middleman reduced the number of exchange transactions from 10 to 5. Had there been ten producing families, the number of transactions would have been reduced from 45 to 10. What would the reduction have been if there were: (a) 50 producing families; (b) 500 producing families?

   Hint: You may have noticed that the number of transactions required in a central market using a marketing middleman is always equal to n, the number of producers in the market. Recall how the number of transactions (T), needed to carry out decentralized exchange was calculated in Question 1. The reduction in transactions (R), which is due to a marketing middleman is simply the difference between the transactions necessary in a decentralized market and the transactions using a middleman, or:

$$R = \frac{n(n - 1)}{2} - n$$

   a) 50 families: $\frac{50 \times (49)}{2} - 50 = (1225 - 50) = 1,175.^{00}$

   b) 500 families: ~~124,250~~ $\frac{500 \times (499)}{2} - 500 = 124,250$

3. Which of the three forms of exchange--decentralized, centralized, or centralized through middlemen--created the greatest amount of economic utility for Tinkerville? Explain your answer.

   Centralized beauce you get time, place + possession utility

4. From a macro-marketing viewpoint, would you say that exchange tends to be carried out *more* or *less* efficiently when it takes place through marketing middlemen rather than directly between producers and consumers? Why?

Question for Discussion

If there are advantages--from a macro-marketing viewpoint--in using marketing middlemen, why do so many people wish to "eliminate the middleman"?

Exercise 1-3

How marketing functions create economic utility

Introduction

Marketing has been defined as the "creation and delivery of a standard of living." In economic terms, marketing contributes to the consumer welfare through the creation of three of the four basic kinds of economic utility--*time, place*, and *possession* utility. Further, marketing may also guide development of *form* utility.

The marketing process does not take place automatically. It requires that certain marketing functions or activities be performed by various marketing institutions--and by *consumers* themselves. The following eight functions are essential to the marketing of all goods: buying, selling, transporting, storing, grading, financing, risk-taking, and market information. No matter how simple or complex the marketing process is, these functions must be performed. Some functions may be performed several times to facilitate the marketing of a given product, while others may be performed only once. At times, the performance of a function may be shifted from one member of a marketing system to another. For example, some modern wholesalers and retailers shift the burden of storing goods back to manufacturers. But, the fact remains that each of the eight functions must be performed by someone at least once before any good can be marketed--none can be eliminated.

Assignment

This assignment illustrates how the performance of marketing functions creates economic utility. Read the following case carefully and then answer the questions that follow in the space provided.

WESTERN RECORD SHOP

Bob and Nancy Anderson were married shortly after graduating from Simon Fraser University--where Bob majored in marketing and Nancy in accounting. After graduation, Bob worked for a while as a salesperson, while Nancy was employed by a local accounting firm. After a few years, they managed to save enough money to finally reach the goal that they had decided upon while still in college--to own and operate their own record shop near the S.F.U. campus.

Records were nothing new to Bob and Nancy--both had been serious record collectors since their early teens. And during their years at S.F.U. they decided that the area lacked a really good record shop with a broad, in-depth selection of records and tapes.

After considering several possible locations, the Andersons leased a former gift shop in a small shopping center very near the S.F.U. campus. The shopping center also contained a Seven-Eleven Food Store, a dry-cleaners and a pizzeria that was very popular with S.F.U. students. Their traffic potential at this location offset one of its disadvantages--a minimum 2-year lease with the first 3 months' rent paid in advance.

Although there were several other record shops in the area, none stocked a very large selection. Thus, Music Vendors, Ltd.--the only record and tape wholesaler in the immediate area--was willing to supply Bob and Nancy with their inventory (which had a retail value of $35,000) and helped them obtain a one-year loan from a local bank--by guaranteeing to buy back unsold records.

The inventory consisted of about 70 percent records and 30 percent tapes, and--based on a survey the Andersons had done as a class project--the inventory was broken down as follows: rock, 30 percent; country, 20 percent; easy listening, 20 percent; classical 20 percent; and miscellaneous, 10 percent.

To announce the grand opening of their record shop, the Andersons placed full-page ads in both the campus newspaper and the city newspaper--as well as placing "spot ads" over local radio stations. In addition to a regular 10 percent discount off suggested list prices for S.F.U. students and faculty, the grand-opening promotion featured a contest offering customers a chance to win an "Elvis Presley Collectors Set" consisting of 25 record albums.

1. What kind(s) of economic utility was created when the records and tapes stocked by the Andersons were first manufactured? _____
    _____ *form utility* _____

2. What kind(s) of economic utility was created by Music Vendors, Ltd. for its customers?
    time, place & possession utility _____

3. What kind(s) of economic utility was created by the Andersons for their customers?
    _____ *time utility* _____

4. The eight basic marketing functions are listed below. Check Yes or No whether each function was performed in the Western Record Shop. If "Yes," explain *when* and *by whom* each function was performed. If "No," explain why not.

    a. Buying: Yes __✓__ No _____ Explain.

    b. Selling: Yes __✓__ No _____ Explain. *by promotional*

    c. Transporting: Yes __✓__ No __✗__ Explain. *(if not returned)* *place utility*

    d. Storing: Yes __✓__ No _____ Explain.

    e. Grading: Yes __✓__ No _____ Explain. *categories*

    f. Financing: Yes __✓__ No _____ Explain.

g.   Risk-taking: Yes ___✓___ No ___✓___ Explain.

h.   Market information: Yes ___✓___ No _____ Explain. *examined traffic flow, location proximity to S.F.U.*

5.   Suppose the Andersons had purchased their inventory directly from various manufacturers instead of from Music Vendors, Ltd. Would *more* or *fewer* marketing functions have been performed in this situation? Explain your answer.

Fewer storage would be eliminated

None can be eliminated - can increase # of functions

6.   Suppose the Andersons had opened their record shop in the Soviet Union instead of Canada. Would *more* or *fewer* marketing functions have been performed in this situation? Explain your answer.

Same amount = universal functions of functions

Question for Discussion

Name a product for which all eight marketing functions do *not* need to be performed by someone somewhere in the marketing system.

Chapter 2
Marketing's role within the firm

What This Chapter Is About

Chapter 2 shows how important micro-marketing can be within a firm. In particular, the "marketing concept" and the evolution of firms from a production to a marketing orientation is explained. Then, the importance of understanding the difference between a production orientation and a marketing orientation is discussed.

The nature of the marketing management process is introduced--and the importance of marketing strategy planning is explained. The four Ps--Product, Price, Place, and Promotion--are introduced as the controllable elements which the marketing manager blends into a marketing mix to satisfy a particular target market. It is very important for you to understand the four Ps--because planning the four Ps is the major concern of the rest of the text.

The chapter gives a very necessary overview to what is coming. Study it carefully so you can understand how the material in the following chapters will fit together.

Important Terms

simple trade era, p. 28
production era, pp. 28-29
sales era, p. 29
marketing department era, p. 29
marketing company era, p. 29
marketing concept, p. 29
production orientation, p. 30
marketing orientation, p. 30
marketing management process, p. 36
strategic (management) planning, p. 37
marketing strategy, p. 38
target market, p. 38
marketing mix, p. 38

target marketing, p. 38
mass marketing, p. 38
channel of distribution, p. 41
personal selling, p. 41
mass selling, p. 41
advertising, p. 41
publicity, p. 41
sales promotion, p. 41
marketing plan, p. 44
implementation, p. 44
operational decisions, pp. 44-45
marketing program, pp. 45-46

True-False Questions

_____ 1. The simple trade era was a time when families traded or sold their "surplus" output to local middlemen who sold these goods to other consumers or distant middlemen.

_____ 2. Marketing departments are usually formed when firms go from the "production era" to the "sales era."

___ 3. A company has moved into the "marketing company era" when, in addition to short run marketing planning, the total company effort is guided by the marketing concept.

___ 4. The marketing concept says that a firm should aim all its efforts at satisfying customers, even if this proves to be unprofitable.

___ 5. The term "marketing orientation" means making products which are easy to produce and then trying to sell them.

___ 6. The three basic ideas included in the definition of the marketing concept are: a customer orientation, a total company effort, and sales as an objective.

___ 7. There are no functional departments in a firm that has adopted the marketing concept.

___ 8. The marketing concept was very quickly accepted, especially among producers of industrial products.

___ 9. In the last decade, service industries have adopted the marketing concept more and more.

___ 10. Because they don't try to earn a profit, the marketing concept is not very useful for nonprofit organizations.

___ 11. The marketing management process consists of (1) planning marketing activities, (2) directing the implementation of the plans, and (3) controlling these plans.

___ 12. Strategic (management) planning is a managerial process of developing and maintaining a match between the resources of the production department and its product opportunities.

___ 13. Marketing strategy planning is the process of deciding how best to sell the products the firm produces.

___ 14. A marketing strategy specifies a target market and a related marketing mix.

___ 15. A target market consists of a group of consumers who are usually quite different.

___ 16. A marketing mix consists of the uncontrollable variable which a company puts together to satisfy a target market.

___ 17. Target marketing aims a marketing mix at some specific target customers.

___ 18. The mass marketing approach is more production-oriented than marketing-oriented.

___ 19. The terms "mass marketing" and "mass marketer" mean the same thing.

___ 20. The problem with target marketing is that it limits the firm to small market segments.

_____ 21. The four "Ps" are: Product, Promotion, Price, and Personnel.

_____ 22. The customer should not be considered part of a "marketing mix."

_____ 23. The Product area is concerned with developing the right physical good, service, or blend of both for the target market.

_____ 24. A channel of distribution must include several kinds of middlemen and specialists.

_____ 25. Personal selling and advertising are both forms of sales promotion.

_____ 26. Price is the most important of the four Ps.

_____ 27. The marketing mix should be set before the best target market is selected.

_____ 28. A marketing plan and a marketing strategy mean the same thing.

_____ 29. Implementation means putting the marketing plan into operation.

_____ 30. Short-run decisions that stay within the overall guidelines set during strategy planning are called implementation decisions.

_____ 31. A marketing program may consist of several marketing plans.

_____ 32. An extremely good marketing plan may be carried out badly and still be profitable, while a poor but well-implemented plan can lose money.

_____ 33. Henry Ford was "production-oriented" because he decided to mass produce cars before he asked whether there was a market for such cars.

_____ 34. In the last decade, the watch industry has become much more marketing-oriented.

_____ 35. Well-planned marketing strategies usually can ignore the uncontrollable variables.

Answers to True-False Questions

1. T, p. 28	13. F, p. 38	25. F, p. 41
2. F, p. 29	14. T, p. 38	26. F, p. 42
3. T, p. 29	15. F, p. 38	27. F, p. 42
4. F, p. 29	16. F, p. 38	28. F, p. 44
5. F, p. 30	17. T, p. 38	29. T, p. 44
6. F, p. 30	18. T, p. 38	30. F, p. 44
7. F, p. 32	19. F, p. 39	31. T, p. 45
8. F, p. 33	20. F, p. 39	32. T, p. 47
9. T, p. 34	21. F, p. 40	33. F, p. 47
10. F, p. 34	22. T, p. 40	34. T, p. 48
11. T, p. 36	23. T, p. 40	35. F, pp. 49-50
12. F, p. 37	24. F, p. 41	

Multiple-Choice Questions (Circle the correct response)

1. A firm that focuses its attention primarily on "selling" its present products in order to meet or beat competition is operating in which of the following "management eras"?

   a. Production era
   b. Sales era
   c. Marketing department era
   d. Marketing company era
   e. Advertising era

2. Based on the following company statements, which company is most likely to be in the marketing company era?

   a. "Our sales force was able to sell middlemen more of our new product than they can resell in all of this year."
   b. "Our marketing manager is coordinating pricing, product decisions, promotion and distribution to help us show a profit at the end of this year."
   c. "The whole company is in good shape--demand exceeds what we can produce."
   d. "Our long range plan--developed by our marketing manager--is to expand so that we can profitably meet the long-term needs of our customers."
   e. "Our new president previously led our marketing effort as Vice President of Sales."

3. Which of the following best explains what the "marketing concept" means:

   a. Firms should spend more money on marketing than they have in the past.
   b. A firm's main emphasis should be on the efficient utilization of its resources.
   c. All of a firm's activities and resources should be organized to satisfy the needs of its customers--at a profit.
   d. A company's chief executive should previously have been a marketing manager.
   e. A firm should always attempt to give customers what they need regardless of the cost involved.

4. The difference between "production orientation" and "marketing orientation" is best explained as follows:

   a. there are no separate functional departments in a marketing-oriented firm.
   b. in a marketing-oriented firm, the total system's effort is guided by what individual departments would like to do.
   c. production-oriented firms usually don't have a marketing manager.
   d. in a marketing-oriented firm, every department's activities are guided by what customers need and what the firm can deliver at a profit.
   e. all major marketing decisions are based on extensive marketing research studies in marketing-oriented firms.

5. Which of the following is one of three basic marketing management jobs?

   a. To direct the implementation of plans
   b. To control the plans in actual operation
   c. To plan marketing activities
   d. All of the above

6. The marketing management process:

   a. includes the on-going job of planning marketing activities.
   b. is mainly concerned with obtaining continuous customer feedback.
   c. involves finding opportunities and planning marketing strategies, but does not include the management tasks of implementing and control.
   d. is called "strategic planning."
   e. Both a and d are true statements.

7. A marketing strategy consists of two interrelated parts. These are:

   a. selection of a target market and implementing the plan.
   b. selection of a target market and development of a marketing mix.
   c. selection and development of a marketing mix.
   d. finding attractive opportunities and developing a marketing mix.
   e. finding attractive opportunities and selecting a target market.

8. Marketing strategy planners should recognize that:

   a. target markets should not be large and spread out.
   b. mass marketing is often very effective and desirable.
   c. firms like General Electric, Sears Roebuck, and Procter & Gamble are too large to aim at clearly defined markets.
   d. target marketing is not limited to small market segments.
   e. the terms "mass marketing" and "mass marketers" mean essentially the same thing.

9. A marketing mix consists of:

   a. policies, procedures, plans, and personnel.
   b. the customer and the "four Ps."
   c. all variables, controllable and uncontrollable.
   d. product, price, promotion, and place.
   e. none of the above.

10. Which of the following statements about marketing mix variables is *false*?

    a. "Promotion" includes personal selling, mass selling, and sales promotion.
    b. The term "Product" refers to services as well as physical goods.
    c. A channel of distribution does not have to include any middlemen.
    d. Generally speaking, "Price" is more important than "Place."
    e. The needs of a target market virtually determine the nature of an appropriate marketing mix.

11. A "marketing plan":

    a. is just another term for "marketing strategy."
    b. consists of several "marketing programs."
    c. includes the time-related details for carrying out a marketing strategy.
    d. is a strategy without all the operational decisions.
    e. ignores implementation and control details.

12. A "marketing program":

    a. is another name for a particular marketing mix.
    b. blends several different marketing plans.

c. consists of a target market and the marketing mix.

d. is primarily concerned with all of the details of implementing a marketing plan.

e. must be set before a target market can be selected.

13. The Ford and General Motors examples in the text all serve to illustrate that:

a. good implementation and control is usually more important than good planning.

b. strategy planning is not relevant for nonmarketing people.

c. an effective marketing strategy guarantees future success.

d. consumers want only high-quality products.

e. creative strategy planning is needed for survival.

Answers to Multiple-Choice Questions

1. b, p. 29	6. a, p. 36	11. c, p. 44
2. d, p. 29	7. b, p. 38	12. b, pp. 45-46
3. c, p. 29	8. d, p. 38	13. e, pp. 47-48
4. d, p. 30	9. d, p. 40	
5. d, p. 36	10. d, p. 42	

Exercise 2-1

Marketing-oriented vs. production-oriented firms

Introduction

Business firms can be classified as either "production-oriented" or "marketing-oriented," depending on whether they have adopted the "marketing concept." The marketing concept is a modern business philosophy which simply states that a firm should aim all its efforts at satisfying its customers--at a profit. This philosophy implies a total management commitment to (1) a customer orientation, (2) a total company effort, and (3) profit, not just sales, as an objective of the firm.

In general, a production-oriented firm tries to get customers to buy what the firm has produced, while a marketing-oriented firm tries to produce and sell what customers need. Actually, the terms "production-oriented" and "marketing-oriented" should be viewed as opposite ends of a continuum along which different firms could be placed. But it is often useful to classify a firm as being *mainly* production- or marketing-oriented.

In practice, however, there is no simple way of identifying the two types of firms. Instead, one must look for subtle "clues" to help decide whether a firm is production-oriented or marketing-oriented. These clues can take many forms, such as the attitudes of management toward customers, the firm's organization structure, and its methods and procedures.

Assignment

This exercise gives you some practice in identifying production-oriented and marketing-oriented firms. You will be given pairs of firms--and a "clue" about each firm. On the basis of these clues, you must decide which one of the two firms is more marketing-oriented and which is more production-oriented.

For each pair of firms, print an *M* before the firm that you think is marketing-oriented and a *P* before the firm that is production-oriented--and then briefly explain your answers. (Note: each set should have an *M* and a *P*--you *must* make a choice.) The first pair is answered for you as an example.

Orientation		Clues

1. *P*   Firm A: "We try to sell the products that we make."

   m   Firm B: "We try to make the products that customers need and want to buy."

Firm A is interested in "doing its own thing," while Firm B has focused its efforts on producing what customers want and need.

2. *P*   Firm A: "As sales manager, my job is to hire sales people who can 'move' as many units as we can produce. After all, the higher the sales, the higher the profits."

   M   Firm B: "As finance manager, my job is to determine how many units it will be profitable for us to sell at the price customers are willing to pay."

3. *M*   Firm A: "What competitive advantage would the proposed new product have in satisfying consumer needs?"

   P   Firm B: "Our competitor's new product is a great idea. Let's see if we can produce and sell it at a lower price."

4. _M_

   _P_

   Firm A: "Our sales have dropped. Let's ask our middlemen why customers have stopped buying our product."

   Firm B: "Our sales are too low. Perhaps we could use our most persuasive salespeople to recruit some new middlemen."

5. _P_

   _M_

   Firm A: "How much money will we save if we wait a year before buying an additional delivery truck?"

   Firm B: "How much will it improve our customer service if we buy an additional delivery truck?"

6. _P_ Firm A: "We've given the people in this city one of the finest symphony orchestras in the world, but hardly anyone attends the concerts. It's a case of misplaced social values--and something must be done about it."

_M_ Firm B: "We've got to find out what it is about our concert series that turns people away. It's a case of needing to do a better job of meeting people's needs--rather than sitting back and waiting for people to see the light."

7. _P_ Firm A: "It costs at least $35.00 to produce a pair of high quality leather shoes."

_M_ Firm B: "Our customers don't always want to pay the high price that usually goes with a pair of really high quality leather shoes."

8. _P_ Firm A: "Our inventory costs are too high. We'll have to reduce our inventory, even if it means that it will take customers longer to get their orders."

_M_ Firm B: "Sure our inventory costs are high. But how many customers would we lose if we were frequently unable to fill orders immediately?"

9. _P_ Firm A: "Our Research and Development group has developed a new type of glue that we could produce at low cost with the excess capacity in our chemical plant. Let's see if the sales force can sell it at a profit."

_M_ Firm B: "Marketing research shows that some customers want glue that dries quicker and adheres better. Let's see if our Research and Development group can develop a product that can meet this need, and at the same time make better use of our excess capacity."

10. _P_ Firm A: "It would cost us too much to lease a store in the shopping center. We'll locate our drugstore a few blocks away where the land is cheaper. We can depend on our low prices and good selection to bring the customers to us."

_M_ Firm B: "People today want the convenience of one-stop shopping and we've got to go where the customers are. It will cost us more to lease a building in the shopping center, but we'll attract more regular customers and that's the key to profit for a drugstore."

11. _MP_ Firm A: "Our sales have nearly doubled since the advertising manager was promoted to president. He's tripled the amount we spend on advertising and personal selling, and he's told the accountants to stick to their balancing the books and leave the marketing budget to him." _not total effort by whole firm_

_PM_ Firm B: "It helps to have an accountant as president. When he took over the company, he found that it was too expensive for a salesperson to visit many of our smaller customers, and now our sales force concentrates its efforts on satisfying those larger accounts that contribute the most to our profits."

Concentrate on what brings in a larger percentage of profit

29

12. _P_   Firm A: "Our profits have been declining. Perhaps we should search for ways to cut costs and make more efficient use of our resources."

     _M_   Firm B: "Our profits have been declining. Perhaps we should search for new opportunities to satisfy unfulfilled needs."

13. _M_   Firm A: "We're getting killed by overseas competitors. We need to improve our quality control and do a better job of meeting customer's expectations."

     _P_   Firm B: "Overseas producers compete unfairly with cheap labor. We need to have our public relations department lobby for tighter import quotas so that we can make a profit."

Question for Discussion

If, as the text emphasizes, it is so important that firms be marketing-oriented, how is it that many production-oriented firms are not only surviving but apparently operating profitably?

Exercise 2-2

Mass marketing vs. target marketing

Introduction

A marketing manager's planning job is to find attractive market opportunities and develop effective marketing strategies. A "marketing strategy" consists of two interrelated parts: (1) a *target market*--a fairly homogeneous group of customers to whom a company wishes to appeal, and (2) a *marketing mix*--the controllable variables which the company puts together to satisfy this target group.

Here, it is important to see the difference between *mass marketing* and *target marketing* in planning marketing strategies.

Production-oriented firms typically assume that everyone's needs are the same. They try to build universal appeals into a marketing mix which--it is hoped--will attract "everyone." This approach we will call "mass marketing." Marketing-oriented firms, on the other hand, recognize that different customers usually have different needs--so they try to satisfy the needs of some particular group of customers--whose needs are fairly similar--rather than trying to appeal to everyone. This "target marketing" approach--a logical application of the marketing concept--simply means that a marketing strategy should aim at *some* target market.

Assignment

This exercise is designed to illustrate the difference between mass marketing and target marketing. Read each of the following cases carefully, and then (1) indicate in the space provided whether each firm is following a mass-marketing or a target-marketing approach and (2) briefly explain your answers.

1. Precision Products Corporation, one of the world's largest producers of keyboards for personal computers, recently introduced a new keyboard design under its "Excel" label. The premium-priced keyboard includes all of the keys found on a typical keyboard, but there is an extra set of special function keys. These keys can be programmed to "remember" a series of key strokes--so that pressing one key executes a complicated series of key strokes. The special function keys will be especially attractive to business analysts, engineers, and others who regularly use the very popular LOTUS 1-2-3 spreadsheet software--since it will make it easier and faster to set up and run analyses. Tests also show that it takes a new computer-user less time to learn to use LOTUS with the new keyboard. The company estimates that within two years 10 percent of current business users of LOTUS will buy the product--because of the productivity savings. The company is working on a new model that offers similar advantages to users of desktop publishing software--one of the fastest growing applications of personal computers.

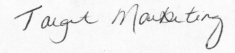

    a) Mass marketing _____ Target marketing __✓__

    b) Comments: _Lotus users - developing separat_
        markts _____

_____

_____

_____

_____

_____

_____

2.   Marie Costana recently retired after 20 years of service as a chef for a luxury cruise line. During her career, she worked on ships that took her to almost every part of the world. In the process, she learned to prepare the favorite dishes of many different countries. Maria and her husband--also an outstanding cook--have decided to use their savings to open an "ethnic" restaurant, but with a difference. Customers will be able to try authentic recipes from all over the world. Maria is sure that their restaurant will be an outstanding success. "After all," she says, "one thing you can count on is that everybody enjoys good food. And where else can people get the variety and quality that we can offer?"

    a) Mass marketing __✓__ Target marketing _____

    b) Comments: _____

_____

_____

_____

_____

_____

_____

3.   Extruded Aluminum Products Co. has just introduced a new product called the "Paradise Chaise Lounge," which is being promoted as the "ultimate in lawn and patio furniture." According to Mac Williams, the company president, the Paradise Chaise Lounge is "absolutely guaranteed to be rust-proof, mildew-proof, and weatherproof." Moreover, "it features a revolutionary new design that makes it the most comfortable folding chaise lounge on the market." Available in several models ranging in price from $30 to $55, the "Paradise Chaise Lounge" is expected to sell "in the millions." "This product is so superior," says Mac Williams, "that no household in Canada will want to be without one."

a) Mass marketing ____✓____ Target marketing _____

b) Comments: _____appealing to everyone - assumes everyone_____

_____needs me_____

_____

_____

_____

_____

_____

4. Consumers may eventually enjoy "personalized" magazines--magazines which are tailored to each individual reader's interests in both editorial and advertising content. By combining detailed survey information about respondents with Can/Stat Inc.'s computerized collating system, consumer and trade magazine publishers may be able to publish magazines which will be read from cover to cover because every article and ad in the magazine will appeal to each reader's self-identified interests. Thus, nonsmokers will never receive a magazine with cigarette ads, while smokers will. And skiers can look forward to a lot of articles about skiing, while camera buffs can look forward to many articles about photography. Because of equipment limitations, the "personalized" magazines would have to be limited to a 300,000-500,000 circulation range.

a) Mass marketing _____ Target marketing __✓__

b) Comments: _____due to segmentation_____

_____

_____

_____

_____

_____

_____

Question for Discussion

"Target marketing" does not guarantee a successful marketing strategy. Selection of a target market is by no means an easy task--as will be discussed in later chapters--and a firm must have the necessary resources and skills to develop an appropriate marketing mix for the target market it selects.

Moreover, a firm's marketing mix must be seen by the target group as being "good" and better than competitive marketing mixes. For example, Gerber's "Singles" failed in the marketplace apparently not because there was no need for such a product--but because consumers rejected the packaging, the brand name, etc. In other words, there will always be some risk inherent in marketing strategy planning--although target marketing certainly will reduce the risk.

Exercise 2-3

Developing a unique marketing mix for each target market

Introduction

Developing a marketing strategy consists of two *interrelated* tasks: (1) selecting a target market and (2) developing the best marketing mix for that target market.

Marketing-oriented firms recognize that not all potential customers have the same needs. Thus, rather than first developing a marketing mix and *then* looking for a market to sell that mix to, marketing-oriented firms first try to determine what kind of mix each possible target market may require. Then they select a target market based on their ability to offer a good marketing mix at a profit.

Assignment

This exercise assumes that different groups of customers in a general market area may have different needs--and therefore may require different marketing mixes. Three possible target markets and alternative marketing mixes are described below for each of four different product types. For each product type, select the marketing mix which would be best for each target market. (*All alternatives must be used, i.e., you cannot use one alternative for two target markets.*) Indicate your selection by writing the letter of the marketing mix in front of the target market you select.

Note: To make it easier for you, each target market consists of only one individual or family, but it should be clear that each individual or family really represents a larger group of potential customers who have similar needs.

I.   Product type: Automobile

Possible Target Markets

b (1) A manager of a real estate firm who uses his company car to show clients the community--and convey a successful business image.

c (2) Middle-aged couple with two children who have just purchased a mountain cabin for use as a family "retreat."

a (3) A student who needs a car to commute to the college campus--and to work a paper route.

Alternative Marketing Mixes

(a) A five-year-old, "for sale by owner" Honda Civic listed in the classified ads of a local newspapaer.

(b) A Buick sedan with luxury features--on a one-year lease from the Buick dealer in a nearby city.

(c) A Jeep Wagoneer purchased with financing arranged by the salesman at a local car dealer--and backed with an extended service warranty.

II.   Product type: Food

Possible Target Markets   *Alternative Marketing Mixes*

_b_ ✓ (1) Airline pilot who has just arrived   (a) A large, hamburger pizza and some
        back from an out-of-town flight at   soft   drinks   delivered   to   the
        8:30 p.m.   house--purchased at "2.00 off the
                                                    regular price" with a coupon from
                                                    an insert in the newspaper.

_a_ ✓ (2) Middle-aged low-income housewife   (b) Nationally   advertised   brand   of
        concerned with feeding her large   frozen "gourmet" dinner on display
        family a well-balanced meal, while   in   the   frozen-food   case   of   a
        operating on a tight budget.   "7-Eleven" convenience food store.

_c_ ✓ (3) Young   mother   who   has   spent   (c) "Market basket" of perishables and
        Saturday afternoon at a part-time   canned goods purchased at a large
        job and has to rush to get her   supermarket that advertises "low
        children dinner before going to a   everyday prices."
        party.

III.   Product type: Computer

Possible Target Markets   *Alternative Marketing Mixes*

_a_ ✓ (1) Young working couple who want   (a) Well known brand of portable laptop
        their child to learn about computers   computer with built in software--
        by using educational game programs.   sold through a dealer who provides
                                                    service and a "loaner" if repairs are
                                                    needed.

_c_ ✓ (2) A local Savings and Loan that has to   (b) Powerful mini-computer leased from
        constantly   update   deposit   and   a   manufacturer--such   as   Digital
        withdrawal information--and prepare   Equipment--that uses knowledgeable
        a variety of company records and   salespeople to help the customer
        reports.   decide on the right equipment.

_b_ ✓ (3) Sales rep who wants to keep   (c) Inexpensive computer sold by a
        records of his sales calls and   mass-merchandiser that advertises
        prepare short reports for the home   its discount prices.
        office while he travels.

IV.   Product type: Wine

Possible Target Markets

b ✓
__a__ (1) Wealthy couple planning a dinner for some socially prominent guests.

✓
__a__ (2) Young college student going to a "bring your own bottle" party at a friend's apartment.

✓
__C__ (3) Young, middle-income, married couple who have invited some friends over for the evening.

Alternative Marketing Mixes

(a) Low-priced, wine cooler, heavily promoted over the radio and sold at a conveniently located party store.

(b) Expensive French wine stocked at a wine store whose owner is a well-known wine expert.

(c) Popular brand of a medium-priced British Columbian wine on display in the wine section of a large supermarket.

V.   Product type: Stereo Equipment

Possible Target Markets

b ✓
__b__ (1) Affluent young executive who wants to install a stereo in her penthouse, but doesn't know much about stereo equipment.

a ✓
__a__ (2) Middle-class married couple who are looking for a stereo that will blend in with their living room furniture.

✓
c __b__ (3) Do-it-yourself enthusiast who wants to add a stereo to the basement recreation room he has just built.

Alternative Marketing Mixes

(a) Popular brand of an AM/FM console stereo with an attractive wood cabinet purchased on credit at a large department store.

(b) Expensive component stereo system, manufactured by a firm with a reputation for high quality and sold by a dealer who specializes in stereo equipment.

(c) Build-it-yourself component stereo kit featured in a catalog published by a large mail-order distributor of electronic equipment.

Question for Discussion

Assuming that a firm cannot satisfy all the needs of all potential customers, what factors should a marketing manager consider before selecting a target market?

Appendix A
Economics fundamentals

What This Chapter Is About

Appendix A is important to understanding how buyers and sellers look at products and markets. Some of the economist's tools are shown to be useful. In particular, demand and supply curves, and their interaction are discussed. Also, elasticity of demand and supply are explained. They help us understand the nature of competition.

The material in this Appendix is not easy--but it is very important. A good marketing manager does not always "win" in every market because consumers' attitudes are continually changing. But an understanding of the nature of demand and competition in different markets will greatly increase your chances for success. Careful study of this Appendix will build a good economics base for this text (especially Chapters 3, 4, 18, and 19).

Important Terms

law of diminishing demand, p. 54
demand curve, pp. 54-55
inelastic demand, p. 57
elastic demand, p. 57
substitutes, p. 58

supply curve, p. 60
inelastic supply, p. 61
elastic supply, p. 61
equilibrium point, p. 61
consumer surplus, p. 62

True-False Questions

_____ 1. Economists usually assume that customers evaluate a given set of alternatives in terms of whether they will make them feel better (or worse) or in some way improve (or change) their situation.

_____ 2. "The law of diminishing demand" says that if the price of a product is raised, a greater quantity will be demanded--and if the price of a product is lowered, a smaller quantity will be demanded.

_____ 3. A demand schedule may indicate that as prices go lower, the total unit sales increase, but the total revenue decreases.

_____ 4. A demand curve is a "picture" of the relationship between price and quantity in a market.

_____ 5. Most demand curves slope upward.

_____ 6. If total revenue would decrease if price were raised, then demand is said to be elastic.

_____ 7. If total revenue would increase if price were lowered, then demand is said to be inelastic.

_____ 8. Unitary elasticity of demand means that total revenue remains the same when prices change, regardless of whether price is increased or decreased.

_____ 9. A demand curve must be entirely elastic or inelastic; it cannot be both.

_____ 10. Whether a product has an elastic or inelastic demand depends on many factors including the availability of substitutes, the importance of the item in the customer's budget, and the urgency of the customer's need in relation to other needs.

_____ 11. When only a small number of good "substitutes" are available, demand tends to be quite inelastic.

_____ 12. A supply curve shows the quantity of products that will be offered at various possible prices by all suppliers together.

_____ 13. An extremely steep or almost vertical supply curve is called elastic because the quantity supplied would not change much if the price were raised.

_____ 14. The intersection of demand and supply determines the size of a market and the market price.

_____ 15. A market is in equilibrium if the quantity and the price that sellers are willing to offer are equal to the quantity and the price that buyers are willing to accept.

_____ 16. "Consumer surplus" is the difference between the value of a purchase and the price the consumer has to pay.

Answers to True-False Questions

1. T, p. 54	7. F, p. 57	13. F, p. 60
2. F, p. 54	8. T, p. 57	14. T, p. 61
3. T, p. 54	9. F, p. 57	15. T, p. 61
4. T, pp. 54-55	10. T, p. 58	16. T, p. 62
5. F, p. 55	11. T, p. 58	
6. T, p. 57	12. T, p. 60	

Multiple-Choice Questions (Circle the correct response)

1. The "law of diminishing demand" says that:

   a. if the price of a product were lowered, a greater quantity would be demanded.
   b. if the price of a product were raised, a greater quantity would be demanded.
   c. the demand for any product will tend to decline over time.
   d. if the price of a product were lowered, a smaller quantity would be demanded.
   e. the more of a product a person buys, the less utility that particular product offers him.

2. A demand curve:

   a. is generally up-sloping from left to right.
   b. is formed by plotting the points from a supply schedule.
   c. shows what quantities would be demanded by potential customers at various possible prices.
   d. shows how total revenue increases as prices decrease.
   e. All of the above are true statements.

3. If a firm's total revenue increases when the price of its product is reduced from $15 to $10, the demand for this product is:

   a. elastic.
   b. inelastic.
   c. unitary elastic.
   d. cannot be determined without looking at the demand curve.

4. Study the following demand schedule:

PRICE	QUANTITY DEMANDED	TOTAL REVENUE
$500	1,000	$500,000
400	2,000	800,000
300	3,000	900,000
200	4,000	800,000
100	5,000	500,000

   This demand schedule shows that the demand for this product is:

   a. elastic.
   b. inelastic.
   c. unitary elastic.
   d. both elastic and inelastic.
   e. This demand schedule cannot be correct because it violates the "law of diminishing demand."

5. The elasticity of demand for a particular product does *not* depend upon:

    a. the availability of substitutes.
    b. the importance of the item in the customer's budget.
    c. the urgency of the customer's need.
    d. how much it costs to produce the product.
    e. All of the above affect the elasticity of demand.

6. Which of the following products would have the most *inelastic* demand for most potential customers?

    a. A home computer
    b. A vacation trip to France
    c. A one-pound package of salt
    d. A pair of designer jeans
    e. A "Big Mac" hamburger

7. A supply curve:

    a. is generally flatter than its supply schedule.
    b. is not affected by production costs.
    c. is generally up-sloping from left to right.
    d. is a picture of the quantities of goods that would be demanded at various possible prices.
    e. All of the above are true statements.

8. Which of the following statements about elasticity of supply is *true*?

    a. If a product's demand curve is elastic, then its supply curve also must be elastic.
    b. A product's elasticity of supply determines its elasticity of demand.
    c. In the short run, the supply curve for most agricultural products is highly elastic.
    d. In the long run, the supply curve for most products is highly inelastic.
    e. None of the above statements are true.

9. Which of the following statements about demand and supply interaction is *true*?

    a. Demand is the sole determiner of price.
    b. A market is said to be in equilibrium when the elasticity of demand equals the elasticity of supply.
    c. The interaction of supply and demand determines the size of the market and the market price.
    d. For a market to be in equilibrium, the price and quantity that buyers are willing to accept must be greater than the price and quantity that suppliers are willing to offer.
    e. All of the above statements are true.

10. Given a situation where there is elastic demand and elastic supply, an *increase* in the quantity suppliers are willing to supply at all possible prices will:

    a. decrease price, but not change quantity demanded.
    b. increase price and decrease quantity demanded.
    c. lower price and increase quantity demanded.
    d. increase price and increase quantity demanded.

11. The term "consumer surplus" means that:

    a.   consumers never get their money's worth in any transaction.

    b.   there are more needs than there are products to satisfy them.

    c.   consumers don't consume all the products they buy.

    d.   some consumers would be willing to pay more than the market equilibrium price if they had to.

    e.   there are more consumers than there are producers.

Answers to Multiple-Choice Questions

1. a, p. 54	5. d, p. 58	9. c, p. 61
2. c, pp. 54-55	6. c, p. 59	10. c, p. 61
3. a, p. 57	7. c, p. 60	11. d, p. 62
4. d, pp. 57-58	8. e, p. 61	

Exercise A-1
Estimating and using demand elasticity

Introduction

"Demand elasticity" is a very useful concept for analyzing the nature of demand and competition in markets. As explained in Appendix A in the text, demand elasticity can be defined in terms of what happens to total revenue when the price of a product is lowered.

a. If total revenue would increase if the price were lowered, then demand is said to be *elastic*.

b. If total revenue would decrease if the price were lowered, then demand is said to be *inelastic*.

c. If total revenue would stay the same if the price were lowered, then we have a special case called *unitary elasticity of demand*.

Different products have different demand elasticities because of factors such as the availability of substitutes, the importance of the item in the customer's budget, and the urgency of the customer's need in relation to other needs.

The elasticity of a firm's demand curve is extremely important to a marketing strategy planner. It provides a shorthand description of the nature of competition and demand facing a firm--often suggesting necessary changes in strategies. For example, a firm with a highly elastic demand curve might have many competitors and would have very little control over the price it could charge for its product. In this case, perhaps the firm should plan a new strategy--one aimed at a different target market with fewer competitors and less elastic demand.

Assignment

This exercise has three parts and is designed to increase your understanding of demand elasticity. The first part focuses on the relationship of demand elasticity to changes in total revenue. The second part shows how demand elasticity can vary in different market situations. The third part shows how product and price are related through demand elasticity.

1. Demand elasticity was defined above in terms of what happens to total revenue when price is lowered. Now complete the following table--showing what happens to total revenue (*TR*) when price is *raised* instead of lowered.

Appendix A

	Elastic demand	*Inelastic demand*	*Unitary elasticity of demand*
Price lowered	TR increases	TR decreases	TR remains the same
Price raised	TR decrease	TR increases	"

2. Figure A-1 shows three demand curves--each with a different degree of elasticity. Each of the demand curves represents *one* of the following situations:

a) The demand for airline fuel during a holiday season.
b) The demand for an individual farmer's strawberry crop.
c) The demand for one firm's "quality" videocassette recorder.

In the space provided, state which of the three situations each demand curve most likely represents. Then briefly explain each answer in terms of the factors which can cause demand elasticity to vary in different market situations.

FIGURE A-1

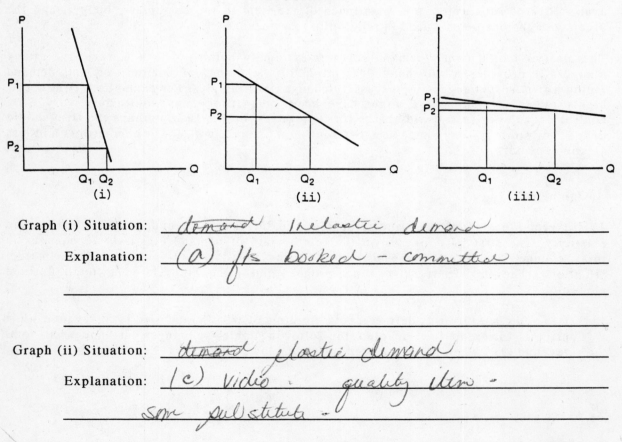

Graph (i) Situation: demand Inelastic demand

Explanation: (a) f/ts booked - committed

Graph (ii) Situation: demand elastic demand

Explanation: (c) vidio . quality item - some substitute .

46

Name: _____ Course & Section: _____

Graph (iii) Situation: *(b) demand very elastic* _____

       Explanation: _____

_____

_____

3. Read the following paragraph and then answer questions (a) through (c).

QC, Ltd. produces and sells quality control instruments that are used by industrial firms to control the production process. QC's management is seeking a larger share of the market. Thus, its objective for the coming year is to increase both its dollar sales volume and its market share for the instruments--which are currently priced at $1,600. QC's estimated demand curve for the next year is shown in Figure A-2.

FIGURE A-2

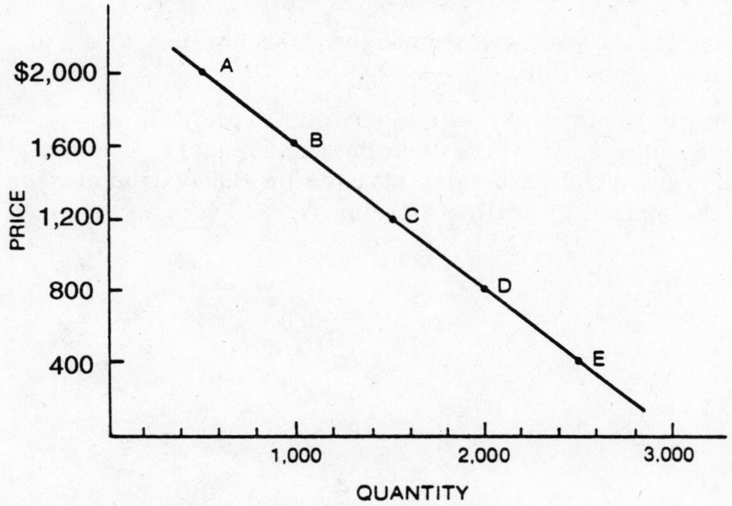

a) Use Figure A-2 to complete the following table:

Demand Schedule of QC's Quality Control Instruments

Points on Graph	Price per unit	Quantity Demanded per unit	Total Revenue per year	
A	$2,000	500	$1,000,000	
B	1,600	*1000*	*1,600,000*	*1.4 m*
C	1,200	*1,400*	*1,800,000*	*1.68 1.8 m —*
D	800	*2,000*	*1,600,000*	*1.6 m*
E	400	*2,450*	*9,800.00*	*1. m*

47

b) Looking at QC's demand curve and demand schedule, would you describe the demand for the firm's instruments as (a) elastic, (b) inelastic, (c) unitary elastic, or (d) both elastic and inelastic? Explain your answer.

_____

_____

c) As president of QC, you have called a meeting of top management to discuss the firm's pricing for the coming year. After explaining the purpose of the meeting, you have asked for comments and suggestions.

"If we want to increase our dollar sales revenue, then we must raise our selling price," suggests your finance manager. *incorrect*

"That may increase our sales revenue," replies your production manager, "but if we want to capture a larger share of the market, then the only answer is to increase our production to its maximum level--while maintaining our current price." *incorrect - not going to increase TR*

"Nonsense," yells your sales manager, "the obvious thing to do is cut our price down as low as possible." *half right - will increase mkt share but decrease total revenue*

Since you have to make the decision, explain how you would resolve the conflicting advice of your department managers. Then state what price QC should charge to increase sales revenue on the instruments *and* capture a larger share of the market by selling more units.

Question for Discussion

Consider the three market situations in Question 2. If a firm's demand curve is elastic, does the demand curve for the industry also have to be elastic? What if the firm's demand curve is inelastic?

Chapter 3

Finding target market opportunities with market segmentation

What This Chapter Is About

In this chapter you will learn how alert marketers find attractive market opportunities--ones that enable them to get a competitive advantage. Creatively defining a firm's markets (product-markets) can suggest many possibilities--and how to do this should be studied carefully. The focus is on how you can use market segmentation to identify possible target markets. Segmenting markets is vital to marketing strategy planning. You will also see how sophisticated segmentation approaches--like clustering and positioning--are used to make better market segmentation decisions.

To improve your understanding, try to apply the segmentation approach to a market in which you actually buy something. Then see how the dimensions in your own market segment affect the marketing mix which is offered to you. There is a logic to marketing strategy planning--marketing mixes flow directly from the characteristics of target markets. Try to get a feel for this interaction as you learn how to segment markets.

This chapter makes it clear why it is important to understand markets--and customers. In later chapters, you will build on this base--as you learn more about the demographic and behavioral dimensions of the consumer market and the buying behavior of intermediate customers.

This is a very important--if difficult--chapter, and deserves careful study. It is difficult because it requires *creative* thinking about markets--but this can also be a challenge, and help you learn how to find your own "breakthrough opportunity."

Important Terms

breakthrough opportunities, p. 67
competitive advantage, p. 67
market penetration, p. 68
market development, p. 68
product development, p. 68
diversification, p. 69
market, p. 69
generic market, p. 70
product-market, p. 70
market segmentation, p. 73
segmenting, p. 75

market segment, p. 75
single target market approach, p. 78
multiple target market approach, p. 78
combined target market approach, p. 78
combiners, p. 78
segmenters, p. 79
qualifying dimensions, p. 83
determining dimensions, p. 83
clustering techniques, p. 90
positioning, pp. 90-91

True-False Questions

_____ 1. Often, attractive opportunities are fairly close to markets the firm already knows and has some chance of doing something about--given its resources and objectives.

_____ 2. "Breakthrough opportunities" are ones which help innovators develop hard-to-copy marketing strategies that will be very profitable for a long time.

_____ 3. A firm with a "competitive advantage" has a marketing mix that the target market sees as better than a competitor's mix.

_____ 4. Marketing opportunities involving present markets and present products are called "market penetration" opportunities.

_____ 5. A "market development" opportunity would involve a firm offering new or improved products to its present markets.

_____ 6. When it comes to choosing among different types of opportunities, most firms tend to be production-oriented and usually think first of diversification.

_____ 7. A market consists of a group of potential customers with similar needs.

_____ 8. A generic market is a market with broadly similar needs and sellers offering various and often diverse ways of satisfying those needs.

_____ 9. A product-market is a market with very similar needs and sellers offering various close substitute ways of satisfying those needs.

_____ 10. A generic market description looks at markets narrowly--and from a producer's viewpoint.

_____ 11. A firm's "relevant market for finding opportunities" should be bigger than its present product-market--but not so big that the firm couldn't expand and be an important competitor in this market.

_____ 12. Just identifying the geographic boundaries of a firm's present market can suggest new marketing opportunities.

_____ 13. A generic market description should include both customer-related and product-related terms.

_____ 14. A segmenter is usually attempting to satisfy a sub-market with its own unique demand curve--and therefore must settle for a smaller sales potential than a combiner.

_____ 15. Customer-related segmenting dimensions are always more effective than situation-related dimensions.

_____ 16. When segmenting markets, "good" market segments are ones which are heterogeneous within, homogeneous between, substantial, and operational.

___ 17. The multiple target market approach combines two or more homogeneous sub-markets into one larger target market as a basis for one strategy.

___ 18. The determining dimensions may help identify the "core features" which will have to be offered to everyone in the broad product-market.

___ 19. Clustering techniques try to find similar patterns within sets of customer-related data.

___ 20. "Positioning" refers to a packaged goods manufacturer's efforts to obtain the best possible shelf or display location in retail stores.

___ 21. Positioning analysis is useful for combining but not for segmenting.

___ 22. The only way to "reposition" a product is to make some physical change in the product.

Answers to True-False Questions

1. T, pp. 66-67
2. T, p. 67
3. T, p. 67
4. T, p. 68
5. F, p. 68
6. F. p. 69
7. F, p. 69
8. T, p. 70

9. T, p. 70
10. F, p. 71
11. T, pp. 71-72
12. T, pp. 71-72
13. F, p. 72
14. T, p. 73
15. F, p. 73

16. F. pp. 76-77
17. F, p. 78
18. F, pp. 83-84
19. T, p. 90
20. F. pp. 90-91
21. F, p. 92
22. F, p. 91

Multiple-Choice Questions (Circle the correct response)

1. Breakthrough opportunities:

   a. are so rare that they should be pursued even when they do not match the firm's resources and objectives.
   b. seldom occur within or close to a firm's present markets.
   c. are especially important in our increasingly competitive markets.
   d. are those which a firm's competitors can copy quickly.
   e. are best achieved by trying to hold onto a firm's current market share.

2. When a firm tries to increase sales by selling its present products in new markets, this is called:

   a. market penetration.
   b. market development.
   c. product development.
   d. diversification.
   e. market integration.

3. A market consists of:

   a. a group of potential customers with similar needs.
   b. various kinds of products with similar characteristics.
   c. sellers offering substitute ways of satisfying needs.
   d. all the firms within a particular industry.
   e. both a and c.

4. A market in which sellers offer various close substitute ways of satisfying the market's needs is called a:

   a. generic.
   b. relevant market.
   c. product-market.
   d. central market.
   e. homogeneous market.

5. Which of the following is the best example of a "generic market"?

   a. The expensive ten-speed bicycle market.
   b. The Canadian college student creative expression market.
   c. The photographic market.
   d. The pet food market.
   e. The teen-age market.

6. A firm's "relevant market for finding opportunities":

   a. should be as large as possible.
   b. should have no geographic limits.
   c. should be no larger than its present product-market.
   d. should always be named in product-related terms.
   e. None of the above is a true statement.

7. Market segmentation:

   a. tries to find heterogeneous sub-markets within a market.
   b. means the same thing as marketing strategy planning.
   c. assumes that most sub-markets can be satisfied by the same marketing mix.
   d. assumes that any market is likely to consist of sub-markets.
   e. All of the above are true statements.

8. Naming broad product-markets is:

   a. an assorting process
   b. a disaggregating process
   c. a segmenting process
   d. an accumulating process
   e. an aggregating process

9. Segmenting:

   a. is essentially a disaggregating or "break it down" process.
   b. assumes that all customers can be grouped into homogeneous and profitable market segments.
   c. tries to aggregate together individuals who have similar needs and characteristics.
   d. usually results in firms aiming at smaller and less profitable markets.
   e. assumes that each individual should be treated as a separate target market.

10. "Good" market segments are those which are:

   a. heterogeneous within.
   b. operational.
   c. homogeneous between.
   d. substantial--meaning large enough to minimize operating costs.
   e. all of the above.

11. Having segmented its market, the Stuart Corp. has decided to treat each of two sub-markets as a separate target market requiring a different marketing mix. Apparently, Stuart is following the _____ target market approach.

   a. single
   b. combined
   c. multiple

12. Segmenting and combining are two alternate approaches to developing market-oriented strategies. Which of the following statements concerning these approaches is *true*?

   a. Combiners treat each sub-market as a separate target market.
   b. Segmenters try to develop a marketing mix that will have general appeal to several market segments.
   c. A combiner combines the demand curve in several markets into one demand curve.
   d. A segmenter assumes that the whole market consists of a fairly homogeneous group of customers.
   e. Both segmenters and combiners try to satisfy some people very well rather than a lot of people fairly well.

13. Customer-related (rather than situation-related) segmenting dimensions include:

    a. benefits offered.
    b. buying situation.
    c. brand familiarity.
    d. family life cycle.
    e. consumption or use patterns.

14. Which of the following types of dimensions would be the most important if one were particularly interested in why some target market was likely to buy a particular brand within a product-market?

    a. Primary dimensions
    b. Secondary dimensions
    c. Qualifying dimensions
    d. Determining dimensions
    e. Both a and c above.

15. Which of the following statements about clustering techniques is *true*?

    a. Clustering techniques try to find dissimilar patterns within sets of customer-related data.
    b. Computers are usually needed to search among all of the data for homogeneous groups of people.
    c. Computers identify the relevant dimensions and do the analysis.
    d. A cluster analysis of the toothpaste market indicated that most consumers seek the same benefits.
    e. All of the above are true.

16. "Positioning":

    a. involves a packaged-goods manufacturer's attempt to obtain the best possible shelf space for its products in retail outlets.
    b. is useful for segmenting but not combining.
    c. helps strategy planners see how customers view various brands or products in relation to each other.
    d. applies only to existing products, not new products.
    e. eliminates the need for subjective decision making in product planning.

17. "Positioning" is concerned with

    a. how current target customers view the products available from one company.
    b. how customers view the competing brands in a market.
    c. an analysis of the design strengths and weaknesses of products in a market.
    d. the economic factors that affect consumer choices among alternative brands.
    e. None of the above is true.

Answers to Multiple-Choice Questions

1. c, p. 67	7. d, p. 73	13. d, p. 82
2. b, p. 68	8. b, p. 74	14. d, pp. 83-84
3. e, p. 69	9. c, p. 75	15. c, p. 90
4. c, pp. 70-71	10. b, p. 77	16. c, pp. 90-91
5. b, p. 71	11. c, p. 78	17. b, p. 92
6. e, pp. 71-72	12. c, pp. 78-79	

Exercise 3-1

Product-markets vs. generic markets

Introduction

A practical first step in searching for breakthrough opportunities is to define the firm's present (or potential) markets. Markets consist of potential customers with similar needs and sellers offering various ways of satisfying those needs.

Markets can be defined very broadly or very narrowly--with either extreme being a potential threat to effective strategy planning. For example, defining its market too broadly as "transportation" could result in General Motors seeing itself in direct competition with manufacturers of airplanes, ships, elevators, bicycles, little red wagons, and perhaps even spaceships! On the other hand, a definition such as "the market for six-passenger motor vehicles with gasoline-powered internal-combustion engines" would be too narrow--and doesn't even identify "potential customers."

While there is no simple and automatic way to define a firm's *relevant* market, marketers should start by defining the relevant generic market and product-market using the 3 and 4 part definitions discussed on pages 70-72 of the text and shown below:

$$
\left.
\begin{array}{c}
\text{Generic} \\
\\
\text{Market Definitions}
\end{array}
\right\{
\begin{array}{c}
\text{Product Type} \\
+ \\
\text{Customer (User) Needs} \\
+ \\
\text{Customer Types} \\
+ \\
\text{Geographic Area}
\end{array}
\left.\right\}
\text{Product-Market Definition}
$$

It often requires a lot of creativity to think in terms of generic markets and product-markets--but failure to do so can cause strategy planners to overlook breakthrough opportunities--and leave themselves exposed to new forms of competition. Just ask the manufacturers of kerosene lamps, buggy whips, and mathematical slide rules!

Assignment

This exercise will give you some practice in naming product-markets and generic markets. It will also require you to be creative and apply your marketing intuition.

Listed below are several generic markets and brand-name products. Using the 3 and 4 part definitions of generic markets and product-markets, suggest possible market names in the blanks. Note: There are no "right answers," but they should be logical and consistent. Generic markets should *not* include any product-related terms. A generic market can have several related product-markets. And a product is offered to a product-market which is a part of a larger generic market. Question 1 is answered to help you get started.

1. Generic market: Security for families in the world

    a) Product-market: <u>Homeowner's insurance for financial security for home-owning families in the United States.</u>
    b) Product-market: <u>Guards for physical security for wealthy families in the world.</u>
    c) Product-market: <u>Smoke alarms for mental security for families in the developed countries.</u>

2. Generic market: Communications systems.

    a. Product-market: _____

    b. Product-market: _____

    c. Product-market: _____

3. Product: Duncan Hines chewy chocolate-chip cookies.

    a. Product-market: _____

    b. Product-market: _____

    c. Generic market: _____

4. Generic market: Entertainment for lower income individuals in Canada.

    a. Product-market: _____

    b. Product-market: _____

    c. Product-market: _____

5. Product: Calvin Klein (label on back pocket) jeans.

    a. Product-market: _____

    b. Product-market: _____

6. Product: Pioneer bi-fi stereo components (medium to high quality and price).

    a. Product-market: _____

    b. Product-market: _____

    c. Generic market: _____

Questions for Discussion

1. How can a firm decide which and how many markets to enter?

2. With the use of the product-market grid illustrated below, explain what strategies gourmet cookie companies in major cities might undertake due to problems of increased competition and decreased sales.

	Present Products	New Products
Present Markets	Market Penetration	Product Development
New Markets	Market Development	Diversification

Exercise 3-2

Using positioning to evaluate marketing opportunities

Introduction

Finding target market opportunities is a continuing challenge for all marketers. Understanding how customers view current or proposed market offerings is often a crucial part of this challenge. And understanding customer perceptions is more difficult when different segments of the market have different needs and different views of how well current or proposed products meet those needs. Developing insights requires that you try to answer questions such as: Are there customer segments with needs which no existing products are satisfying very well? Could our existing product be modified to do a better job of satisfying the needs of some segment? Could promotion be used to communicate to consumers about aspects of the product--so that target customers would "see" it in a different way?

There are no easy answers to such questions, but *positioning* approaches can help. As explained in the text (pp. 90-93), positioning uses marketing research techniques which measure customer views of products of brands according to several product features (e.g., do consumers think of a brand of detergent as "gentle" or "strong" relative to other brands?). Usually, customers are also asked to decide the amount of each feature that would be "ideal" (e.g., how strong a detergent do you want?).

The results are plotted on a two- or three-dimensional diagram--called a "product space." Each dimension represents a product feature which the customers feel is important. The diagram shows how each product or brand was rated on each of the dimensions. In other words, it shows how the various products or brands are "positioned" relative to each other--and relative to the "ideal" products or brands of different segments of customers. Usually, circles are used to show segments of customers with similar "ideal points" along the dimensions.

The mechanics of how all this is done are beyond the scope of this course. But you should know that positioning research techniques produce a very useful graphic aid to help marketing managers do their job better. Looking at a product space for a market, a marketing planner may see opportunities to "reposition" existing products or brands through product and/or promotion changes. Or he may spot an empty space which calls for the introduction of a new product. Often, he may be quite surprised to see that customer views of market offerings differ a great deal from his own ideas.

FIGURE 3-1
Product Space for Ready-to-Eat Breakfast Cereal

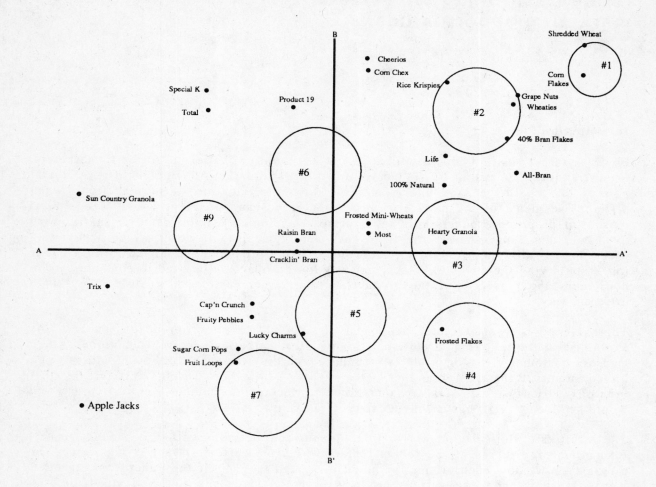

Assignment

Figure 3-1 is a fictional "product space" diagram for ready-to-eat breakfast cereal. The diagram shows how target customers rated several brands of cereal along two product dimensions which have been identified only as Dimension A and Dimension B. The diagram also shows 8 segments of customers grouped together on the basis of similar "ideal points." For example, customers in segment #8 desire very little of attribute B and a lot of attribute A.

1. a) Based on your interpretation of Figure 3-1, what product feature does Dimension AA' appear to represent?

    _____

    b) Based on your interpretation of Figure 3-1, what product feature does Dimension BB' appear to represent?

    _____

2. What opportunities for "repositioning" *existing* products do you see in Figure 3-1? Be specific, and indicate the segment(s) to which you want to target your appeal(s).

3. What opportunities for introducing *new* products do you see in Figure 3-1? Be specific, and indicate the segment(s) whose needs you would want to satisfy.

4. If you were interested in targeting customers in segment #8, which existing brands would be your most direct competitors?

5. If you were the marketing manager for Frosted Mini-Wheats brand cereal and you were thinking about using the combined target market approach to two different segments, which segments would be the likely target for your marketing strategy? Briefly explain your choice.

6. Are the two product dimensions shown in Figure 3-1 the two most important dimensions in choosing a brand of breakfast cereal? If not, what dimensions are most important?

7. Do all potential customers agree as to which two dimensions are the most important dimensions in choosing a brand of breakfast cereal? If not, what are the implications for using "positioning" as an aid in evaluating market opportunities?

Question for discussion

Is positioning an art or a science? Why?

Exercise 3-3
Segmenting multidimensional markets

Introduction

Marketing-oriented business managers realize that what is often considered as the mass market may actually consist of many smaller more homogeneous market segments. Thus, market segmentation becomes a crucial step in the development of a successful marketing strategy.

Market segmentation can be illustrated graphically through the use of "market grids." The grid approach pictures a market as a large box that is divided up into smaller boxes on the basis of the relevant needs and characteristics of potential customers. Each smaller box within the larger box represents a smaller, more homogeneous market segment--and a potential target market.

For example, a watch manufacturer who believed that sex and social class were the most relevant customer dimensions for his product-market might construct the following market grid.

FIGURE 3-2
Market Grid for the Watch Market

	Upper-Class	Middle-Class	Lower Class
Male			
Female			

In looking at Figure 3-2 however, you should keep in mind that sex and social class are only two of many possible dimensions that might be used to segment the watch market. As discussed in the text, possible segmenting dimensions include geographic dimensions, demographic dimensions, need or attitude dimensions, life-style dimensions, benefit dimensions, usage patterns, brand familiarity, and buying situations.

In other words, market segmentation is complicated by the fact that markets can be defined in many different ways. In keeping with the marketing concept, markets should be defined in terms of the needs and characteristics of potential customers. But this still remains a difficult task because customers are *multi-dimensional* and typically display many similarities and differences--only some of which may be relevant for a particular market situation.

The task of deciding which dimensions are relevant for segmenting a particular market is further complicated by the need to distinguish between qualifying and determining dimensions. *Qualifying dimensions* include *any factors which qualify one as a potential customer*, while *determining dimensions* include only those factors which *determine which type of product or even which brand may be purchased*. For example, any person who needs to know the correct time and can afford the price of a watch presumably would qualify as a potential customer. But these dimensions would not be sufficient to determine which type of watch (e.g., calendar watch, digital watch, pocket watch, etc.) or which brand a person might purchase.

This exercise is designed to familiarize you with some of the different types of dimensions that are often used to segment markets--and to emphasize the need for considerable management judgment in deciding which dimensions are most relevant for a particular market.

FIGURE 3-3
Alternative Market Grids for the Canadian Breakfast Food Market

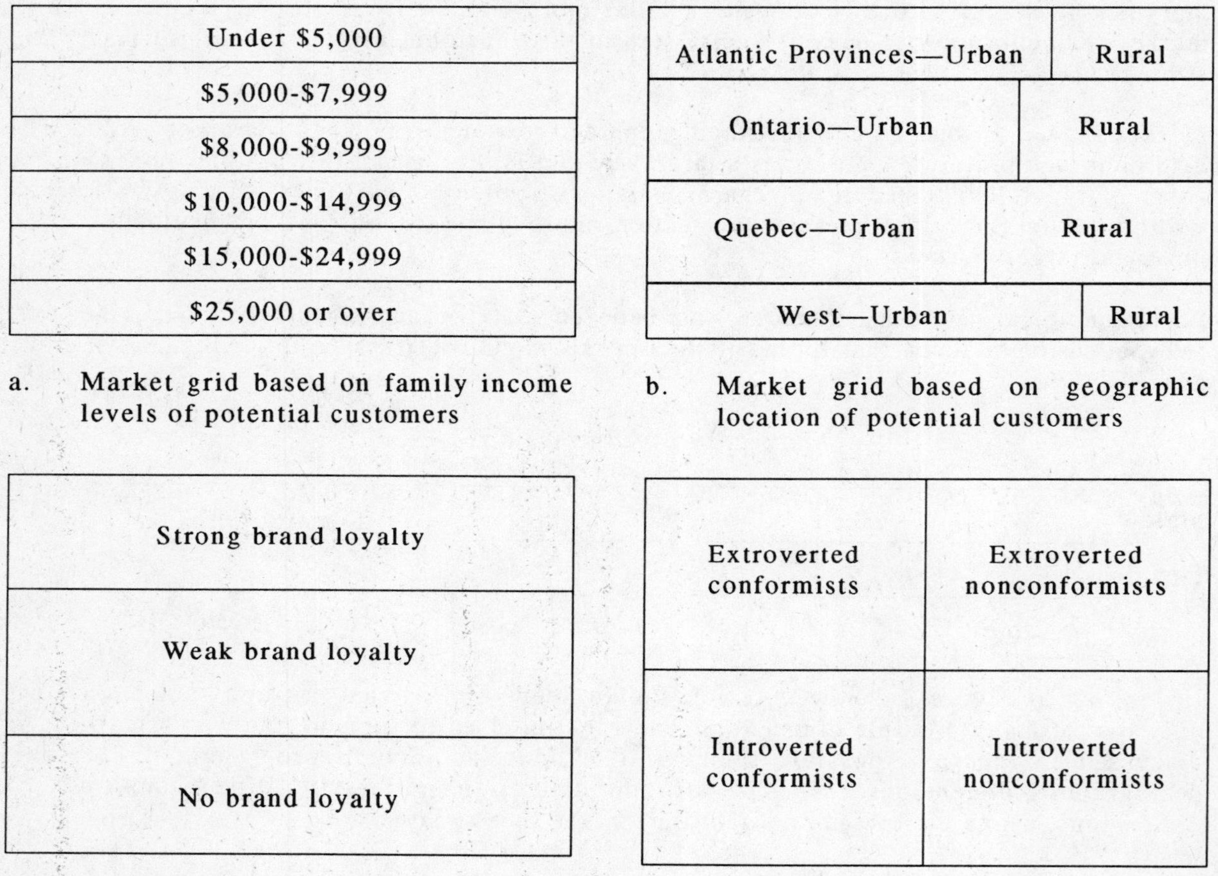

Under $5,000
$5,000-$7,999
$8,000-$9,999
$10,000-$14,999
$15,000-$24,999
$25,000 or over

a. Market grid based on family income levels of potential customers

Atlantic Provinces—Urban	Rural
Ontario—Urban	Rural
Quebec—Urban	Rural
West—Urban	Rural

b. Market grid based on geographic location of potential customers

Strong brand loyalty
Weak brand loyalty
No brand loyalty

c. Market grid based on "brand loyalty" of potential customers

Extroverted conformists	Extroverted nonconformists
Introverted conformists	Introverted nonconformists

d. Market grid based on personality traits of potential customers

Harried Commuters	Working Mothers
Snack Servers	Calorie Counters

e. Market grid based on potential customers' needs and benefits sought*

Harried commuters—Busy career people who need a source of energy and nutrition—but who don't have time to prepare and eat a complete breakfast.

Working mothers—The women whose work schedules prevent them from making sure their children eat a full and nutritious breakfast.

Snack servers—Homemakers who see to it that their children eat a full and balanced breakfast—but who also want to provide them with nutritious and good-tasting snacks.

Calorie counters—Dieters looking for tasty, filling, and nutritious meal substitutes.

Assignment

Assume that you are the marketing manager for a firm that is about to introduce a new instant breakfast food which is considered superior to anything already on the market in terms of taste and convenience. The product comes in a relatively expensive multiple-unit package, looks and tastes like a chocolate brownie, requires no preparation, and can be used either as a nutritious meal substitute, a snack, or a diet food.

As marketing manager, it is your job to develop a successful marketing strategy for the new product--starting with the selection of a target market. Therefore, you have asked your marketing research staff to analyze the breakfast food market and describe the various market segments that make up the overall market. However, as it turned out, there was considerable disagreement among the researchers as to which dimensions should be used to segment the market. Unable to reach any consensus among themselves, they therefore submitted five different market grids for the breakfast food market--as shown in Figure 3-3.

1. Of the five market grids shown in Figure 3-3, which one do you think would be most relevant and effective for segmenting the breakfast food market? Why?

2. Given your answer to Question 1, which of the following approaches would you recommend in selecting a target market for the instant breakfast food: (a) the single target market approach, (b) the multiple target market approach, or (c) the combined target market approach? In answering this question, specify your recommended target market and explain why.

Question for Discussion

What criteria should marketing managers use to judge whether or not the segmenting dimensions they are using are relevant and effective for marketing strategy planning?

Chapter 4

Evaluating opportunities in uncontrollable environments

What This Chapter Is About

In the last chapter, you learned that finding opportunities takes a real understanding of customers. But marketing managers can not select target markets or plan strategies in a vacuum. Uncontrollable environments affect the attractiveness of possible opportunities. And opportunities need to be carefully evaluated and screened--to identify the really attractive ones.

A company's objectives can guide this process--and its resources may limit the search for opportunities, or alternatively give the firm a competitive advantage.

This chapter treats the competitive environment in some depth (building on the economic concepts reviewed in Appendix A, which follows Chapter 2). The marketing manager can't control competitors--but he can try to avoid head-on competition--or plan for it when it is inevitable.

The economic and technological environment can change rapidly. These shifts may require changes in marketing strategies.

The political and legal environment is given special attention because of its possible impact on the marketing manager. Further, the evolution of legislative thinking is outlined as a foundation for discussion in later chapters.

The cultural and social environment concerns the number of people and how they live and behave. A marketing manager must understand his markets--and cultural and social environments affect the way people buy.

Finding *attractive* opportunities requires screening and evaluation--and various approaches are presented towards the end of the chapter.

Important Terms

competitive environment, p. 103
pure competition, p. 104
equilibrium price, p. 104
oligopoly, p. 105
monopolistic competition, p. 106
economic and technological
    environment, p. 107

technological base, p. 110
consumerism, p. 112
cultural and social environment, p. 118
strategic business unit (SBU), p. 125
portfolio management, p. 125

True-False Questions

____ 1. Consumerism is a social movement seeking to give sellers as much power and legal rights as buyers and consumers.

____ 2. Canada has not been as ideologically committed as the United States to protecting either competition or the existence of a large number of small firms.

____ 3. A business firm's only objective should be to earn enough profit to survive.

____ 4. Trying to maximize short-run return on investment may not be good in the long run.

____ 5. Winning a larger market share necessarily leads to greater profitability.

____ 6. Company objectives should lead to a hierarchy of marketing objectives.

____ 7. Attractive opportunities should make use of a firm's resources and its unique strengths.

____ 8. A large producer with economies of scale always has a competitive advantage over smaller firms.

____ 9. A patent owner has a 20-year monopoly to develop and use its new product, process, or material as it sees fit.

____ 10. Although the marketing manager cannot control the competitive environment, he can choose strategies that will avoid head-on situations.

____ 11. In pure competition, both the industry demand curve and the individual firm's demand curve are horizontal.

____ 12. Except for oligopolies, most industries tend to become more competitive--that is, move toward pure competition.

____ 13. Oligopoly situations develop when a market has a few sellers of essentially homogeneous products and a fairly elastic industry demand curve.

____ 14. In oligopoly situations, individual firms are faced with a "kinked" demand curve.

____ 15. In monopolistic competition, there is only one seller and that seller has complete control over the price of its unique product.

____ 16. The technological base includes the technical skills and equipment which affect the way the resources of an economy are converted to output.

____ 17. Changes in the technological environment could be rejected by the cultural and social environment--through the political and legal environment--even though such changes might help the economic environment.

____ 18. Nationalism may affect marketing strategy planning by determining to whom and how much a firm may sell.

___ 19. The political environment may either block or promote new marketing opportunities.

___ 20. Recent trends indicate a major shift in traditional thinking about buyer-seller relations from "let the seller beware" to "let the buyer beware."

___ 21. Because the cultural and social environment tends to change slowly, firms should try to identify and work with cultural attitudes rather than trying to encourage big changes in the short run.

___ 22. Product-market screening criteria should be mainly quantitative in nature, because qualitative criteria are too subjective.

___ 23. Forecasts of the probable results of implementing whole strategic plans are needed to apply quantitative screening criteria.

___ 24. The profit potentials of alternative strategic plans can be evaluated at the same time only if the plans are very similar.

___ 25. The General Electric "strategic planning grid" forces company managers to make three-part judgments (high, medium, and low) about the business strengths and industry attractiveness of all proposed or existing products of businesses.

___ 26. The G.E. "stop-light" evaluation method is a very objective approach because G.E. feels there are too many possible errors if it tries to use subjective criteria for judging "attractiveness" or "strength."

___ 27. The G.E. approach favors opportunities which are high in industry attractiveness and low in business strengths over opportunities which are high in business strengths and low in industry attractiveness.

___ 28. SBU's are small businesses which try to compete with major divisions of larger multiproduct companies.

___ 29. Portfolio management tends to emphasize current profitability and return on investment, often neglecting the long run.

Answers to True-False Questions

1. T, p. 112	11. F, p. 104	21. T, p. 118
2. T, p. 113	12. T, p. 105	22. F, p. 121
3. F, p. 98	13. F, p. 105	23. T, p. 122
4. T, p. 99	14. T, p. 105	24. F, p. 122
5. F, p. 100	15. F, p. 106	25. T, p. 123
6. T, p. 100	16. T, p. 110	26. F, p. 124
7. T, pp. 100-101	17. T, p. 111	27. F, p. 124
8. F, pp. 101-102	18. T, p. 113	28. F. p. 125
9. F, p. 102	19. T. p. 113	29. T. pp. 125-126
10. T, p. 103	20. F, p. 117	

Multiple-Choice Questions (Circle the correct response)

1. In the short run at least, which of the following is usually *beyond* the control of the marketing manager?

   a. Political and legal environment
   b. Economic and technological environment
   c. Cultural and social environment
   d. Competitive environment
   e. All of the above.

2. The recent decline in the Canadian birth rate has forced manufacturers of baby food, clothing, and toys to reconsider their marketing strategies. Which of the following uncontrollable variables does this trend illustrate?

   a. Economic and technological environment
   b. Cultural and social environment
   c. Existing business situation
   d. Political and legal environment
   e. Resources and objectives of the firm

3. Which of the following was *not* included in Bill C2?

   a. Existing federally-incorporated cooperatives were provided with a legal framework.
   b. Matters pertaining to competition policy were brought under civil jurisdiction.
   c. Protection for the consumer in the area of warranties was increased.
   d. Services were brought under the Combines Investigation Act.
   e. Bid-rigging was made an indictable offense.

4. In Canada, provincial and city laws are in existence to regulate:

   a. minimum prices and the setting of prices.
   b. the conditions necessary for setting up a business.
   c. the granting of credit.
   d. the rights of the consumer against deceptive trade practices.
   e. all of the above.

5. The purpose of provincial "trade practices" legislation is to:

   a. reduce price-cutting practices at the retail level.
   b. protect consumers from price-discrimination practices.
   c. create inter-provincial standards for trade practices.
   d. protect the consumer from unconscionable and deceptive practices.
   e. allow price-fixing arrangements between manufacturers and small retailers.

6. Which of the following objectives of a business is the *most* important?

   a. To engage in some specific business activity which will perform a socially and economically useful function.
   b. To develop an organization to carry on the business and implement its strategies.
   c. To earn enough profit to survive.
   d. All three of the above are equally important, because a failure in any one could lead to a total failure of the business.

7. Of the following, the *last* objectives that a firm should specify are its:

   a. company objectives.
   b. marketing objectives.
   c. promotion objectives.
   d. advertising objectives.
   e. price objectives.

8. A first step in evaluating marketing opportunities is to:

   a. decide which markets the firm wishes to enter.
   b. consider the objectives and resources of the firm.
   c. hire a "futurist" as a marketing consultant.
   d. estimate market and sales potentials.
   e. find out if potential competitors are larger.

9. In which of the following situations would an individual firm be most likely to face a horizontal demand curve?

   a. Oligopoly
   b. Pure competition
   c. Monopoly
   d. Monopolistic competition
   e. None of the above--demand is always downward sloping.

10. Oligopoly situations are generally characterized by:

    a. essentially heterogeneous products.
    b. relatively few sellers, or a few large firms and perhaps many smaller firms.
    c. fairly elastic industry demand.
    d. a and b above--but not c.
    e. All of the above.

11. In an oligopoly situation:

    a. an individual firm's demand is inelastic above the "kink" and elastic below the kink.
    b. the market price is usually somewhere above the "kink."
    c. price wars usually increase profits for all competitors.
    d. price fluctuations may occur despite the kinked demand curve faced by each firm.
    e. All of the above are true statements.

12. A particular market is characterized by different (heterogeneous) products in the eyes of some customers and sellers who feel they do face some competition. This product-market is an example of:

    a. oligopoly.
    b. monopoly.
    c. monopolistic competition.

13. Which of the following statements about the competitive environment is *true*?

    a. The industry demand curve in a pure competition situation is horizontal.
    b. Monopolistic competition is characterized by downsloping demand curves due to the lack of any substitute products.
    c. In a pure competition situation, an individual firm is faced with a very inelastic demand curve.
    d. Since a monopolistic competitor has a downsloping demand curve just like a pure monopolist, it has some control over its price.
    e. All of the above are true statements.

14. Which of the following is *not* an example of how the economic and technological environment may affect marketing strategy planning?

    a. The price of bicycles is rising because of inflation.
    b. Bicycle manufacturers are finding it difficult to keep up with the growing demand for bicycles because of raw material shortages.
    c. Because of exchange rates, imported bikes are cheaper than those made in Canada.
    d. Computer-controlled assembly lines can turn out a new bike every three and one-half seconds.
    e. The demand for bikes is increasing because consumers are becoming more health conscious.

15. The recent interest in physical fitness has forced producers of food, clothing, and other products to reconsider their marketing strategies. Which of the following uncontrollable variables does this trend illustrate?

    a. economic and technological environment.
    b. cultural and social environment.
    c. existing business situation.
    d. political and legal environment.
    e. resources and objectives of the firm.

16. Product-market screening criteria should be:

    a. quantitative.
    b. qualitative.
    c. realistic and achievable.
    d. all of the above.
    e. all of the above *except* b.

17. Which of the following is a quantitative screening criteria?

    a. increase sales by $100,000.
    b. earn 25 percent return on investment.
    c. break even within one year.
    d. all of the above are quantitative criteria.

18. General Electric's "strategic planning grid":

    a. substitutes precise quantitative estimates for management judgment and intuition.
    b. places too much emphasis on industry attractiveness, almost ignoring the firm's own business strengths.
    c. emphasizes market share and market growth rate.
    d. is oversimplified in that it assumes all opportunities must be either "good" or "bad."
    e. None of the above is a true statement.

19. GE's Planning Grid approach to evaluating proposed and existing plans and businesses

   a. considers how profitable opportunities are likely to be.
   b. reflects the corporation's objectives.
   c. helps managers see why some ideas are supported and others are not.
   d. can use quantitative data but it is basically a qualitative approach.
   e. All of the above are true.

20. Organizational units within a larger company which focus their efforts on selected product-markets and are treated as separate profit centers are called:

   a. portfolios.
   b. strategic business units.
   c. BTUs.
   d. functional departments.
   e. basing points.

Answers to Multiple-Choice Questions

1. e, p. 98	8. b, p. 98	15. b, p. 120
2. b, pp. 118-120	9. b, p. 104	16. d, p. 122
3. a, pp. 114-115	10. b, p. 105	17. d, p. 122
4. c, p. 115-116	11. d, p. 105	18. e, p. 123
5. d, p. 115-116	12. c, p. 106	19. e, p. 123
6. d, p. 98	13. d, p. 106	20. b, p. 125
7. d, pp. 98-99	14. e, p. 107	

Exercise 4-1

How uncontrollable variables affect marketing strategy planning

Introduction

Marketing managers are not free to choose *any* marketing strategy they please. On the contrary, their choice of strategies is usually affected by variables related to the:

1. Cultural and social environment
2. Economic and technological environment
3. Competitive environment
4. Political and legal environment
5. Resources and objectives of the firm

These variables are called "uncontrollable" because, in the short run, they are beyond the control of marketing managers--although in the long run, marketing managers may be able to influence some or all of these variables.

In the short run, at least, these uncontrollable variables may force marketing managers to change their present strategies--or even to choose less-than-ideal strategies. On the other hand, trends in the uncontrollable environments often create new opportunities for alert marketing strategy planners.

Assignment

This exercise is intended to stimulate your thinking about how uncontrollable variables such as the cultural and social environment, economic and technological environment, or the political and legal environment might affect marketing strategy planning. More emphasis on how the competitive environment plays a role is analyzed in the following exercise of this chapter. Read and answer each of the following questions.

1. The number of single-adult households in Canada continues to increase. This has had a big impact on some industries. How do you think a food manufacturer's marketing strategy might be influenced by this trend?

    _____

    _____

    _____

2. The economic environment also affects the choices made in marketing strategy planning. A marketing manager must attempt to anticipate, understand and deal with such changes, as well as changes in the technological base underlying this economic environment. Compare and contrast the marketing strategies of firms facing the following situations:

    a. The manufacturer of Mercedes Benz cars during a recession versus a period of economic growth.

    b. A chain grocery store during a recession versus a period of economic growth.

    c. A fashion designer in a recession versus a period of economic growth.

3. In recent years, various federal and local agencies, environmental groups, and consumer advocates have been promoting greater concern for the environmental impact of solid waste, especially disposable products and packaging. Consequently, many communities now have active "recycling" programs, and some consumers have begun to switch away from products or packages that are not biodegradable. What effect do you think these trends might have on the marketing efforts of a fast-food restaurant? On a consumer package goods company like Procter and Gamble?

4. Choices made in marketing strategy planning are also affected by aspects of the political and legal environments.

    a. In the past decade, the government of Quebec issued a law prohibiting advertisements directed at children. Describe how this change would affect the marketing strategy planning of a firm such as Fischer-Price in Quebec?

    b. How would it affect the marketing strategy of a cereal manufacturer in the same province?

5. Comment on the purpose of the Consumer Packaging and Labeling Act. Do you agree with the viewpoint that Canadian consumers are rational and capable of deciding what are deceptive marketing activities without government interference? Justify your position.

Question for Discussion

How can marketers deal effectively with changing trends and developments in their uncontrollable environments?

Exercise 4-2

Analyzing the competitive environment

Introduction

Marketing managers do not always enjoy a full range of alternatives when planning a marketing mix. Their choices may be largely determined by the nature of the competitive environment.

For example, a firm might be able to use almost any marketing mix in a *pure monopoly* situation, while a firm's mix might be entirely determined by market forces in a *pure competition* situation. In an *oligopoly* situation, a firm would have some control over its marketing mix, but it might find it difficult to differentiate its product and any price-cutting could lead to a "price-war." Of course, most firms find themselves in a *monopolistic competition* situation where their control over their marketing mix can range from a lot to a little--depending on how competitive the monopolistic competition is.

It is not always easy to identify the nature of a firm's competitive environment. In general, one must consider many factors--besides just the number and size of competitors.

Perhaps the most important factor is how the target market is defined--an important topic discussed in Chapter 3. Other factors that should be considered include: (a) the similarity of competing products and marketing mixes--as seen by the target customers, (b) barriers to entry for new firms, and (c) seller concentration--(i.e., the extent to which a few large sellers control the bulk of industry sales).

Assignment

This exercise will give you some practice in analyzing the competitive environment. Read the following cases carefully and for each of them:

a)   Indicate the nature of the competitive environment, taking into consideration the probable target market.

   Use the following terms to identify the nature of competition: Pure competition, monopolistic competition, monopoly, and oligopoly.

Note: The term "monopolistic competition" can be used to describe situations ranging from near-monopoly to almost pure competition. Try to distinguish between "moderately competitive monopolistic competition" situations and those which may be "extremely" or only "slightly" competitive--by labeling the latter as either "monopolistic competition approaching pure monopoly" or "monopolistic competition approaching pure competition."

b)   Briefly explain your answer, taking into account the various factors which were discussed above.

The first case has been answered for you as an example.

1.   Don's Truck Stop is a combination gasoline station-restaurant-motel which caters to long-distance truck drivers. It is located at the intersection of two major highways near a city of about 150,000 people. There are no other truck stops in the immediate area.

   a)   Nature of competition: <u>Monopolistic competition approaching pure monopoly.</u>

   b)   Explanation: <u>Although Don's Truck Stop probably gets a large share of the long-distance truckers' business, it does not have a pure monopoly because truckers can go into the city or on to the next truck stop. Further, there is nothing to prevent a potential competitor from locating nearby--which may very well happen if Don's is enjoying unusually high profits.</u>

2.   Tom Knappe is one of the thousands of farmers who grow large crops of sunflower seeds to use in making cooking oil, baked goods, and snack foods--as well as for birdfeeding. Tom's crop is just a very small fraction of the nation's total crop of sunflower seeds. But like other farmers, he has increased the size of his crop in recent years as increasing demand has raised market prices. Now he plans to increase his crop even more, given the strong likelihood of rising international demand for sunflower seeds.

   a)   Nature of competition: _____

   b)   Explanation: _____

   _____

   _____

   _____

3.   Among the many passing trends in Canada is the once-common practice of using store-front symbols, such as the pharmacist's familiar mortar and pestle, to identify various types of merchants and craftsmen. Rapidly becoming extinct, for example, are the red, white, and blue barber poles which once adorned the front of virtually every barbershop in the country. Many barbers (or "hairstylists" as some now refer to themselves) are now opting for more individualized store signs or relying mainly on telephone directories and printed business cards to promote their businesses. Consequently, a once-prosperous industry has all but faded away, and today the Marvy Company in Hamilton is the only remaining firm in all of Canada that still manufactures barber poles. Marvy has managed to stay in business by producing several modern styles of barber poles in addition to the one standard style which used to be the proud symbol of all barbers.

   a)   Nature of competition: _____

b) Explanation: _____

_____

_____

_____

_____

_____

4. The Toronto metropolitan area is supplied by five regional manufacturers of bricks. The bricks are used in constructing homes and office buildings as well as for other purposes (decorative walls, patios). Three of these firms account for more than 80 percent of all the bricks sold in the area. The bricks are purchased either in standardized sizes or according to buyer specifications, and all five firms charge almost identical prices. When bricks are in short supply, a few buyers have purchased some bricks from other firms located outside the region, but high transportation costs make this an extremely expensive alternative. Two manufacturers have announced plans to boost their production capacity, and all five manufacturers have announced price increases of at least 6 percent for the coming year.

a) Nature of competition: _____

b) Explanation: _____

_____

_____

_____

_____

5. Racket World, Inc. operates the only privately-owned indoor racket ball court facility in Mason City--a northern city with a population of 340,000. It runs a full program of racket ball lessons, tournaments, and public play. It is also the "sponsor" of local "high school racket ball"--trading practice time for a share of the gate. Its only "indoor" competition is from the state university courts--which are only three miles away. The university athletic department does not run competing programs--because its primary role is to serve the students and intramural teams. However, it does have a large amount of "extra time" and regularly sells blocks of time to groups (for example, businessmen who come to town for conferences at local hotels). The athletic department usually charges such groups prices that are below Racket World's prices (by 10-40 percent) and probably way below its variable costs of operating the facility.

a)Nature of competition: _____

b)   Explanation: _____

_____

_____

_____

Question for Discussion

Have the firms described in the above cases achieved any "competitive advantage" over their competitors? If not, what steps might they take in the future to achieve some competitive advantage?

Chapter 5

Getting information for marketing decisions

What This Chapter Is About

Marketing managers need information to plan effective marketing strategies. Chapter 5 stresses that getting good information for marketing decisions involves much more than just surveys.

Many managers now rely on marketing information systems to help meet their recurring information needs. But marketing managers must also deal with ever-changing needs in dynamic markets. So you should understand how marketing research can help marketing managers solve problems--and make better decisions.

A scientific approach to marketing research is explained and illustrated. This approach can help marketing managers solve problems--not just collect data.

This chapter also shows that the text's strategy planning framework is especially helpful in identifying marketing problems. This framework, along with a "scientific approach," can be very helpful in solving real problems. Often, small bits of information available *now* are far more valuable than an extensive research report which cannot be available for several months.

Try to understand how to go about a scientific approach to problem solving--just finding the right problem is sometimes half the job. This is something you should be able to do by the end of the text--even though you do not have all the tools and skills needed to do a formal research project. Specialists can be hired to do that part of the job if you--as the marketing manager--have correctly identified what information is needed to make the marketing strategy decisions.

Important Terms

marketing information system (MIS), p. 131
decision support system (DSS), p. 132
marketing model, p. 132
marketing research, p. 134
scientific method, p. 135
hypotheses, p. 135
marketing research process, p. 135
situation analysis, p. 137
secondary data, p. 138
primary data, p. 138
research proposal, p. 139

qualitative research, p. 140
focus group interview, p. 140
quantitative research, p. 140
response rate, p. 142
experimental method, p. 144
statistical packages, p. 145
population, p. 145
sample, p. 145
random sampling, p. 146
confidence interval, p. 146
validity, p. 148

True-False Questions

_____ 1. A marketing information system is an organized way of using "one-shot" research projects to gather and analyze information that will help marketing managers make better decisions.

_____ 2. The key advantage in using an MIS is that it makes available information accessible.

_____ 3. A decision support system (DSS) is a computer program that makes it easy for a marketing manager to get and use information as he is making decisions.

_____ 4. Decision support systems that include marketing models allow the manager to see how answers to questions might change in various situations.

_____ 5. Marketing research is best defined as a set of techniques applied by specialists in survey design or statistical methods.

_____ 6. Marketing research details may be handled by staff or outside specialists, but the marketing manager must know how to plan and evaluate research projects.

_____ 7. The scientific method is a decision-making approach that focuses on being objective and orderly in testing ideas before accepting them.

_____ 8. Hypotheses are statements of fact about relationships between things or what will happen in the future.

_____ 9. The marketing research process is a five-step application of the scientific method that includes: defining the problem, analyzing the situation, getting problem-specific data, interpreting the data, and solving the problem.

_____ 10. Defining the problem--although usually the easiest job of the marketing researcher--is also the most important job.

_____ 11. Developing a list that includes all possible problem areas is a sensible start to the situation analysis step.

_____ 12. Gathering primary data about the problem area is part of analyzing the situation.

_____ 13. Secondary data is information which is already collected or published.

_____ 14. _The Canada Year Book_ is a good source of primary data.

_____ 15. A written research proposal is a plan that specifies what marketing research information will be obtained and how.

_____ 16. The two basic methods for obtaining information about customers are questioning and observing.

_____ 17. Qualitative research seeks in-depth, open-ended responses.

_____ 18. A focus group interview involves interviewing 6 to 10 people in an informal group setting.

_____ 19. It is typical to use quantitative research in preparation for doing qualitative research.

_____ 20. Quantitative research seeks structured responses that can be summarized in numbers--like percentages, averages, or other statistics.

_____ 21. A common quantitative research approach to summarize consumers' opinions and preferences is to have respondents indicate how much they agree or disagree with a questionnaire statement.

_____ 22. The response rate is the percent of people contacted who complete a questionnaire.

_____ 23. Mail surveys are economical per questionnaire--if a large number of people respond.

_____ 24. A mail survey is the best research approach if you want respondents to expand on particular points and give in-depth information.

_____ 25. With the observation method, the researcher avoids talking to the subject.

_____ 26. The use of computer scanners to observe what customers actually do is changing research methods for many firms.

_____ 27. With the experimental method, the responses of groups which are similar, except on the characteristic being tested, are compared.

_____ 28. The experimental method is the most widely used marketing research method because managers want and need quantitative information to make better decisions.

_____ 29. Statistical packages are easy-to-use computer programs that help analyze data.

_____ 30. In regard to marketing research, *population* means the total group that responds to a survey.

_____ 31. In most marketing research studies, only a sample--a part of the relevant population--is surveyed.

_____ 32. Random sampling is sampling in which each member of the population does not have the same chance of being included in the sample.

_____ 33. With random samples, researchers can narrow confidence intervals by increasing sample sizes.

___34. Validity concerns the extent to which data measures what it is intended to measure.

___35. Conducting and interpreting a marketing research project should be left entirely to the researcher because most marketing managers have no training in this area.

___36. One should always seek to obtain as much marketing information as possible before making a decision.

Answers to True-False Questions

1. F, p. 131	13. T, p. 138	25. T, p. 142
2. T, p. 132	14. F, p. 138	26. T, p. 143
3. T, p. 132	15. T, p. 139	27. T, p. 144
4. T, p. 132	16. T, pp. 139-140	28. F, p. 144
5. F, p. 134	17. T, p. 140	29. T, p. 145
6. T, p. 134	18. T, p. 140	30. F, p. 145
7. T, p. 135	19. F, p. 140	31. T, p. 145
8. F, p. 135	20. T, p. 140	32. F, p. 146
9. T, pp. 135-136	21. T, p. 141	33. T, p. 146
10. F, p. 136	22. T, p. 142	34. T, p. 148
11. T, p. 137	23. T, p. 142	35. F, p. 148
12. F, p. 138	24. F, p. 142	36. F, p. 149

Multiple-Choice Questions (Circle the correct response)

1. Which of the following statements about marketing information systems is *true*?

   a. Marketing information systems are used to gather and analyze data from intracompany sources, while marketing research deals with external sources.
   b. Most firms can or could generate more market-related data than they could possibly use.
   c. Computerized marketing information systems tend to increase the quantity of information available for decision making but not without some corresponding decrease in quality.
   d. The value of decision support systems is limited because the manager can't use them while he is actually making his decisions.
   e. All of the above are true statements.

2. Marketing research:

   a. requires a market research department in the company.
   b. consists mainly of survey design and statistical techniques.
   c. should be planned by research specialists.
   d. is needed to keep isolated marketing planners in touch with their markets.
   e. All of the above are true.

3. In small companies,

    a. there is no need for marketing research.
    b. there should be a marketing research department--or there will be no one to do marketing research.
    c. the emphasis of marketing research should be on customer surveys.
    d. salespeople often do what marketing research gets done.

4. The scientific method is important in marketing research because it:

    a. forces the researcher to follow certain procedures, thereby reducing the need to rely on intuition.
    b. develops hypotheses and then tests them.
    c. specifies a marketing strategy which is almost bound to succeed.
    d. Both a and b are correct.
    e. All of the above are correct.

5. The most important--and often the most difficult step--of the marketing research process is:

    a. analyzing the situation.
    b. collecting data.
    c. observation.
    d. defining the problem.
    e. interpreting the data.

6. When analyzing the situation, the marketing analyst:

    a. sizes up the situation by talking with executives in competitive companies.
    b. seeks information that is already available in the problem area.
    c. begins to talk informally to a random sample of customers.
    d. talks to experts in data analysis at trade association meetings.
    e. All of the above.

7. A small manufacturing firm has just experienced a rapid drop in sales. The marketing manager thinks that he knows what the problem is and has been carefully analyzing secondary data to check his thinking. His next step should be to:

    a. conduct an experiment.
    b. develop a formal research project to gather primary data.
    c. conduct informal discussion with outsiders, including middlemen, to see if he has correctly defined the problem.
    d. develop a hypothesis and predict the future behavior of sales.
    e. initiate corrective action before sales drop any further.

8. Which of the following is a good source for locating secondary data:

    a. a focus group interview.
    b. personal interviews with customers.
    c. *the Canada Year Book*.
    d. a marketing research survey.
    e. none of the above.

9. A marketing analyst would *not* use which of the following research methods when gathering primary data?

   a. Observation
   b. Experiment
   c. Mail survey
   d. Library search
   e. Personal interviews

10. With regard to getting problem-specific data:

   a. the observation method involves asking consumers direct questions about their observations.
   b. telephone surveys are declining in popularity.
   c. focus group interviews are usually more representative than a set of personal interviews.
   d. mail surveys are limited to short, simple questions--extensive questioning cannot be done.
   e. None of the above is a true statement.

11. To be effective, marketing research should be:

   a. quantitative.
   b. qualitative.
   c. either or both--depending on the situation.

12. Experimental method research:

   a. is often hard to use in "real world" markets.
   b. always uses observing rather than questioning.
   c. is more popular than focus group interviews.
   d. is used to compare groups for differences.
   e. all of the above.

13. A statistical package is most likely to be used for a marketing research project that:

   a. used focus group interviews.
   b. relied on secondary data.
   c. included a mail survey.
   d. consisted of open-ended questions in a personal interview.
   e. was based on qualitative research.

14. Using random samples:

   a. guarantees that the findings will be valid.
   b. is stressed by theoretical statisticians--but usually is unnecessary in marketing research.
   c. guarantees that the sample will have the same characteristics as the population.
   d. allows the researcher to use confidence intervals to evaluate estimates from the sample data.
   e. All of the above are true statements.

15. At the step when data are interpreted, a marketing manager should:

    a. leave it to the technical specialists to draw the correct conclusions.
    b. realize that statistical summaries from a sample may not be precise for the whole population.
    c. know that quantitative survey responses are valid, but qualitative research may not be valid.
    d. be satisfied with the sample used as long as it is large.
    e. All of the above are correct.

16. Which of the following statements about marketing research is *false*?

    a. A low response rate may affect the accuracy of results.
    b. You never can get all of the information which might be useful.
    c. Getting more or better information is not always worth the cost.
    d. Because of the risks involved, marketing managers should never base their decision on incomplete information.
    e. A marketing manager should evaluate *beforehand* whether research findings will be relevant.

Answers to Multiple-Choice Questions

1. b, p. 131	7. c, p. 138	13. c, p. 145
2. d, p. 134	8. c, p. 138	14. d, p. 146
3. d, p. 134	9. d, p. 138	15. b, p. 145
4. d, p. 135	10. e, pp. 139-140	16. d, p. 149
5. d, p. 136	11. c, p. 140	
6. b, p. 138	12. e, p. 144	

Exercise 5-1

Problem definition in marketing research

Introduction

Perhaps the most important step in researching a marketing problem is defining the problem correctly. The marketing manager must clearly define the problem to be researched before the marketing researcher can develop an effective research design. This means that the marketing manager should direct the efforts of the researcher, rather than simply asking for some "marketing research" when a problem arises.

The strategic planning framework that is used throughout the text can be of great help in defining marketing problems. (See pages 38-40 of the text.) For instance, the problem may be caused by rapid changes in the uncontrollable variables--especially the economic, competitive, or legal environments--or the firm may have lost sight of its objectives. The problem could also be that the firm has neglected to select a target market, or that the needs and attitudes of its target market have changed. Finally, one or more of the "four Ps" may be inappropriate for the rest of the marketing mix.

Where more than one problem has been identified, it is generally desirable to start with the broadest or highest level problems. For example, a marketing manager should not be concerned with strategy planning until the firm's objectives have been made clear. Some marketing problems may require whole new strategies, while other problems may involve only one of the four Ps if all other elements of the firm's marketing strategy seem to fit together well. For example, changes in the economic environment may call for a whole new marketing strategy, while only some "minor" product change may be needed if the target market's needs have changed slightly or the product was not exactly what consumers wanted.

Assignment

This exercise will give you some practice in defining marketing problems which might require some research. Read the following cases and, for each one, clearly state the nature of the problem and explain why the problem might require some marketing research. If you feel there are several problems in the particular case, list them in the order of their importance and indicate which problems you would research first.

Note: Most managers would like to know more about "everything," but generally it is not practical to research every detail of a case. Therefore, in doing this exercise, it may be necessary for you to make some reasonable assumptions--based either on the facts of the case or your knowledge of the marketplace--in order to focus the problem and subsequent research on issues that really make a difference in the case.

The first case is presented with an answer, as an example.

1. The Atlantic Hamburger shop opened on a lot adjoining a nationally-franchised hamburger shop which had been in operation about one year. During its grand opening, the Atlantic attracted large crowds of curious people wishing to try the products of this new business. However, after about ten days of operation, the number of customers coming into the Atlantic seemed to be declining.

   By the end of the first month, very few customers were coming in. At the same time, business next door at the franchised hamburger shop seemed to be prospering. The Atlantic offered all the items that the nationally-franchised shop offered, as well as several other items which were not on the menu of its franchised competitor. Prices were about the same at both shops.

   Sample Answer

   Since the Atlantic located its shop right next door to a nationally-franchised competitor, it apparently hopes to make a profit catering to the same target market (whatever that is!) as its competitor. Since the franchise operation is prospering, Place does not appear to be the problem. There are many shops of this type competing at about the same price level with similar products, so Price is probably not the problem either. And the large crowds during the Atlantic's grand opening may rule out Promotion.

   Potential customers did "sample" the product, and apparently are not returning for more. Therefore, the problem may be in the *Product* area, and this possibility should be researched first. Target customers may not like the taste or appearance of the products, or they may not like the Atlantic's service (e.g., waiting time, cleanliness, appearance, the employees' attitudes, etc.). Marketing research can be used to determine if the Atlantic's product/service is really the problem and what changes are likely to be effective.

2. The Torch Club, now a restaurant-dance floor-bar combination, is located about one mile from the edge of Eastern Provincial University and two miles from the downtown district of a city of about 150,000. The Club is large and could seat over 500 people comfortably. The business has been losing money for four years. In this period various things have been tried.

   First, the major emphasis was on indoor golfing with some food. After about six months, the emphasis was changed to a night club, emphasizing record playing, and go-go dancing--while at the same time retaining some of the golfing facilities. After several months of this, the emphasis was changed to family-style restaurant, featuring roasted chicken. Six months later, the business tried to become more attractive by featuring country and western, and sometimes rock'nroll music. About six months later, a number of billiard tables were installed in an effort to become a fancy billiard parlor.

   Currently, there is a small dance floor, and a band plays soft rock music on Wednesday, Friday, and Saturday nights. The record player has no special emphasis and the Club still has some of the golf facilities, billiard tables, a small sit-down bar, and a small restaurant area. At no time during its operation has it been profitable.

Answer

3. The Bronson Company, a leading manufacturer of breakfast cereals, has developed a new ready-to-eat breakfast cereal which is expected to become very popular among pre-school children. The cereal will be called "Kermits" and will be manufactured in frog-shaped pieces which look like the "Kermit the Frog" character that has become a big hit on children's television shows. The new cereal is also expected to appeal to health-conscious parents because it contains no sugar and tests conducted by an independent laboratory have shown it to be very nutritious.

Unfortunately, Bronson's new product is being introduced at a time when the government is trying to discourage the use of television advertising aimed at children under eight years old, and is also thinking of banning the use of cartoon characters such as "Tony the Tiger" to help sell products to children. Furthermore, many parent groups are in an uproar about commercial attempts to "manipulate" their children's minds. In particular, ready-to-eat breakfast cereals have received so much bad publicity from mass media sources that Bronson is not sure if parents will believe its claim about the nutritional benefits of "Kermits."

Answer

Question for Discussion

What kinds of business problems are most apt to require marketing research? Why?

Exercise 5-2

Evaluating marketing research

Introduction

Marketing managers need good information to develop effective marketing strategies. They need to know about the uncontrollable environment, about possible target customers, and about the marketing mix decisions they can make.

Sometimes the only way to get needed information is with marketing research. When this is the case, the manager can sometimes get help--perhaps from marketing research specialists in the firm or from outside specialists. But, marketing managers must be able to explain what their problems are--and what kinds of information they need. They should also know about some of the basic decisions made during the research process--so they know the limitations of the research. They need to be able to see if the results of a research project will really solve the problem!

It is true that marketing research can involve many technical details--that is why specialists are often involved. But, often a marketing manager can use "common sense"--and knowledge of marketing strategy planning--to improve marketing research.

Assignment

In this exercise you are presented with short cases that involve marketing research. You are asked to identify and comment about the possible limitations of the research. The cases are accompanied by questions that will help to get your thinking started.

You will need to know about the marketing research ideas discussed in Chapter 5 to evaluate the cases. But, remember that the idea here is not just to memorize the points from the text. Rather, you should really think about the problem, and use common sense along with the information from the book to evaluate the case situation.

A sample answer is provided to the first case--to give you an example of the type of thinking that might be helpful. But--before you read the answer--think about how you would answer the question yourself.

1. A marketing manager for a big industrial equipment company wanted to get ideas about new products he could develop. A salesman suggested that they conduct a few focus group interviews with some "friendly" customers--to get some ideas. This seemed like a good idea, so an outside marketing specialist was hired to set up and videotape two focus group sessions.

After the sessions, the specialist presented a short summary report. His main conclusion was that 40 percent of the participants wanted a certain type of machine, and urged the company to develop one quickly "since the market will be large." He also said that from watching the tapes he was certain that the customers were unhappy with the products they had been getting from the firm. This left the marketing manager quite concerned and wondering what to do.

a) Is a focus group interview a good basis for drawing the type of conclusions offered by the outside researcher? Why or why not?

Sample Answer

The conclusion probably is not justified. A focus group interview includes relatively few customers, and they may not be representative. Also, trying to provide quantitative summaries of the qualitative results might be really misleading. The new product might be a good idea, but just because a few people in a focus group mentioned it does not mean that there will be a large market. That will require more study.

b) Should the manager hire the marketing research firm to do a large survey to see if customers are really unhappy, as he suggests based on the focus groups? Why or why not?

Sample Answer

It is too early to be thinking about rushing out to do a big expensive survey. After all, conclusions reached by watching a focus group interview can vary a lot depending on who watches it. As a start, the marketing manager might watch the tapes of the focus groups and see if he draws the same conclusions. Other views might be sought as well. Even if the conclusion seems correct, it would be best to define the problem more specifically, and do a situation analysis to get a better idea about what research is needed.

2. A marketing manager for a bank wants to survey potential customers to see if they know about the bank's new drive-in window services. An outside marketing research specialist tells the manager that for $5,000 the research firm can send out a mail survey to 500 people, tabulate the results, and present a report. He explains that the bank will need to provide a computer mailing list of people who have accounts at the bank--to save costs in developing the sample. He concludes by pointing out that the research will be quite inexpensive: "We will give you results from a representative sample of 500 people, at only $10 per respondent. And you can be confident with a sample of 500 that the statistics are accurate."

a) Is the proposed sample well-suited to the manager's problem? Why or why not?

People from mailing list able to comment on existing service but will not give him what he wants

b) Is the researcher's concluding statement misleading? (*Hint*: Think about the response rate issue.) Why or why not?

Based on a full 100% ~~proxy~~ participation rate is variable

3. A marketing manager for a Mercedes dealership is trying to decide how many cars to order during the coming year--to be sure to have enough on hand to meet demand. He decides that it would be useful to do a survey of customers to whom he has sold Mercedes in the last year. He wants to know how satisfied they are with their current car, and he wants to know how many want to buy another Mercedes from him in the coming year. He would also like to know if they could afford another expensive car so soon. He decides to have salesmen call the customers and ask the following questions:

(1) How do you feel about the car you bought from us? Are you very satisfied, or only moderately satisfied?

(2) Do you plan to buy another Mercedes from us during the coming year? Yes, you plan to buy; or no, you don't plan to buy. *closed end - may feel pressured*

Why-

(3) I have one final question, and your response will be strictly confidential and used only in statistical summaries with answers from other respondents. Would you please tell us your annual income? $ _____

   a) Do you think that customers will give a valid response to the second question? Why or why not?

No, what do mean by income
ie. dual income, income before taxes, commissions,

   b) Do you think that customers will give a valid response to the last question? Why or why not?

- no rapport built up, no trust

   c) What is there about the way that the first question is worded that might keep the manager from getting valid information about how satisfied a customer really is? (*Hint*: Read the whole question several times carefully from the point-of-view of different customers.)

doesn't give enough ~~they~~ options
- not accurate, market is probably also a first-time buyer, as opposed to owners of one year

4. Louise Rimer, a marketing manager for Southern Pools, a swimming pool maintenance service firm, is concerned that profits have dropped, and she has noticed that many customers who once were regulars are no longer calling for service. She decides to send out a questionnaire to a sample of old customers, using addresses from her mailing list. She wrote a letter asking customers to respond to her questionnaire. She also provides a postage paid envelope for return of the completed forms. The instructions on the short questionnaire were:

(1) Please discuss the things you liked most about our service the last time you called to have work done on your pool. *unstructured question, involves lots of work for customer*

(2) Please explain what you liked least about our services. Please discuss anything that bothered you. *same as above*

(3) Please tell us what other pool services you may have used, and what is it about each service that you liked the most?

    a) Is a mail survey useful for questions like these? Why or why not?

        Not really, not structured enough

    b) What would you recommend if Louise Rimer asked you for ideas on how to get better information about her problems?

        - telephone survey is better

        - if mail survey needs to be more structured

Question for Discussion

How do the limitations of qualitative research differ from the limitations of quantitative research?

Chapter 6

Demographic dimensions of the Canadian consumer market

What This Chapter Is About

Chapter 6 is the first of a group of three chapters about customers and their buying behavior. Actually, we know a great deal about potential customers. Therefore, there is no reason for relying on common and *often erroneous stereotypes* and generalizations.

Here you will see that the Canadian population is growing and that disparities in income distribution are great. At the same time, however, expenditure patterns vary considerably by age, stage in family life cycle, and other dimensions. This data will provide background for our analysis of target markets. Try to get a "feel" for relationships. Don't just memorize a lot of "facts." Demographic relationships are enduring--and a good understanding of these relationships will help you avoid mistakes when decisions about the size of potential markets must be made quickly.

Important Terms

Census Metropolitan Area (CMA), p. 169
"mosaic", p. 172
birth rate, p. 177

disposable income, p. 185
discretionary income, p. 185
empty nesters, p. 190
senior citizens, p. 190

True-False Questions

_____ 1. The first and most basic question which must be answered about any potential market is: what are its relevant segmenting dimensions?

_____ 2. It is predicted that the population will increase by over 200,000 each year due to immigration.

_____ 3. Canada's population growth has slowed dramatically and ranks among the slow growth countries of the world.

_____ 4. Disposable income is the income remaining after taxes and savings have been subtracted.

_____ 5. Most discretionary income is spent on necessities.

_____ 6. While income has a direct bearing on spending patterns, other demographic dimensions--such as age and stage in family life cycle--may be just as important to marketers.

___ 7. "Empty nesters" are an important group of highly mobile individuals who do not maintain a regular place of residence and thus are a very difficult group to track.

___ 8. Many firms cater to the senior citizen market--although older people generally have reduced incomes.

___ 9. More than 50 percent of families have more than one wage earner.

___ 10. Since 1965, the poorest 20 percent of families have never received more than 6.4 percent of total family income.

Answers to True-False Questions

1. T, p. 167   5. F, p. 185   8. T, p. 190
2. F, p. 172   6. T, p. 187   9. T, p. 181
3. T, p. 177   7. F, p. 190   10. T, pp. 182-183
4. F, p. 185

Multiple-Choice Questions (Circle the correct response)

1. When analyzing a potential product-market, a marketing planner should decide:

   a. what its relevant segmenting dimensions are.
   b. where it is.
   c. how big it is.
   d. All of the above.

2. According to the text, which of the following provinces had the largest percentage increase in population between 1972 and 1987?

   a. Ontario
   b. New Brunswick
   c. Alberta
   d. Saskatchewan
   e. British Columbia

3. Which of the following are the most receptive to new products and new brands?

   a. Young people
   b. Senior citizens
   c. Empty nesters
   d. Middle-aged people
   e. All are equally receptive

4. Disposable income is defined as:

   a. total market value of goods and services produced.
   b. gross national product per capita.
   c. income available after taxes.
   d. income available before taxes.
   e. income available after taxes and "necessities."

5. Which of the following stages in the family life cycle can be described as follows: Financially even better off as husband earns more and more wives work. May replace durables and furniture and buy cars, boats, dental services, and more expensive recreation and travel. May buy bigger houses.

   a. Newly married couples with no children
   b. Empty nest
   c. Full nest III--older couples with dependent children
   d. Senior citizens I--older married couple, no children living with them, head retired.
   e. Full nest I--youngest child under 6

Answers to Multiple-Choice Questions

1. d, p. 167   3. a, p. 187   5. c, p. 189
2. c, p. 168   4. c, p. 185

Exercise 6-1

How demographic trends affect marketing strategy planning

Introduction

A common approach to identifying markets uses "demographic" characteristics of customers--such as age, sex, race, education, occupation, geographical location, income, marital status, and family size. The popularity of demographics is due to the fact that such characteristics are easily measured, easily understood, and readily available in published form. Demographic characteristics are very useful for identifying market segments, planning appropriate marketing mixes and estimating market potential.

This exercise will stress another major use of demographics--to monitor changes and trends in the uncontrollable cultural and social environments to help find new marketing opportunities.

We will focus on four major demographic trends:

1. The maturing of the post-World War II "baby boom" generation
2. The increasing number and age of elderly people
3. The increasing number of women in the labor force
4. The trend toward smaller family units

You will be asked to evaluate the likely positive or negative effects of these four trends on three major industries.

Assignment

Listed below are three major industries in Canada. In the space provided, discuss the likely positive and/or negative effects of the above-mentioned demographic trends on *each* of the three industries. Base your answers on the text discussion and your general knowledge--DO NOT DO ANY LIBRARY OR FIELD RESEARCH. Use your head instead--to apply what you already know!

Industries

Apparel	Health care	Leisure time

1. Industry: <u>Apparel</u>

   a) Effects of baby boom generation maturing:

      apparel more money # $

   b) Effects of more elderly persons:

      comfort, easy care, spend less

   c) Effects of more working women:

      Spend more $
      better quality

   d) Effects of smaller family units:

      upscale

2. Industry: <u>Health care</u>

    a) **Effects of baby boom generation maturing:**

        not a major shift / more family oriented

    b) **Effects of more elderly persons:**

        large consumers, little education,
        2nd opinion
        nursing, chronic

    c) **Effects of more working women:**

    d) **Effects of smaller family units:**

3.   Industry: <u>Leisure Time</u>

    a)   Effects of baby boom generation maturing:

family oriented, value oriented

    b)   Effects of more elderly persons:

more $$

    c)   Effects of more working women:

– health oriented

– culture oriented

    d)   Effects of smaller family units:

Question for Discussion

Name some other important demographic trends. How might these trends affect the three industries discussed in the exercise?

Exercise 6-2
Family life cycle

Introduction

The products consumers purchase tend to change as they grow older. Factors other than buying decisions are also affected by age: number of children, ages of children, and marital status. In an attempt to develop a theory of buying behavior, marketers have combined such factors into the concept of the family life cycle. Stages in the family life cycle are used by marketers as guidelines when defining their target markets and are used to develop appropriate marketing strategies.

Assignment

Using the ten-stage family life cycle outlined in Exhibit 6-13 of your text, identify the appropriate stages of the cycle that each of the following products would appeal to:

1.   Denture cleanser:

   a.   Stages of life cycle:

   b.   Justification:

2.   Mercedes Benz sports car:

   a.   Stages of life cycle:

   b.   Justification:

3.   Bryan Adams record album:

   a.   Stages of life cycle:

   b.   Justification:

4.   Life insurance:

   a.   Stages of life cycle:

   b.   Justification:

5. Children's toys:

    a. Stages of life cycle:

    b. Justification:

6. Motorcycle:

    a. Stages of life cycle:

    b. Justification:

7. House:

    a. Stages of life cycle:

    b. Justification:

8. McDonald's hamburgers:

    a. Stages of life cycle:

    b. Justification:

9. Diamond ring:

    a. Stages of life cycle:

    b. Justification:

10. Sailboat:

    a. Stages of life cycle:

    b. Justification:

Chapter 7

Behavioral dimensions of the consumer market

What This Chapter Is About

Chapter 7 focuses on the contribution of the behavioral sciences to our understanding of consumer behavior. As we saw in Chapter 6, demographic analysis does not fully explain *why* people buy or *what* they buy.

The importance of considering several behavioral dimensions at the same time is stressed. This is not easy because there are many psychological and sociological theories. Nevertheless, marketing managers must make decisions based on their knowledge of potential target markets. They must do their best to integrate the various theories and findings. This chapter is intended to get you started on this task.

Several buyer behavior models are presented to help organize your thinking. Then their interrelation is suggested in a "big" model of the consumer's problem solving process. Try to find a way of integrating these models together for yourself. Behavioral science findings can be a great help, but you still must add your own judgment to apply the various findings in particular markets. These findings coupled with "market sense" can take you a long way in marketing strategy planning.

Important Terms

Stimulus-response model, p. 194
economic men, p. 194
needs, p. 196
wants, p. 196
drive, p. 197
physiological needs, p. 198
safety needs, p. 198
social needs, p. 198
personal needs, p. 198
economic needs, p. 198
selective exposure, p. 199
selective perception, p. 199
selective retention, p. 199
learning, p. 200
cues, p. 200

response, p. 200
reinforcement, p. 200
attitude, p. 201
belief, p. 201
psychographics, p. 202
life-style analysis, p. 202
social class, p. 205
reference group, p. 207
opinion leader, p. 208
culture, p. 208
extension problem solving, p. 217
limited problem solving, p. 217
routinized response behavior, p. 217
low involvement purchases, p. 217
adoption process, p. 218
dissonance, p. 218

True-False Questions

____ 1. Because demographic analysis isn't of much value in predicting which products and brands will be purchased, many marketers have turned to the behavioral sciences for insight and help.

____ 2. The "black box" model of buyer behavior is based on the stimulus-response model--and explains why consumers behave the way they do.

____ 3. Behavioral scientists suggest that the "black box" works in a more complicated way than the "economic-man" model.

____ 4. A drive is a strong need that is learned during a person's life.

____ 5. Motivation theory suggests that people have hierarchies of needs, and that they never reach a state of complete satisfaction.

____ 6. The PSSP needs are power, security, social acceptance, and prestige.

____ 7. The basic needs (PSSP) can help explain what we buy--but the economic needs can help explain why we buy specific product features.

____ 8. Economic needs include things such as convenience, efficiency in operation or use, dependability in use, and economy of purchase or use.

____ 9. Selective perception refers to a person's ability to screen out or modify ideas, messages, or information that conflict with previously learned attitudes and beliefs.

____ 10. Learning is a change in a person's thought processes caused by prior experience.

____ 11. Reinforcement of the learning process occurs when a cue follows a response and leads to a reduction in the drive tension.

____ 12. An attitude is a person's point of view towards something.

____ 13. Advertising is so powerful that changing consumers' negative attitudes is usually the easiest part of the marketing manager's job.

____ 14. Personality traits have been very useful to marketers in predicting which products or brands target customers will choose.

____ 15. Life-style analysis refers to the analysis of a person's day-to-day pattern of living--as expressed in his activities, interests, and opinions.

____ 16. Social influences are concerned with how an individual interacts with family, social class, and other groups who may have influence on the buying process.

____ 17. Buying responsibility and influence within a family vary greatly--depending on the product and the family.

____ 18. The social class system in Canada is usually measured in terms of income, race, and occupation.

____ 19. More than half of our society is *not* middle class.

____ 20. Middle-class consumers tend to be more future-oriented and self-confident than lower-class consumers.

____ 21. A person normally has several reference groups.

____ 22. "Opinion leaders" are generally higher income people and better educated.

____ 23. The attitudes and beliefs that we usually associate with culture tend to change slowly.

____ 24. Different purchase situations may require different marketing mixes--even when the same target market is involved.

____ 25. A grid of evaluative criteria can be used to help managers think about how customers evaluate a marketing mix.

____ 26. A homemaker doing weekly grocery shopping is more likely to use extensive problem-solving than limited problem-solving or routinized response behavior.

____ 27. Low involvement products are products which are seldom purchased by the target market.

____ 28. In the adoption process, the evaluation step usually comes before the trial step.

____ 29. Dissonance might cause a consumer to pay more attention to automobile advertisements after a new car is purchased than before the purchase.

____ 30. Knowing how a target market handles the problem-solving process, the adoption process, and learning can aid marketing strategy planning.

Answers to True-False Questions

1. T, p. 194	11. F, p. 200	21. T, p. 207
2. F, p. 194	12. T, p. 201	22. F, p. 208
3. T, p. 194	13. F, p. 201	23. T, p. 208
4. F, p. 197	14. F, p. 202	24. T, p. 214
5. T, p. 198	15. T, pp. 202-203	25. F, p. 216
6. F, p. 198	16. T, p. 203	26. F, p. 217
7. T, p. 198	17. T, p. 205	27. F, p. 217
8. T, p. 199	18. F, p. 205	28. T, p. 218
9. T, p. 199	19. T, p. 206	29. T, pp. 218-219
10. T, p. 200	20. T, p. 207	30. T, p. 219

Multiple-Choice Questions (Circle the correct response)

1. According to the text, the consumer "black box" model:

   a. is controlled by social influences.
   b. is a stimulus-response model.
   c. reveals that we all behave like "economic men."
   d. is controlled by psychological variables.
   e. explains why people behave the way they do.

2. Which of the following is *not* a psychological variable?

   a. Social class
   b. Motivation
   c. Perception
   d. Attitudes
   e. Learning

3. A good marketing manager

   a. knows that only a few basic needs explain almost all consumer product choices.
   b. doesn't have to understand consumer needs if his product has some design improvements over his competitor's product.
   c. should find ways to create internal drives in consumers.
   d. knows that consumer needs in product-markets are probably much more specific than those in a related generic market.
   e. will make fewer strategy planning mistakes if he uses the "economic men" model.

4. According to motivation theory, the *last* needs a family would usually seek to satisfy would be:

   a. safety needs.
   b. personal needs.
   c. physiological needs.
   d. social needs.

5. Motivation theory suggests that:

   a. lower-level needs must be completely satisfied before higher-level needs become important.
   b. a particular good or service might satisfy different levels of needs at the same time.
   c. all consumers satisfy needs in the same order.
   d. self-esteem is an example of a social need.
   e. All of the above are true statements.

6. Why customers select specific product features may be best explained by:

   a. physiological needs.
   b. safety needs.
   c. personal needs.
   d. economic needs.
   e. social needs.

7. When consumers screen out or modify ideas, messages, and information that conflict with previously learned attitudes and beliefs, this is called:

   a. selective retention.
   b. selective exposure.
   c. selective perception.
   d. selective dissonance.
   e. selective cognition.

8. A change in a person's thought processes caused by prior experience is called:

   a. learning
   b. attitude change
   c. belief change
   d. response
   e. reinforcement

9. Which of the following is not a major element in the learning process?

   a. Drive
   b. Cues
   c. Dissonance
   d. Reinforcement
   e. Response

10. An attitude:

    a. is easily changed.
    b. is a person's point of view toward something.
    c. is the same as opinion and belief.
    d. is a reliable indication of intention to buy.
    e. All of the above are true statements.

11. The AIO items used in life-style analysis include:

    a. activities, interests, and opinions.
    b. attitudes, interests, and opinions.
    c. activities, intentions, and opinions.
    d. attitudes, intentions, and opinions.
    e. attitudes, income, and opinions.

12. Which of the following is *not* a social influence?

    a. Culture
    b. Social class
    c. Family
    d. Reference group
    e. Personality

13. According to the text, social class is usually measured in terms of:

    a. income.
    b. occupation, education, and housing arrangements.
    c. income, occupation, and education.
    d. race, religion, and occupation.
    e. income, occupation, and religion.

14. Jack Simmons, now an account representative responsible for selling computer systems to some of ABC Corporation's major accounts--has been with ABC since graduating from McGill University in 1965. Jack's father was a plumber, but Jack is a professional--one of ABC's top five salespeople--and earns about $70,000 a year in salary and commissions. Jack is a member of the _____ social class.

    a. upper
    b. upper-middle
    c. lower-middle
    d. upper-lower
    e. lower-lower

15. Which of the following statements about social class is NOT true?

    a. The various classes tend to shop in different stores.
    b. The upper class tends to avoid shopping at mass-merchandisers.
    c. Upper-middle class consumers tend to buy quality products which will serve as symbols of their success.
    d. Lower-class buyers often want guidance from a salesperson about what choice to make.
    e. Lower class consumers are more likely to save and plan for the future than middle class consumers.

16. For which of the following products would reference group influence probably be *least important*?

    a. Clothing
    b. Cigarettes
    c. Furniture
    d. Canned peaches
    e. Wine

17. Qpinion leaders are:

    a. usually better educated.
    b. usually reference group leaders.
    c. not necessarily opinion leaders on all subjects.
    d. usually wealthy, middle- or upper-class people.
    e. All of the above are true statements.

18. Behavioral scientists recognize different *levels* of consumer problem solving. Which of the following is *not* one of these levels?

    a. Routinized response behavior
    b. Limited problem solving
    c. Rational problem solving
    d. Extensive problem solving
    e. All of the above are recognized levels of problem solving.

19. Which of the following gives the proper *ordering* of the stages in the "adoption process"?

    a. Awareness, interest, trial, evaluation, decision, dissonance
    b. Awareness, interest, trial, decision, evaluation, confirmation
    c. Awareness, interest, evaluation, trial, decision, confirmation
    d. Interest, awareness, trial, decision, evaluation, dissonance
    e. Awareness, interest, evaluation, decision, trial, confirmation

20. Dissonance is:

    a. a type of cue.
    b. a form of laziness commonly observed among low-income consumers.
    c. a type of positive reinforcement.
    d. tension caused by uncertainty about the rightness of a decision.
    e. none of the above.

21. The present state of our knowledge about consumer behavior is such that:

    a. the behavioral sciences provide the marketing manager with a complete explanation of the "whys" of consumer behavior.
    b. we still must rely heavily on intuition and judgment to explain and predict consumer behavior.
    c. relevant market dimensions can be easily identified and measured using "psychographics."
    d. marketing research can't tell us much more about specific aspects of consumer behavior.
    e. All of the above are true statements.

Answers to Multiple-Choice Questions

1. b, p. 194	8. a, p. 200	15. e, p. 207
2. a, p. 195	9. c, p. 200	16. d, p. 207
3. d, p. 197	10. b, p. 201	17. c, p. 208
4. b, p. 198	11. a, pp. 202-203	18. c, p. 217
5. b, p. 198	12. c, p. 203	19. c, p. 218
6. d, pp. 198-199	13. b, p. 205	20. d, pp. 218-219
7. c, p. 199	14. b, p. 206	21. b, p. 219

Exercise 7-1

Psychological variables and social influences affect consumer buying behavior

Introduction

To plan good marketing strategies, marketing managers must try to improve their understanding of buying behavior. Ideally, marketers would like to know *how* and *why* individual consumers buy the way they do. Then it might be possible to group individual consumers with similar needs and buying behavior into homogeneous market segments for which suitable marketing mixes could be developed.

This is easier said than done, however, because human behavior is very complex. Traditional demographic analysis, for example, can be used to study basic trends in consumer spending patterns, but it is of little use in explaining *why* people like, choose, buy, and use the products and brands they do.

For this reason, many marketers have turned to the behavioral sciences for help in understanding how and why consumers behave as they do. However, there is no "grand theory" available right now which ties together all the behavioral theories and concepts in a way which will explain and predict all aspects of human behavior. Therefore, marketers must try to understand the various behavioral theories and concepts. Then they can put them together into a model of consumer behavior which works in their own particular situation.

Hopefully, the complex decision-making processes which take place within the consumer's "black box" are clearer to you after reading Chapter 7 of the text. Although the simplified model of buyer behavior presented in the text can't explain or predict consumer behavior, it does provide a useful framework which identifies the major variables which influence consumer behavior.

This exercise should improve your understanding of various psychological variables and social influences which may affect a consumer's behavior. You will recall from Chapter 7 that psychological variables focus on the individual while social influences involve relations with others.

Assignment

In the short cases which follow, a variety of psychological variables and social influences are operating to influence a consumer's response. For each case, identify the relevant psychological variables and social influences and briefly explain how each item is illustrated in the case. The first case has been completed for you as an example.

1. Joan and Paul Davis and their two children are considering the purchase of a recreational vehicle. Paul is enthusiastic because, he argues, the RV would be perfect for family camping trips, as well as fishing trips with his friends. Joan is less in favor of the purchase. She is nervous about camping in remote locations--and wonders how they would get help in emergencies. She also remembers a report that RVs get low gas mileage and are, therefore, expensive to run. Paul is quick to point out that the same report described the large potential savings of a week-long vacation in an RV compared to staying at a hotel or motel.

    a. Psychological variables

        1) <u>PSSP hierarchy</u>   Explanation: <u>Joan is afraid of being isolated--</u>

            <u>safety needs.</u>

        2) <u>Selective Processes</u>   Explanation: <u>Joan only remembers the part of the</u>

            <u>report that supports her viewpoint.</u>

    b. Social influences

        1) <u>Family</u>   Explanation: <u>Paul wants to take family camping</u>

            <u>vacations, but Joan is concerned about the family's safety.</u>

        2) <u>Reference Group</u>   Explanation: <u>Paul wants to take his friends on a</u>

            <u>fishing trip in "his" RV.</u>

2. Robert Ezzell just returned from a year in France as an exchange student. To see his old friends, he is planning a dinner party with a French menu. As he is shopping for the necessary supplies, he recalls his first experience with escargot--a delicacy of broiled snails he plans to serve at his party. When Robert was told by his host family what he had been served, he was not sure he would be able to eat it. Nothing in his Canadian upbringing had prepared him to eat snails. However he did not want to offend his hosts, so he smiled bravely and downed the escargot. To his amazement it was delicious, and he now enjoys escargot frequently. He is sure he will have to be very persuasive to overcome his friends' initial reactions.

    a. Psychological variables

        1) _____   Explanation: _____

            _____

        2) _____   Explanation: _____

            _____

    b. Social influences

        1) _____ Explanation: _____

               _____

        2) _____ Explanation: _____

               _____

3.   Pat Marshall is planning to buy a VCR, but is unsure where she wants to shop or what brand she wants to buy. She has asked her boss, whom everyone considers an "electronic nut," for his advice, and she has started noticing magazine ads about the various features. She is most interested in a JVC brand unit that has a 7 day timer--since she is often away from home during the week on business trips and the timer would allow her to tape her favorite programs while she is gone. It also comes with a remote control unit that makes it easy to speed past commercials. An added plus is that the VCR's remote control unit would also work with her JVC brand TV, which she has had for a year and found very satisfactory. In addition, her boyfriend thinks that the JVC offers "a good value for the price," although it is more expensive than what she had originally expected to spend.

    a. Psychological variables

        1) _____ Explanation: _____

               _____

        2) _____ Explanation: _____

               _____

    b. Social influences

        1) _____ Explanation: _____

               _____

        2) _____ Explanation: _____

               _____

4.   Mindy Petrucci is planning a vacation, but is unsure where she wants to go or what she wants to do. She has asked her "well traveled" boss for his advice, and has started noticing magazine articles about the various possibilities. She is most interested in a Club Med package to the Caribbean. It offers an "all-inclusive package of food, drink, organized activities and instruction, and free use of all facilities--including swimming, tennis, wind-surfing, sailing, water-skiing, snorkeling, scuba-diving, ping-pong, crafts, games--as well as nightly entertainment." All this is available in one, informal, self-contained place. Mindy is an outdoors-type who enjoys sports and excitement. She hates getting dressed up and is very interested in meeting new people. She remembers that two of her friends went last year and had a great time.

a. Psychological variables

1) _____ Explanation: _____

_____

2) _____ Explanation: _____

_____

3) _____ Explanation: _____

_____

b. Social influences

1) _____ Explanation: _____

_____

2) _____ Explanation: _____

_____

3. Howard Rocker has had a cold--and all of the typical symptoms that come with it--for almost a week. At first he hadn't taken any medicine. He had always felt that there wasn't anything you could do about a cold. However, while he was playing cards at the home of some friends they kidded him about his runny, red nose. When they offered him a Benadryl cold tablet, he figured it wouldn't hurt to try it. To his surprise, he felt much better after taking the tablet. The next morning, he stopped at a drugstore on his way to work and bought a package of the medicine. Howard had never heard of Benadryl before, but while driving home from work that evening he noticed a large billboard for Benadryl.

a. Psychological variables

1) _____ Explanation: _____

_____

2) _____ Explanation: _____

_____

3) _____ Explanation: _____

_____

b. Social influences

1) _____ Explanation: _____

_____

2) _____ Explanation: _____

_____

Question for Discussion

Which items--psychological variables or social influences--have the most influence over consumer behavior and thus are more important for the marketing strategy planner?

Exercise 7-2

Consumer behavior is a problem-solving process

Introduction

While consumer behavior may often appear to be quite irrational to the casual observer, most behavioral scientists agree that consumers are *problem solvers* seeking to relieve tension caused by their unsatisfied needs. How an individual consumer goes about solving problems depends on the intra-personal and inter-personal variables that affect that individual. In general, however, most consumers tend to follow the following five-step problem-solving process:

1. Becoming aware of--or interested in--the problem.
2. Gathering information about possible solutions.
3. Evaluating alternative solutions--perhaps trying some out.
4. Deciding on the appropriate solution.
5. Evaluating the decision.

The length of time it takes to complete the problem-solving process and how much attention is given to each of the five steps depends, of course, on the nature of the problem and how much experience an individual has had in trying to solve this particular kind of problem. To understand the process better, it helps to recognize three levels of problem solving: *extensive problem solving, limited problem solving*, and *routinized response behavior*.

The purpose of this exercise is to illustrate the three levels of consumer problem solving by relating the problem-solving process to *your* problem-solving experiences in the marketplace.

Assignment

Think of *three* recent purchases that *you* made that involved extensive problem solving, limited problem solving, and routinized response behavior. For each of these purchases, outline the problem-solving process that you used. You may wish to follow the five-step process listed above, indicating how you went about performing each of the five steps.

1. Routinized response behavior: Product _____

   Explanation:

2.   Limited problem-solving: Product _____

      Explanation:

3.   Extensive problem-solving: Product _____

      Explanation:

Question for Discussion

Which of the three levels of problem solving offers marketers the most opportunity? The least opportunity? Why?

Chapter 8

Industrial and intermediate customers and their buying behavior

What This Chapter Is About

Chapter 8 discusses the buying behavior of the important industrial and intermediate customers who buy for resale or for use in their own businesses. They buy more goods and services than final customers! There are many opportunities in marketing to producers, to middlemen, to government, and to nonprofit organizations--and it is important to understand how these organizational customers buy.

Organizations tend to be much more economic in their buying behavior than final consumers. Further, some must follow pre-set bidding and bargaining processes. Yet, they too have emotional needs. And sometimes a number of different people may influence the final purchase decision. Keep in mind that industrial and intermediate customers are problem solvers too. Many of the ideas in Chapter 7 carry over--but with some adaptation.

This chapter deserves careful study because your past experience as a consumer is not as helpful here as it was in the last few chapters. Intermediate customers are much less numerous. In some cases it is possible to create a separate marketing mix for each individual intermediate customer. Understanding these customers is necessary to plan marketing strategies for them. Try to see how they are both similar and different from final customers.

Important Terms

intermediate customers, p. 224
standard industrial classification
  (SIC) codes, p. 227
new-task buying, p. 228
straight rebuy, p. 228
modified rebuy, p. 228
purchasing agents, p. 229
vendor analysis, p. 229
multiple buying influence, p. 230
buying center, p. 232
inspection buying, p. 233
sampling buying, p. 233

description (specif.) buying, p. 234
competitive bids, p. 234
negotiated contract buying, p. 234
requisition, p. 235
"just in time" delivery, p. 237
reciprocity, p. 237
open to buy, p. 240
resident buyers, p. 240
contract farming, p. 242
agribusiness, p. 242
marketing boards, p. 243

True-False Questions

____ 1. Intermediate customers are wholesalers or retailers, but not buyers who buy to produce other goods and services.

____ 2. Since sellers usually approach each intermediate customer directly through a sales representative, it is possible that there can be a special marketing strategy for each individual customer.

____ 3. Retailers are the largest group of intermediate customers.

____ 4. Manufacturers tend to be concentrated by geographic location and industry, and the majority of them are quite small.

____ 5. Two-digit SIC code breakdowns start with broad industry categories, but more detailed data may be available for three-digit and four-digit industries.

____ 6. When the majority of a company's purchases involve straight rebuy buying, these purchases occupy most of an effective buyer's time.

____ 7. A salesperson usually must see the industrial buyer or purchasing agent first, before any other employee in the firm is contacted.

____ 8. "Vendor analysis" involves formal rating of suppliers on all relevant areas of performance.

____ 9. Emotional needs are often quite relevant for the typical purchasing agent, and therefore a marketing mix should seek to satisfy both the buyer's company needs and the buyer's individual needs.

____ 10. Strong multiple-buying influence is most likely to be involved when there is new-task buying.

____ 11. Multiple-buying influence makes the promotion job easier.

____ 12. A buying center consists of all the people who participate in or influence a purchase.

____ 13. Buying by inspection would probably be necessary for a firm that wanted to purchase a large supply of nuts and bolts.

____ 14. As products become more standardized, perhaps because of more careful grading and better quality control, sampling buying becomes possible.

____ 15. Services are usually purchased by description.

____ 16. Negotiated contracts commonly are used for products which can be described sufficiently well that suppliers know what is wanted and can submit definite prices or bids.

____ 17. Even if a firm has developed the best marketing mix possible, it probably will not get all of the business of its industrial customers.

____ 18. A requisition is a request to buy something.

____ 19. Industrial buyers typically do not even see a sales rep for straight rebuys.

_____ 20. Buyers who delegate routine buying to a computer might be more favorably impressed by a new company's offer of an attractive marketing mix, perhaps for a whole line of products, rather than just a lower price for a particular order.

_____ 21. "Just-in-time" delivery means reliably getting products there before or very soon after they are needed.

_____ 22. Purchasing agents tend to resist reciprocity, but it may be forced on them by their sales departments.

_____ 23. Compared to manufacturers, services firms are more numerous, smaller, and more spread out.

_____ 24. Most retail and wholesale buyers see themselves as selling agents for manufacturers.

_____ 25. The large number of items bought and stocked by wholesalers and retailers makes it imperative that inventories be watched carefully.

_____ 26. The retail buyer is "open-to-buy" whenever his cost of merchandise is less than his forecasted sales.

_____ 27. Resident buyers are employees of retail stores whose job it is to reach the many small manufacturers in central markets who cannot afford large sales departments.

_____ 28. Committee buying by retailers will probably force better strategy planning by wholesalers and manufacturers, instead of relying just on persuasive salespeople.

_____ 29. All government customers are required by law to use a mandatory bidding procedure which is open to public review.

_____ 30. Government buyers avoid the use of negotiated contracts whenever there are a lot of intangible factors.

Answers to True-False Questions

1. F, p. 224	12. T, p. 232	23. T, p. 238
2. T, p. 225	13. F, p. 233	24. F, p. 239
3. T, p. 224	14. T, p. 233	25. T, p. 239
4. T, p. 225	15. T, p. 234	26. F, p. 240
5. T, p. 227	16. F, p. 234	27. F, pp. 240-241
6. F, p. 228	17. T, p. 235	28. T, p. 241
7. T, p. 229	18. T, p. 235	29. T, p. 244
8. T, p. 229	19. T, p. 235	30. F, p. 244
9. T, p. 230	20. T, p. 237	
10. T, p. 230	21. F, p. 237	
11. F, pp. 231-232	22. T, p. 238	

Multiple-Choice Questions (Circle the correct response)

1. The bulk of all buying done in Canada is not by final consumers--but rather by intermediate customers. Which of the following is an intermediate customer?

    a. a manufacturer.
    b. a retailer.
    c. a wholesaler.
    d. a government agency.
    e. All of the above are intermediate customers.

2. Which of the following SIC codes would provide the most specific information about a sub-category of an industry?

    a. 3
    b. 31
    c. 314
    d. 3142
    e. Cannot be determined without additional information.

3. A large manufacturer is about to purchase a large supply of an unfamiliar chemical that will be used in the production of an important new product. What kind of buying would the company be most likely to do?

    a. New-task buying
    b. Straight rebuy buying
    c. Modified rebuy buying

4. In comparison to the buying of final consumers, the purchasing of industrial buyers:

    a. is strictly economic and not at all emotional.
    b. leans heavily toward patronage, especially in new products.
    c. leans basically toward economy, quality, and dependability.
    d. is even less predictable.
    e. Both a and c are true statements.

5. Today, many agricultural commodities and manufactured items are subject to rigid control or grading. As a result, the buying and selling of these goods can be done at a low cost by:

    a. inspection.
    b. sampling.
    c. description.
    d. negotiated contracts.

6. An automobile manufacturer's practice of buying some of its raw materials from other manufacturers who in turn buy from it is an example of:

    a. tying contracts.
    b. vendor analysis.
    c. buying by description.
    d. being "open to buy."
    e. reciprocity.

7. As contrasted with manufacturers, producers of services are:

    a. more geographically spread out.
    b. more numerous.
    c. less well represented by SIC data.
    d. all of the above.
    e. None of the above.

8. A plastics manufacturer is selecting a new supplier. People from sales, production, quality control, and finance are working with the purchasing department on the decision. The sales manager wants to select a supplier that is also a customer for some of the firm's own products. The sales manager

    a. is a gatekeeper.
    b. may not get his way because the government frowns on such deals.
    c. is trying to use vendor analysis to his advantage.
    d. is not a member of the buying center, so he can be ignored.
    e. none of the above.

9. Which of the following statements about retail buying is *false*?

    a. In most retail operations, a "resident buyer" runs his own department--and his decision is final.
    b. Retail buyers may be responsible for supervising the salesclerks who sell the merchandise they buy.
    c. Retail buyers make most purchases as straight rebuys.
    d. A retail buyer is usually "open to buy" only when he has not spent all of his budgeted funds.
    e. In large retail stores, buyers tend to specialize in certain lines.

10. Which of the following statements about bidding for government business is *true*?

    a. Government buying needs are hard to identify--and their primary concern is with finding the lowest price.

    b. Government buyers avoid using negotiated contracts since they must purchase at a pre-set price.

    c. A government buyer may be forced to accept the lowest bid whether he wants the goods or not.

    d. The biggest job of the government buyer is to locate enough potential suppliers so the bidding procedure works effectively.

    e. All of the above are true statements.

Answers to Multiple-Choice Questions

1. e, p. 224	5. c, p. 234	8. b, p. 238
2. d, p. 227	6. c, pp. 237-238	9. a, p. 240
3. a, p. 228	7. d, p. 238	10. c, p. 244
4. c, p. 229		

Exercise 8-1
Analyzing industrial buying behavior

Introduction

Some people see industrial buying and consumer buying as two very different processes. Industrial buying is thought of as "economic," while consumer buying is seen as "emotional." In fact, closer study of buying processes suggests that industrial and consumer buying may be quite similar in many ways. For example, like consumers, industrial buyers are *problem solvers*. And while their problems may be very different, both consumer and industrial buyers seem to use three levels of problem solving. In Chapter 7, we saw that consumer buyers do extended, limited, and routinized problem solving. Similarly, industrial buyers do *new-task, straight rebuy,* and *modified rebuy buying*.

Recognition of the three levels of problem solving by industrial buyers *and* the different problem solving steps they pass through has important implications for market analysis. It suggests that industrial markets can be segmented not only in terms of product-related needs, industry categories, and geographic location--but also in terms of similarities and differences in buying behavior. *Each level of problem solving may require a different marketing mix*--especially in regard to the promotion variable--even when identical goods or services are involved. Knowing the nature of buying behavior at each level helps to determine the proper ingredients for a marketing mix.

This exercise shows how knowledge of industrial buying behavior can improve marketing strategy planning--in three "case" situations. You will be asked to identify the problem solving level for an industrial product. Then you will discuss likely buying behavior and how this might affect a firm's marketing strategy planning.

Assignment

Assume the role of marketing manager for a large chemical manufacturing firm. Your firm produces a variety of chemicals for use as ingredients in your customers' finished products. These same chemicals are typically available from several competing suppliers, including some large and some smaller firms. While some slight differences in quality may exist, all of the suppliers produce chemicals that meet the minimum specifications set by the customers' research departments. With few exceptions, the prices charged by all suppliers tend to be almost identical.

Recently, you learned--from your salesforce--of three potential customers whose needs might be satisfied by a chemical commonly known as "silico." Read each of the three buying situations described below, and then:

a.   Determine which level of problem solving--new-task buying, straight rebuy, or modified rebuy--applies to each situation.

b.   Discuss in detail the probable nature of the firm's buying behavior in each situation. Which of the five problem solving steps in Chapter 7 (page 214) would be most important in each situation? Why? Which is the next most important? Why? How important would multiple buying influence be in each situation?

c.   Explain how your firm might vary its marketing mix to satisfy the potential customer's needs in each situation.

Situation 1:

The potential customer has been producing a successful product for several years. But, the government has just informed the company that a chemical used as a key ingredient in the product can be dangerous. The potential customer thinks that "silico" could possibly be used instead of the current chemical.

a)   Level of problem solving: _____

b)   Nature of buying behavior:

c)   Marketing mix:

Situation 2:

The customer has been purchasing "silico" from one of your firm's competitors for several years. But it is dissatisfied with the technical support and delivery service provided by its present supplier.

a)   Level of problem solving: _____

b)   Nature of buying behavior:

c)   Marketing mix:

Situation 3:

The customer has been purchasing "silico" from one of your customers on a regular basis for several years. No change in this procedure is expected.

a)   Level of problem solving: _____

b)   Nature of buying behavior:

c)   Marketing mix:

Question for Discussion

In which of the three buying situations would emotional needs be most important? Least important? To what extent does this depend on the overlap between individual buyer needs and company needs?

Exercise 8-2

Using SIC codes to analyze industrial markets

Introduction

Compared to the final consumer market, industrial markets have a smaller number of customers and much of the buying potential is concentrated among a relatively few large firms. Further, firms within the same industry tend to cluster together by geographic location. For these reasons it may be less difficult to analyze industrial markets than consumer markets.

Much published data is available to help the marketing manager analyze industrial markets. The most important source of information is the federal government, which regularly collects data on the number of establishments, their sales volumes, and number of employees for a large number of industry groups. The data is reported for Standard Industrial Classification (SIC) code industries--broken down by region, province, county, and Census Metropolitan Area. As explained in Chapter 8 of the text, the SIC system combines and classifies industrial firms on the basis of product produced or operation performed into 85 major industry groups designated by two-digit codes--code 20, for example, identifies the "food and kindred products" industry. Each major industry is then subdivided into about 596 three-digit industries (e.g., code 202, "dairy products") which in turn are subdivided further into about 976 four-digit industries (e.g., code 2021, "creamery butter"). However, four-digit detail is not available for all industries in every geographic area because *Statistics Canada* will not disclose an individual firm's data.

Unfortunately, some firms are hard to classify because of the diversity of their products, and SIC codes may not exist for new industries formed through technological breakthroughs. Therefore, most companies usually find it necessary to modify the SIC system. For example, some measure of the size of firms is often added to provide some indication of the complexity of the buying decision process, the degree of specialization in buying, and so on.

This exercise illustrates the usefulness of SIC-coded data for analyzing industrial markets. *Note:* You may find it helpful to read pages 225-227 in the text before doing this exercise.

Assignment

Read the following case carefully and answer the questions as they appear.

BAKER MANUFACTURING COMPANY

The Baker Manufacturing Company produces a large line of electrical products for industrial markets. Baker's recently-appointed consulting manager is currently in the process of reevaluating the firm's marketing strategy for an important product, "electric widgets," which he suspects may not be realizing its full sales potential. In particular, he feels that Baker has been following a "mass-marketing" approach for this product and has neglected to identify which markets the product appeals to and their relative importance.

The marketing manager began his analysis by attempting to determine which four-digit SIC industries may have some need for electric widgets. First, he analyzed past sales records for the product and assigned SIC codes to previous and present customers. Next, he asked his sales manager to go through the SIC manual and check off the four-digit industries which he believed would be relevant for the product. Finaliy, to make sure that other potential customers were not being overlooked, he conducted a survey of companies falling under other SIC categories to find out whether they might have any possible use for the product. As a result of this analysis, a total of 12 industries were identified as potential target markets for electric widgets. These industries are listed in columns 1 and 2 of Table 8-1.

Having identified 12 potential target markets for electric widgets, the marketing manager then conducted another survey of a sample of firms belonging to each industry to determine the market potential for each industry. Included in the data he collected were the amount of each firm's annual dollar purchases for the product and the number of production workers employed. This data is summarized in columns 3 and 4 of Table 8-1. From the sample data for each SIC industry, the marketing manager then calculated the average dollar purchases per production worker. The results are shown in column 5.

1.   Complete column 5 of Table 8-1 by calculating the average dollar purchases per worker for SIC industry N3611--electric measuring instruments. Show your calculations below.

In order to project the sample data to the entire Canadian market, Baker's marketing manager turned to *Statistics Canada* to find the national total of production workers employed by each industry. From this data, shown in column 6, he was then able to estimate the national market potential for each SIC industry by multiplying column 6 by column 5. These estimates are shown in column 7.

2.   Complete column 7 of Table 8-1 by calculating the national market potential for SIC industry N3611. Show your calculations below.

Finally, because Baker's sales territories were aligned according to provinces, the marketing manager proceeded to estimate the market potential for each industry in each state. For example, he again turned to *Statistics Canada* to determine the number of production workers employed in the province of Saskatchewan. The results, computed by multiplying column 8 by column 5, are shown in column 9.

3.   Complete column 9 of Table 8-1 by calculating the market potential in Saskatchewan for SIC industry N3611. Show your calculations below.

Table 8-1

Calculation of Market Potential for "Electric Widgets" Using Market Survey Approach for National and Saskatchewan Markets

		Market Survey Results			National Market Number of Production Workers (1,000)	Estimated National Market Potential ($1,000)	Saskatchewan Market Number of Production Workers (1,000)	Estimated Saskatchewan Market Potential ($1,000)
SIC Code (1)	Effective Industries (2)	Product Purchases (3)	Number of Production Workers (4)	Average Purchases per Worker (5)	(6)	(7)	(8)	(9)
3611	Electric measuring instruments	$ 6,400	3,200	$ 2.00	35.1	$ 70.2	2.8	$ 5.6
3612	Transformers	50,150	4,616	10.86	37.6	408.3	3.8	41.3
3621	Motors and generators	28,400	10,896	2.61	78.3	204.4	3.0	7.8
3622	Industrial controls	40,100	4,678	8.57	30.8	264.0	3.2	27.4
3631	Household cooking equipment	2,600	2,104	1.24	16.9	21.0	3.9	4.8
3632	Household refrigerators and freezers	149,600	5,215	28.69	40.1	1,153.3	—	—
3633	Household laundry equipment	35,200	3,497	10.07	17.8	179.2	3.7	1.4
3634	Electric housewares and fans	1,200	3,208	0.37	40.3	14.9	—	—
3635	Household vacuum cleaners	1,875	402	4.66	7.5	35.0	—	—
3636	Sewing machines	600	912	0.66	4.9	3.2	—	—
3661	Telephone and telegraph apparatus	65,500	6,451	10.15	101.6	1,031.2	—	—
3662	Radio and TV communication equipment	132,100	6,889	19.18	185.7	3,561.7	7.5	143.8
	Total	$508,925				$6,946.5		$232.1

Column:

(1), (2) Four-digit SIC industries making up the industrial market for "electric widgets."

(3) Dollar value, classified by industries, of purchases of "electric widges" as reported by those firms included in the survey.

(4) Number of production workers as reported by those firms included in the survey.

(5) Average dollar value of "electric widget" purchases per production worker for each SIC industry. Computed by dividing column 3 by column 4.

(6) Number of production workers for the entire Canadian market for the given SIC industries.

(7) The resultant estimated national market potential for the total market. Computed by multiplying column 6 by column 5.

(8) Number of production workers for Saskatchewan trading area for the given SIC industries. Note: Blanks in column 8 indicate either that there are no firms in Saskatchewan for a particular SIC industry, or that there are only a few firms and Saskatchewan has withheld the data in order to protect the confidentiality of the firms in question. Same source as column 6.

(9) The resultant estimated Saskatchewan area market potential. Computed by multiplying column 8 by column 5.

Source: Adapted with considerable modification from Francis E. Hummel, *Market and Sales Potentials* (New York: The Ronald Press Co., 1961), pp. 110, 112.

4. a. *For all industries combined*, what percentage of the total national market potential for electric widgets is represented by the province of Saskatchewan? Show your work below.

    b. *For SIC industry* N3611 only, what percentage of the national market potential for electric widgets is represented by the province of Saskatchewan? Show your work below.

5. Suppose Baker's marketing manager learned that his firm's electric widget sales to SIC industry N3611 amounted to about 20 percent of its national market potential for that industry--while sales to the other 11 industries ranged from 5-10 percent. Suppose further that he then decided that the firm should aim at achieving 20 percent of its national market potential in each of the 12 SIC industries--and set his sales quotas accordingly. Is it likely that Baker could achieve these sales quotas? Why or why not? Comment on this approach to marketing strategy planning.

6. Which of the 12 SIC industries would you select as your target market(s) for the electric widgets if you were Baker's marketing manager? Why?

    a. For the national market:

    b. For the Saskatchewan market:

Question for Discussion

After selecting its target market(s), how could Baker then go about identifying and reaching those firms which make up the target market(s)? What other information would be needed and how could the information be obtained?

Chapter 9
Elements of product planning

What This Chapter Is About

Chapter 9 introduces the idea of a "product"--which usually includes more than just a physical good, and may be no physical good at all!

Then, the need for goods classes--to relate products to marketing mix planning is explained. Two sets of goods classes--for consumer goods and industrial goods--are introduced. Notice that the same product might be classified in two or more ways at the same time--depending on the attitudes of potential customers.

These goods classes should be studied carefully. They are an important thread linking our discussion of marketing strategy planning. In fact, these goods classes can be a shorthand way of describing how customers look at Products--and this has a direct bearing on Place (how the Product will get to them) and Promotion (what the seller should tell them).

Chapter 9 also discusses two important aspects of Product--branding and packaging.

Branding is concerned with identifying the product. A good brand can help improve the product's image and reinforce the firm's effort to increase the product's degree of brand familiarity.

The advantages and disadvantages of both dealer and manufacturer branding should be studied carefully. They will help you understand the "battle of the brands"--and why some markets are so competitive.

Packaging can actually improve a product--perhaps making it more appealing and/or protecting it from damage. Packaging can also complement promotion efforts by making the whole product more attractive or carrying a promotion message.

By the end of the chapter you should see that wise decisions on packaging and branding can improve any marketing mix--and may help a firm avoid extremely competitive--or even pure competition--situations.

Important Terms

product, p. 250
product assortment, p. 254
product line, p. 254
individual product, p. 254
consumer products, p. 255
industrial products, p. 255
convenience products, p. 255
staples, p. 256
impulse goods, p. 256

emergency products, p. 256
shopping products, p. 257
homogeneous shopping products, p. 257
heterogeneous shopping products, p. 257
specialty products, p. 257
unsought products, p. 258
new unsought products, p. 258
regularly unsought products, p. 258
derived demand, p. 259

True-False Questions

1. A "product" may not include a physical good at all.

2. A product line should be thought of as a firm's product assortment.

3. An individual product is a particular product within a product line and is usually differentiated by brand, size, price, or some other characteristic and identified with its own stockkeeping number.

4. Industrial products are products meant for final consumers.

5. Consumer product classes are based on how consumers think about and shop for a product.

6. Convenience products are products a consumer needs but isn't willing to spend too much time or effort to shop for.

7. Because customers are not willing to spend much time or effort shopping for staples, branding is of little importance for such products.

8. Impulse products are items that the customer decides to purchase on sight, may have bought the same way many times before, and wants "right now."

9. The marketing mix for emergency products will be different from the mix for staples--at least regarding where the products are placed.

10. Shopping products are those products that customers feel are worth the time and effort to compare with competing products.

11. If customers see a product as a homogeneous shopping product, they will base their purchase decisions on the one variable they feel is or can be different--price.

F 12. Price is considered irrelevant for products that the customer sees as heterogeneous shopping products.

F 13. ✓ Specialty products are expensive and unusual products that customers insist upon having and generally have to travel far to find.

T 14. ✓ Specialty products are characterized by brand insistence and relatively inelastic demand curves.

F 15. Unsought products are those items that have no potential value for customers.

T 16. A consumer product must be either a convenience product, a shopping product, or a specialty product--it cannot be all three.

F 17. ✓ In times of recession, a good marketing mix aimed at intermediate customers may not be very effective unless it has some impact on final consumer demand, because the demand for final consumer products is derived from the demand for industrial products.

F 18. ✓ The fact that the demand for most industrial products is derived means that industry demand will be fairly elastic, although the demand facing individual firms may be extremely inelastic.

T 19. ✓ Since industrial products buyers do relatively little shopping compared to consumer products buyers, the industrial products classification system is determined by how buyers see products and how they are to be used.

F 20. ✓ Installations include only buildings and land rights--such as factories, farms, stores, office buildings, mining deposits, and timber rights.

F 21. ✓ Because installations are bought quite often, buying needs are basically economic.

T 22. ✓ Although accessory equipment consists of capital items, purchasing agents have more say in buying accessories--and different marketing mixes would be needed --than for installations.

F 23. ✓ Because raw materials are expensive items, they usually are purchased routinely by purchasing agents--no multiple-buying influence is involved.

F 24. ✓ Most farm products have an elastic market (industry) demand, even though the many small producers are in nearly pure competition.

T 25. ✓ In contrast to farm products, natural products are produced by fewer and larger companies that are quite responsive to market demands and inclined to limit supply to maintain stable prices.

F 26. ✓ Component parts and materials are capital items which have had more processing than raw materials.

T 27. ✓ Although the industry and individual firms' demand may be fairly inelastic for components, there often are many suppliers--so buyers operate in a fairly competitive market.

T 28. A product originally considered a component part when it was sold in the OEM market might become a consumer product for the replacement market--and probably would require a different marketing mix.

F 29. Supplies are commonly described as MRO items, meaning that "More Rational Ordering" procedures are normally followed for them.

T 30. High-level executives may negotiate contracts for some important operating supplies that are needed regularly and in large amounts.

T 31. Maintenance items are similar to consumers' convenience products--and branding may become important for such products.

F 32. Demand for repair items is quite inelastic--and the market is seldom very competitive.

T 33. Services are expense items, and often the cost of buying them outside the firm is compared with the cost of having company personnel do them.

F 34. The terms branding, brand name, and trademark all mean about the same thing--and can be used interchangeably.

F 35. All over the world, branding assures high or at least consistent quality--and encourages repeat purchasing.

F 36. Branding is advantageous to customers--but not to manufacturers.

F 37. Despite the many advantages of branding, a marketing manager would probably be wise to avoid spending large amounts on branding unless (1) the product quality being offered is better than that being offered by all competitors, and (2) the quality can be easily maintained.

F 38. Brand recognition will usually make it easy for the firm to sell its product.

F 39. A firm whose products have reached the brand insistence stage will enjoy a more inelastic demand curve than a firm whose products have achieved brand preference.

F 40. Family brands are also called "fighting brands" because several different products can carry the same brand name.

T 41. A licensed brand is a well-known brand which different sellers pay a fee to use.

F 42. Dealer brands should be used only if they can be priced lower and achieve a faster turnover than manufacturers' brands.

T 43. Generic products are products which have no brand at all other than identification of their contents and the manufacturer or middleman.

T 44. The chances of a middleman being successful with a dealer brand are increased if manufacturers' brands are overpriced.

T 45. Eventually, dealer-branded products may win the "battle of the brands," perhaps because dealers are closer to customers and they can choose to promote their own brands more aggressively.

F 46. While packing is concerned with protecting the product, packaging refers only to promotion.

T 47. When a firm decides to use a new package for its product--to appeal to additional market segments, it is, in effect, adopting a new marketing strategy or strategies.

F 48. Better protective packaging is more important to final consumers than to manufacturers and middlemen.

F 49. A firm should adopt a more expensive package only when the overall effect will be to reduce the total distribution cost for its product.

T 50. Unit-pricing involves placing the price per ounce (or some other standard measure) on or near a product.

T 51. Large supermarket chains have been eager to use the universal product code system--to speed the checkout process and eliminate the need for marking the price on every item.

T 52. A warranty explains what a seller promises about its product.

Answers to True-False Questions

1. T, p. 252	19. T, p. 259	36. F, p. 268
2. T, p. 254	20. F, p. 260	37. F, p. 268
3. T, p. 254	21. F, p. 261	38. F, p. 270
4. F, p. 255	22. T, p. 261	39. F, p. 270
5. T, p. 255	23. F, p. 262	40. F, p. 271
6. T, p. 255	24. F, p. 263	41. T, p. 272
7. F, p. 256	25. T, p. 263	42. F, p. 274
8. T, p. 256	26. F, p. 263	43. T, p. 272
9. T, p. 256	27. T, p. 263	44. T, p. 274
10. T, p. 257	28. T, p. 263	45. T, p. 274
11. T, p. 257	29. F, p. 265	46. F, p. 274
12. F, p. 257	30. T, p. 265	47. T, p. 274
13. F, p. 257	31. T, p. 265	48. F, p. 275
14. T, p. 258	32. F, p. 266	49. F, p. 275
15. F, p. 258	33. T, p. 266	50. T, p. 278
16. F, p. 256	34. F, p. 267	51. T, p. 278
17. F, p. 259	35. F, p. 267	52. T, p. 279
18. F, p. 259		

Multiple-Choice Questions (Circle the correct response)

1. According to the text, the word "product" means:

   a. any tangible item that satisfies needs.
   b. goods but not services.
   c. the need-satisfying offering of a firm.
   d. any item that is mass produced by a firm.
   e. all of the above.

2. Marketing mix planning for services

   a. is easier than for physical goods because services don't need to be stored.
   b. is more likely to be influenced by economies of scale.
   c. must consider where the service is produced.
   d. All of the above are true.
   e. None of the above is true.

3. The set of all products a firms sells is called its:

   a. product line.
   b. individual products.
   c. product assortment.
   d. tangible products.

4. The text's consumer product classes are based upon:

   a. methods of distribution.
   b. SIC codes.
   c. the nature of the products.
   d. the way people think about and buy products.
   e. the way firms view their products.

5. Which of the following is *not* included as a product class in the classification system for consumer products given in the text?

   a. Convenience products.
   b. Staple products.
   c. Specialty products.
   d. Shopping products.
   e. Durable products.

6. As Mary Allen was doing her weekly supermarket shopping, she walked down the cat food aisle to pick up her usual six cans of brand "X." However, she came upon a special display of a new, highly advertised brand and decided to try it instead. In this case, the cat food she bought is:

   a. an impulse product.
   b. a specialty product.
   c. an unsought product.
   d. a homogeneous shopping product.
   e. a staple product.

7. You are stranded in your automobile during a snowstorm. You decide to walk to the closest service station for tire chains. In this case you would consider the tire chains as:

   a. emergency products.
   b. staple products.
   c. impulse products.
   d. shopping products.
   e. specialty products.

8. Mr. Collins feels that most people are too emotional and status-minded concerning their automobile purchases. "An automobile's only function is transportation," he says, "and those high-priced 'chrome-wagons' can't do anything that most lower priced cars won't do." Collins only considers Fords, Chevrolets, and Plymouths when he looks around for a new car. For him automobiles are:

   a. a specialty product.
   b. a homogeneous shopping product.
   c. a convenience staple product.
   d. a heterogeneous shopping product.
   e. a staple product.

9. Specialty products would best be described as having:

   a. brand insistence and inelastic demand.
   b. brand preference and inelastic demand.
   c. brand insistence and elastic demand.
   d. brand preference and elastic demand.
   e. a relatively high price and durability.

10. Which of the following statements about consumer products is *true*?

   a. Convenience products are those that customers want to buy at the lowest possible price.
   b. Shopping products are those goods for which customers usually want to use routinized buying behavior.
   c. Specialty products are those that customers usually are least willing to search for.
   d. Unsought products are not shopped for at all.
   e. None of the above statements are true.

11. Motels are a good example of:

   a. convenience products.
   b. shopping products.
   c. specialty products.
   d. unsought products.
   e. Could be any of the above.

12. Which of the following is *not* a general characteristic of most industrial products?

   a. Buyers tend to buy from only one supplier.
   b. Their demand is derived from the demand for final consumer products.
   c. Industry demand may be inelastic while each company's demand may be elastic.
   d. Buying is basically concerned with economic factors.
   e. All of the above are characteristics for most industrial products.

13. Tax regulations affect industrial buying decisions because:

   a. expense items are depreciated.
   b. capital items are written off over several years.
   c. installations are expensed in one year.
   d. capital items are expensed in one year.

14. According to the text, industrial product classes should be based on:

    a. the shopping behavior of the buyer.
    b. how sellers view their product.
    c. how the products are to be used.
    d. All of the above.
    e. Both b and c.

15. Which of the following is not one of the industrial product classes in the text?

    a. Services
    b. Farm products
    c. Component parts
    d. Accessory equipment
    e. Fabrications

16. Which of the following industrial products to be purchased by a firm is most apt to involve top management?

    a. Raw materials
    b. Accessory equipment
    c. Operating supplies
    d. Installations
    e. Component parts

17. Which of the following should not be classified as accessory equipment?

    a. Office typewriters
    b. Filing cabinets
    c. Portable drills
    d. Accounting machines
    e. All of the above might be accessory equipment

18. Raw materials are usually broken down into two broad categories which are:

    a. domestic animals and crops.
    b. farm products and natural products.
    c. forest products and mineral products.
    d. crops and animal life.
    e. farm products and chemicals.

19. A marketing manager for a firm which produces component parts should keep in mind that:

    a. most component buyers prefer to rely on one reliable source of supply.
    b. the replacement market for component parts generally requires the same marketing mix as the one used to serve the original equipment market.
    c. any product originally sold as a component part becomes a consumer product when sold in the replacement market.
    d. the original equipment market and the replacement market for component parts should be viewed as separate target markets.
    e. All of the above statements are true.

20. Which of the following would not be considered as a component part by an auto manufacturer?

    a. Automobile batteries
    b. Steel sheets
    c. Automobile jacks
    d. Tires
    e. All of the above can be considered component parts, except when they are sold in the replacement market.

21. Supplies may be divided into three main categories. Lubricating oils and greases for machines on the production line would be classified as:

    a. maintenance items.
    b. production items.
    c. operating supplies.
    d. repair supplies.
    e. OEM items.

22. Which of the following statements about the strategic importance of packaging is *false*?

    a. A package may have more promotional impact than a firm's advertising efforts.
    b. A new package can become the major factor in a new marketing strategy by significantly improving the product.
    c. Packaging is concerned with both protection and promotion.
    d. Better packaging always raises total distribution costs.
    e. A package should satisfy not only the needs of consumers but also those of intermediate customers.

23. A "brand name" is:

    a. any means of product identification.
    b. a word used to identify a seller's goods.
    c. the same thing as "branding."
    d. the same thing as "trademark."
    e. All of the above.

24. Which of the following conditions would not be favorable to branding?

    a. Dependable and widespread availability will be possible
    b. Economies of scale in production
    c. Fluctuations in product quality due to inevitable variations in raw materials
    d. Product easy to identify by brand name or trademark
    e. Large market with a variety of needs and preferences

25. A manufacturer has achieved what degree of brand familiarity if, when various "name" brands are available, the firm's particular brand will be chosen out of habit or past experience?

    a. Brand rejection
    b. Brand preference
    c. Brand recognition
    d. Brand insistence
    e. Nonrecognition of brand

26. A firm that has decided to brand all of its products under one label is following a policy of:

   a. using "fighting brands."
   b. dealer branding.
   c. generic branding.
   d. family branding.
   e. individual branding.

27. The best reason for dealer branding by wholesalers is:

   a. to utilize manufacturers' excess capacity.
   b. to protect against channel changes by manufacturers or retailers.
   c. to protect against fickle consumers.
   d. to encourage competition with other wholesalers.
   e. to eliminate need to handle manufacturer brands.

28. Which of the following statements about manufacturer or dealer brands is *true*?

   a. Dealer brands are distributed only by chain-store retailers.
   b. Dealer brands may be distributed as widely or more widely than many manufacturers' brands.
   c. Dealer brands are always priced lower than manufacturers' brands.
   d. Manufacturer brands are sometimes called private brands.
   e. Manufacturer brands usually have widespread distribution in contrast to dealer brands which are only distributed locally or regionally.

29. Which of the following statements regarding the "battle of the brands" is *true*?

   a. It is pretty well over as the dealers now control the marketplace.
   b. In the future, retailer-controlled brands will seek narrower distribution due to increasing promotion costs.
   c. If the present trend continues, manufacturers will control all middlemen.
   d. Manufacturer brands may be losing ground to dealer brands.
   e. By and large, consumers clearly prefer manufacturer brands over dealer brands.

Answers to Multiple-Choice Questions

1. c, p. 250	11. e, p. 258	21. c, p. 265
2. c, p. 253	12. a, p. 259	22. d, p. 275
3. c, p. 254	13. b, p. 259	23. b, p. 267
4. d, p. 256	14. c, p. 259	24. c, p. 268
5. e, p. 254	15. e, p. 260	25. b, p. 268
6. a, p. 256	16. d, p. 260	26. d, p. 271
7. a, p. 256	17. e, p. 261	27. b, p. 273
8. d, p. 257	18. b, p. 262	28. b, p. 273
9. a, p. 258	19. d, p. 265	29. d, p. 274
10. d, p. 258	20. b, p. 263	

Exercise 9-1

Classifying consumer products

Introduction

Consumer product classes are based on the way people think about and buy products. However, different groups of potential customers may have different need and buying behavior for the same product. Thus, the same product could be placed in two or more product classes--depending on the needs and behaviors of target customers. Therefore, product planners should focus on specific groups of customers (i.e., market segments) whose needs and buying behavior are relatively homogeneous.

This exercise will give you some practice in using consumer product classes. As you do the exercise, you will see that the product classes have very little meaning unless they are related to specific target markets.

Assignment

The buying behavior of several customers or potential customers is described below for Canon Sureshot Ace cameras.* Assume in each situation that the customer being described is representative of a particular group of customers--all possessing the same needs and exhibiting similar buying behavior. Then: (a) indicate in which consumer product class the product should be placed based on the characteristics of each group of customers and (b) state why you placed the product in this class. Use the following classes which are described on pages 256-258 in the text.

Staple convenience product   Heterogeneous shopping product
Impulse convenience product   Specialty product
Emergency convenience product   New unsought product
Homogeneous shopping product   Regularly unsought product

The first situation has been answered for you as an example.

Situation 1.　　Mary Wang, a college student, wished to purchase a camera as a birthday gift for her boyfriend. Although Mary could only afford to spend about $70, she wanted a camera of reasonable good quality--but also one which would be easy to operate. Knowing very little about cameras, Mary asked a salesperson at the Campus Camera Shop for his advice. He recommended that she buy a Canon Sureshot Ace camera because of its low price and many convenient features.

Product class: Heterogeneous shopping product.

Reason: Customer spends time and effort to compare quality and features, has little concern for brand, and is not too concerned about price as long as it's within her budget.

The Canon Sureshot Ace camera is a relatively small ("pocket"), easy-to-operate camera which takes "good pictures" using 35 mm film. It features built-in automatic flash and can take "close-in" pictures. The suggested retail price is $79.95.

Situation 2. While deep-sea fishing off the coast of Hawaii, Vic Shaw caught a large swordfish. He decided that his friends back home would never believe his "fish story" if he didn't have pictures. But he did not have a camera. As soon as the boat got back to the dock, Vic went to a nearby tourist shop. He was pleased to see a display of Canon Sureshot Ace cameras, but was sorry to see a much higher price than the same camera sold for in his hometown. He bought one anyway, because he wanted to take some pictures right away before the fish was taken away to the fish market.

Product class: ___Impulse_____

Reason: _____

_____

_____

_____

_____

_____

_____

_____

Situation 3. Maury Schmidt walked into a Consumers Distributing Co. store and told the clerk at the camera counter that he wanted to buy a pocket camera with a built-in flash. The clerk said the store carried several such cameras, including the Canon Sureshot Ace. "I'll take the one with the lowest price," Maury told the clerk.

Product class: ___heterogeneous_____

Reason: _____

_____

_____

_____

_____

_____

_____

Situation 4. Bob Goff teaches high school science courses. He spends most of his leisure time with amateur photography. In fact, he enjoys photography so much that for several years he has volunteered to teach the advanced photography workshop offered by the city recreation department. He has won several awards for his photographs of mountain landscapes. Bob has even earned extra cash by selling some of his photos to companies that print postcards. Several of his friends have encouraged him to turn professional, but he prefers using his talents mainly as a hobby.

Product class: ___Specialty___

Reason: _____

_____

_____

_____

Situation 5. While Mrs. Lotz was shopping in her local supermarket, she came upon a special display of Canon Sureshot Ace cameras. At first, she doubted the product quality because they were priced quite low compared to her friend's Minolta camera. But remembering all the Canon advertisements she had seen on television and in magazines, she decided to buy one to take photographs of her grandchildren who were visiting for the week.

Product class: ___Impulse___

Reason: _____

_____

_____

_____

_____

Situation 6. Ellen Pierce was at her cousin's house and saw some photographs that her cousin had taken with a Canon Sureshot Ace camera. She was so impressed by the quality of the pictures that she decided to purchase the same camera. The next day she went to a nearby camera store and found that the store did not have the camera in stock--although it did have other "pocket cameras" in stock in the same price range. The salesperson in the store assured her that the others were just as good. But Ellen ignored this advice and tried two other stores that were also out of stock. Getting frustrated, Ellen was ready to drive downtown to a large camera store when she came upon a display of Canon Sureshot Ace cameras in a nearby department store. She quickly bought one--even though she felt the price would probably be lower at the camera store.

Product class: _____Specialty_____

Reason: _____

_____

_____

_____

Question for Discussion

What implications do your answers to the above exercise have for Canon when planning its marketing strategies? Be specific.

Exercise 9-2
Classifying industrial products

Introduction

Compared to consumer product buyers, industrial product buyers do relatively little shopping. The accepted practice is for the seller to come to the buyer. This means that industrial product classes based on shopping behavior are *not* useful. The industrial product classes are determined by *how buyers think about products* and *how the products are to be used.*

The industrial product classes may be easier to use than consumer product classes, because industrial buyers tend to have similar views of the same products. Another reason is that the way a purchase is treated for tax purposes affects its classification. The treatment is determined by Revenue Canada rather than the buyer--so little variation is possible.

However, it is possible that a product may be placed in different classes by two buyers because of how they view the purchase. A "small" truck might be classified as an "accessory" by a large manufacturer, while a small manufacturer would view the same truck as an important "installation." Thus, how the customer sees the product is the determining factor--and it will affect marketing mix planning!

Assignment

This exercise focuses on the essential differences between industrial product classes. After carefully reading the following cases, indicate which type of industrial product each case is *primarily* concerned with. Use the following classes:

installations	component materials
accessories	supplies
raw materials	professional services
component parts	

Then explain your answers, taking into consideration the various characteristics of each type of product as explained in the text on pages 258-266. The first case is answered for you as an example.

1. The Perry Company produces a wide variety of metal coil and flat springs for use by many types of industrial customers--including manufacturers of watches, toys, ballpoint pens, weighing scales, office equipment, garage doors, and automobiles. The springs are generally shipped finished and ready for assembly, although minor processing is sometimes required later. Perry faces stiff competition for most of its products, which are mass-produced and processed to commonly accepted standards. Since price and quality often vary only slightly between Perry and its competitors, the company stresses availability and prompt delivery in its selling appeals. Recently, Perry started an aggressive promotion campaign to find new customers for custom-made springs--in an effort to increase profits through the sale of higher-margin products.

a) Product Class: <u>Component parts.</u>

b) Reason: <u>Springs become a part of the finished product--with little or no further processing required--and are treated as expense items. Since they go into the final product, a replacement market could develop. As repair items, the springs would then be "supplies" or some kind(s) of consumer products.</u>

2. Owosso Elevator Company buys the wheat crops of hundreds of small farmers in its area. The wheat is accumulated, sorted, stored until it's sold to flour mills and cereal manufacturers.

a) Product class: _____ raw _____

b) Reason: _____

_____

_____

_____

_____

3. Sue Traykus has worked for XYZ Co. as a purchasing agent for nearly ten years and reacts rather strongly when people refer to purchasing as dull, routine work. "Purchasing is an extremely demanding field," she argues. "A purchasing agent can have a tremendous effect on corporate profits." She recently purchased several new IBM typewriters to be used by the accounting office. Ordinarily she would order something like the typewriters as soon as a requisition slip was submitted to her through proper channels. Due to the company's current cost-cutting program, however, she was required to pass the requisition along to a special top-level budget committee for further approval. Almost a month passed before the order was finally sent to a supplier. "An amazing amount of attention for such a standardized product," said Sue Traykus.

a) Product class: _____ surplus _____

b) Reason: _____

_____

_____

_____

_____

4. Bryon Tang is the service manager for General Mfg. Company's car and truck garage. Tang is responsible for making sure that General's fleet of cars and trucks is in good operating condition at all times. One of his duties is to maintain an adequate inventory of repair parts and equipment, such as mufflers, fan belts, and spark plugs. His parts department is larger than that of many new automobile dealers, and the department is more difficult to manage because General uses several different makes of cars and trucks. Thus, Tang must order a large variety of parts from many suppliers--along with large quantities of lubricating oils, grease, and gasoline.

   a) Product class: _____ Component materials _____

   b) Reason: _____

   _____

   _____

   _____

   _____

5. MARKIT is a marketing research company that helps clients improve their management and marketing decision making--through data collection and evaluation. The firm employs specialists in consumer, industrial, transportation, medical, and government research. It offers clients national field surveys, consumer mail panels, test marketing facilities, shopping center interviews, group interviewing facilities, and a telephone interviewing center--in addition to sophisticated computer and data analysis programs.

   a) Product class: _____ pro. serv. _____

   b) Reason: _____

   _____

   _____

   _____

   _____

6. Tim Vane manages Bob's Service Station, one of three gasoline stations in the rural community of Mason. Until two years ago, Tim was chief mechanic for the station and--according to local residents--was responsible for making Bob's the most popular service station in town. When Bob retired, he made Tim manager and sales have climbed steadily ever since, despite unfavorable economic conditions. Nevertheless, Tim feels the station is not meeting its full potential because it owns only one old wrecker which is suitable for light towing. He would like to purchase a new heavy-duty wrecker to improve his road service. However, Bob (the owner) wants to postpone the purchase until the business cycle takes an upswing.

    a) Product class: _____Installation_____

    b) Reason: _____

    _____

    _____

    _____

    _____

7.   The Universal Steel Supply Company distributes steel and other metals to steel fabricators and tool-and-die shops in the Capital City area. Universal faces stiff competition from approximately 10 other steel wholesalers, including branch warehouses, operated by a few large steel manufacturers. The firm often experiences large sales fluctuations, since many of its customers do work which is related to the automotive industry. Universal's sales force of three salespersons solicits orders for products which have been produced (at the factory) to widely accepted standards. In addition, the company employs a metallurgical engineer to help buyers with their metal working problems. John Carson, the company's president, often assumes personal responsibility for negotiating potentially large orders.

    a) Product class: _____

    b) Reason: _____

    _____

    _____

    _____

    _____

Question for Discussion

Which types of products would most likely be associated with the following kinds of buying: (a) new-task buying, (b) straight rebuy, (c) modified rebuy? Why? Illustrate with examples from Exercise 9-2.

Exercise 9-3
Achieving brand familiarity

Introduction

In hopes of developing a strong "customer franchise," Canadian firms spend billions of dollars annually to promote brands for their products. Nevertheless, many brands are, for practical purposes, valueless because of their *nonrecognition* among potential customers. And while obtaining *brand recognition* may be a significant achievement--given the many nondescript brands on the market--this level of brand familiarity does not guarantee sales for the firm. To win a favorable position in monopolistic competition, a firm may need to develop *brand preference* or even *brand insistence* for its products.

Why are some firms more successful than others in their branding efforts? The reasons are not always clear. Unfortunately, brand loyalty, like many aspects of buying behavior, remains a rather mysterious phenomenon. In general, a firm probably must produce a good product and continually promote it, but this alone may not ensure a high level of brand familiarity--particularly if the firm does not direct its efforts toward some specific target market.

This exercise gets at some important problems in branding--such as conditions favorable to branding--and the difficulty of achieving brand familiarity for certain types of products. As you do the exercise, you may begin to wonder if brands are really relevant for some product classes. You may also wish to speculate about how much effort is spent promoting brands to consumers who have no use for the product in question--or for whom brand names are meaningless.

Assignment

1. List *from memory* (DO NOT DO ANY "RESEARCH") up to five brand names for each of the following product types. List the first brands that come to mind. If you cannot think of *any* brands for a particular product type, write "none" on the first line.

    a) Jams:
    ED Smith
    Kraft
    P.C Loblaws
    Laura Secord
    Robertson

    b) Shampoo:
    Pears
    Sirmack
    Pert
    Pantene PV

c) Glue: _____   e) Crayons: _____
    _____   _____
    _____   _____
    _____   _____

d) Upholstered _____   f) Dishwashers: _____
    furniture: _____   _____
    _____   _____
    _____   _____
    _____   _____

2. What level of brand familiarity do you think exists among the majority of consumers for each of the following products?

       Product Types   *Level of Brand Familiarity*

a) Jams: _____

b) Shampoo: _____

c) Glue: _____

d) Upholstered furniture: _____

e) Crayons: _____

f) Dishwashers: _____

3. From the product types listed in questions 1 and 2, indicate for which one branding would be *most appropriate* and explain what conditions make branding so favorable for that product type.

Product type: _____

Conditions:

4. From the product types listed in questions 1 and 2, indicate for which one branding would be *least appropriate* and explain what conditions make branding so unfavorable for that product type.

Product type: _____

Conditions:

Question for Discussion

Does a firm have a right to use any brand name it chooses?

Exercise 9-4

Comparing branded product offerings

Introduction

Most manufacturers of consumer products use *manufacturers' brands* (often called "national brands") to try to develop a loyal group of customers for their products. At the same time, more and more wholesalers and retailers are offering consumers *dealer brands* (sometimes called "private brands") to try to develop channel and store loyalty. As a result, millions of dollars are spent each year for promotion in a "battle of the brands."

The "battle of the brands" takes many forms--and attitudes toward brands vary a lot both among consumers and marketers. Some retailers tend to stock mainly manufacturers' brands. Meanwhile, some manufacturers--particularly in the shoe industry--have opened up their own retail outlets to promote their own brands.

To add to the "battle of the brands," many food retailers are now carrying *generic products*--unbranded products in plain packages (or unpackaged!)--to appeal to price-conscious consumers. This gives consumers even more products to choose from--but may make it more difficult and confusing to determine the "best buy."

This exercise is designed to give you additional insight into the "battle of the brands." You are asked to make price comparisons between manufacturers' brands, dealer brands, and generic products--and then decide which is the "better buy."

Assignment

1. Visit a large chain supermarket and record the prices of the items listed on the next page. For each item, select one manufacturer brand, one dealer brand, and one generic product. If no generic product is available, write the price of the dealer brand in the generic column. If the store carries neither a dealer brand nor a generic product, write the price of the manufacturer brand in all three columns. Each column must be completely filled out so that you can compare the totals for all three columns.

2. Which do you think is the "better buy"--manufacturer brands, dealer brands, or generic products? Why? What factors did you take into consideration in deciding which is the better buy?

PRICE COMPARISON CHART

Name and location of store: _____

Date visited: _____

Item and Approximate Size	Manufacturer Brand	Dealer Brand	Generic Product
Ketchup (14-oz. bottle)			
Instant coffee (8-oz. jar)			
Corn flakes (12-oz. box)			
Peanut butter (1-lb. 2-oz. jar)			
White vinegar (1 qt.)			
Tomato soup (10-oz. can)			
Bathroom tissue (4-pack)			
Cream style corn (17-oz. can)			
Sliced yellow cling peaches (29-oz. can)			
Tomato juice (46-oz. can)			
Bar soap (bath size)			
Shortening (3-lb. can)			
White flour (5-lb. bag)			
Chocolate cake mix (1-lb. 3-oz. package)			
Liquid detergent for dishes (32-oz. container)			
Facial tissue (box of 400 or 200 double)			
Mouthwash (12-oz. bottle)			
Liquid bleach (1 gal.)			
Powdered detergent (3-lb. box)			
Total cost of a basket of goods			

Question for Discussion

For what reason(s) would a supermarket want to stock dealer brands or generic products when heavily-advertised manufacturer brands are available?

Chapter 10

Product management and new-product development

What This Chapter Is About

Chapter 10 introduces product life cycles--and shows the need for managing products and developing new products.

Modern markets are dynamic--and the concepts introduced in this chapter should deepen your understanding of how and why markets evolve. Product life cycles should be studied carefully--to see how marketing strategies must be adjusted over time. In later chapters you will get more detail about how the marketing mix typically changes at different stages of the life cycle. So now is the time to build a good base for what is to come.

This chapter is one of the most important in the text, because new products are vital for the continued success of a business. Yet, a large share of new products fail. Such failures can be avoided by using the new-product development process discussed in the text. Think about this process carefully, and try to see how you could help develop more satisfying and profitable products. Creativity in product planning--perhaps seeing unsatisfied market needs--could lead to breakthrough opportunities!

Important Terms

product life cycle, p. 284
market introduction, p. 284
market growth, p. 284
market maturity, p. 285
sales decline, p. 286
fashion, p. 287
fashion cycle, p. 288
distinctiveness stage, p. 288
emulation stage, p. 288

economic emulation stage, p. 288
fad, p. 289
new product, p. 294
The Hazardous Products Act, p. 299
product liability, p. 300
concept testing, p. 300
product managers, p. 304
brand managers, p. 304

True-False Questions

_F_ 1. The product life cycle is divided into four major stages: market introduction, market growth, market maturity, and market saturation.

_T_ 2. A firm's marketing mix usually must change--and different target markets may be appealed to--as a product moves through the different stages of its life cycle.

F 3. Industry sales and profits tend to rise and fall together as a product moves through its life cycle.

F 4. The market introduction stage is usually extremely profitable due to the lack of competitors.

T 5. Industry profits tend to reach their peak and start to decline during the market growth stage--even though industry sales may be growing rapidly.

T 6. Industry profits decline throughout the market maturity stage because aggressive competition leads to price cutting and increased expenditures on persuasive promotion.

F 7. During the sales decline stage, new products replace the old--and all firms remaining in the industry find themselves operating at a loss.

F 8. In general, product life cycles appear to be getting longer due to a decline in product innovation.

T 9. A fashion is the currently accepted or popular style.

T 10. In the distinctiveness stage of the fashion life cycle, buyers with a need for individuality are willing to pay for products that are different than those that satisfy the majority.

T 11. The emulation stage of a fashion life cycle is like the early market growth stage of the product life cycle.

T 12. A fad is an idea that is fashionable only to certain groups who are enthusiastic about it--but so fickle that it is even more short-lived than a regular fashion.

T 13. Target marketers should recognize that each market segment may have its own product life cycle.

F 14. Once a firm introduces a product to a market, it has no other choice but to watch its product move through the remaining stages of the product life cycle.

T 15. Strategy planning can sometimes extend product life cycles, delaying the move from market maturity to sales decline.

F 16. While a lot of strategy planning is necessary to introduce a new product, no strategy is required to get rid of a dying product.

T 17. According to the text, a new product is one that is new in any way for the company concerned--including offering an existing product to a new market.

T 18. Twelve months is the longest time that any product may be called "new" according to Consumer and Corporate Affairs Canada.

F 19. Since new products are vital to the survival of most firms, the objective of the new-product development process should be to approve as many new-product ideas as possible.

F 20. Product planners should consider long-term welfare in addition to immediate satisfaction--and therefore should offer "pleasing products" instead of "desirable products."

F 21. The idea generation and screening steps of the new-product development process are very subjective--only qualitative evaluation criteria can be employed because no physical product exists.

T 22. Product liability means the legal obligation of sellers to pay damages to individuals who are injured by defective or unsafe products.

T 23. Concept testing is done before any tangible product has been developed--and involves marketing research to determine potential customers' attitudes towards the new-product idea.

F 24. The development step (in new-product development) involves the testing of physical products as well as test marketing--something that must be done for all products prior to commercialization.

T 25. The specific organization arrangement for new-product development may not be too important--as long as there is top-level support.

T 26. Product managers sometimes have profit responsibilities and much power, but often they are "product champions" who are mainly involved in planning and getting promotion done.

Answers to True-False Questions

1. F, p. 284
2. T, p. 284
3. F, p. 284
4. F, p. 284
5. T, p. 284
6. T, p. 285
7. F, p. 286
8. F, p. 286
9. T, p. 287

10. T, p. 288
11. T, p. 288
12. T, p. 289
13. T, p. 290
14. F, p. 292
15. T, p. 292
16. F, p. 293
17. T, p. 294
18. T, p. 294

19. F, p. 294
20. F, p. 299
21. F, p. 298
22. T, p. 300
23. T, p. 300
24. F, p. 301
25. T, p. 303
26. T, p. 304

Multiple-Choice Questions (Circle the correct response)

1. The product life cycle has four stages. Which of the following is *not* one of these?

   a. Market introduction
   b. Market growth
   c. Market maturity
   d. Economic competition
   e. Sales decline

2. During the *market introduction* stage of the product life cycle:

   a. considerable money is spent on promotion while place development is left until later stages.
   b. products usually show large profits if marketers have successfully carved out new markets.
   c. most potential customers are quite anxious to try out the new-product concept.
   d. funds are being invested in marketing with the expectation of *future* profits.
   e. product and promotion are more important than place and price.

3. Which of the following statements regarding the *market growth* stage of the product life cycle is *false*?

   a. Innovators still earn profits--but this stage is less profitable for them than the previous stage.
   b. This is the time of peak profitability for the industry.
   c. The sales of the total industry are rising fairly rapidly as more and more customers buy.
   d. Monopolistic competition is common during this stage.

4. In planning for different stages of the product life cycle, strategy planners must be aware that:

   a. losses can be expected during the market introduction stage.
   b. the life cycles of mature product-markets can be extended through strategic product adjustments.
   c. offering the product to a new market segment may start a whole new life cycle.
   d. products can be withdrawn from the market before the sales decline stage--but even here a phase-out strategy is usually required.
   e. All of the above are true statements.

5. Regarding product life cycles, good marketing managers know that:

   a. all competitors lose money during the sales decline stage:
   b. they are getting longer.
   c. industry sales reach their maximum during the market growth stage.
   d. firms earn their biggest profits during the market introduction stage.
   e. industry profits reach their maximum during the market growth stage.

6. A particular industry is experiencing no real sales growth and declining profits in the face of oligopolistic competition. Demand has become quite elastic--as consumers see competing products as almost homogeneous. Several firms have dropped out of the industry, and there has been only one recent new entry. Firms in the industry are attempting to avoid price-cutting by budgeting huge amounts for persuasive advertising. In which stage of the product life cycle are firms in this industry competing?

   a. Market maturity
   b. Sales decline
   c. Market growth
   d. Market introduction

7. Marketing managers should recognize that:

   a. product life cycles appear to be getting longer.
   b. every segment within a market has the same product life cycle.
   c. the product life cycle describes the sales and profits of individual products, not industry sales and profits.
   d. firms that enter mature markets have to compete with established firms for declining industry profits.
   e. None of the above is a true statement.

8. Which of the following statements about fashions and fads is *false*?

   a. A fad is an idea that is fashionable only to certain enthusiastic but perhaps fickle groups.
   b. A fashion refers to the currently accepted or popular style.
   c. In the economic emulation stage, many consumers want the currently popular fashion--but at a lower price.
   d. Fashion cycles usually lead the relevant product life cycle.
   e. How a particular fashion gets started is not well understood.

9. With regard to the new-product development process:

   a. the objective should be to "kill" all ideas that probably will not be profitable.
   b. screening criteria should be entirely quantitative--as qualitative criteria tend to allow for too much subjectivity and bias.
   c. the idea evaluation step involves product-usage tests by potential customers to determine if the concept is appealing.
   d. market tests are essential for all products prior to commercialization.
   e. concept testing is usually done as soon as a product has been developed and can be put into consumers' hands.

10. Which of the following types of products provides low immediate satisfaction but high long-run consumer welfare?

   a. Salutary products
   b. Pleasing products
   c. Desirable products
   d. Deficient products

11. A firm should attempt to estimate the ROI on a new product during the _____ step of the new-product development process.

    a. screening
    b. idea evaluation
    c. development
    d. commercialization
    e. all of the above

12. Product or brand managers are commonly used when a firm:

    a. has several different kinds of products or brands.
    b. wants to eliminate the job of the advertising manager.
    c. has one or a few products--all of which are important to its success.
    d. wants to eliminate the job of sales manager.
    e. wants one person to have authority over all the functional areas that affect the profitability of a particular product.

Answers to Multiple-Choice Questions

1. d, p. 284	5. e, p. 285	9. d, p. 300
2. d, p. 284	6. a, p. 285	10. a, p. 299
3. a, pp. 284-285	7. d, p. 285	11. a, p. 300
4. e, p. 285	8. d, pp. 287-289	12. e, p. 304

Exercise 10-1

Identifying a product's stage in the product life cycle

look from industry life cycle

Introduction

This exercise is designed to improve your understanding of the product life cycle--a valuable model for marketing strategy planning. For example, the product life cycle can help decide if and when it will be to a company's advantage to add, change, or drop a given product. Further, where a product is along its life cycle suggests a workable blend of the "four Ps."

Assignment

Read the following five cases carefully and for each one:

a)   Decide which stage of the product life cycle best describes the situation in the case--considering the relevant product-market.

b)   Briefly explain your answer, including such factors as profitability, number of competitors, place, promotion, and pricing.

1.   Necci Stereo Systems is just entering the fast-growing, but increasingly competitive compact disc player market. The Necci marketing manager is confident that he can capture a profitable share of the market because his firm's player has--as a standard feature--a remote control unit that is an extra cost option on players from well-known competitors like Pioneer and Sony. To attract support from traditional retailers of home electronics products, Necci is offering a very low wholesale price. Even at the very low suggested retail price, this will make the Necci player very profitable for the retailers. Necci's marketing manager says that this very aggressive pricing will pay off. He predicts that in the next decade compact discs will replace cassette tapes--and that already prices of the discs are dropping rapidly. He says that this will stimulate even faster growth in the disc player market.

a)   Stage of product life cycle: ___Market growth___ ✓

b)   Explanation: _some competitors, promotion of incl. feature high_
     will be a key factor, pricing low but volume should high -
     should climb steadily volume

2. Sony recently announced a new VHS format videocassette recorder. Sony was one of the first firms to offer a cassette player, but its Beta format cassettes never proved to be as popular as VHS. While Sony stuck to its Beta format machines, many other firms enjoyed rapid sales growth with their VHS equipment. Now, prices on VHS equipment have dropped and profit margins have thinned. Even so, Sony anticipates a good market share because it believes the new recorder will have better sound reproduction than the dozens of other brands of VHS recorders on the market. Sony also hopes that the new model--and consumer familiarity with the Sony name--will allow the firm to obtain greater distribution through a variety of electronics stores, catalog stores, department stores, and mass-merchandisers.

   a) Stage of product life cycle: _Product introduction Mkt Maturity_

   b) Explanation: _Many competitors but better quality, familiarity c Sony name key, some profits but generally low, higher initial price_

3. Body Beautiful, Inc., one of the nation's largest producers of personal care products, has just announced plans to sell a new shampoo called Tender-Care. The company is spending heavily on magazine and TV ads that will promote Tender-Care as "The shampoo that everyone can use daily. No other shampoo is as gentle on your hair or provides as clean and natural a scent." Free samples of Tender-Care will be attached to packages of other Body Beautiful products, and magazine ads will include cents-off coupons. Despite intense competition, Body Beautiful expects its new product to capture a 5 percent share of the slowly growing shampoo market.

   a) Stage of product life cycle: _Product intro. Mkt Maturity_

   b) Explanation: _Promotion heavy, low profit, higher retail price._

4. Monsanto has recently received Food and Drug Administration approval to market Simplesse, a low-calorie, low-cholesterol product that can be used as a fat substitute in a variety of frozen dessert products. Monsanto hopes that Simplesse will meet the needs of health-conscious consumers--and the food producers who serve them. However, the cost of promotion to build awareness of the benefits of Simplesse will be very significant, and the investment in research and development is already high. Furthermore, other firms--including Procter and Gamble and Kraft--are developing products that will compete for the same market.

   a) Stage of product life cycle: _Mkt growth introduction_

   b) Explanation: _Many competitors,_

5. General Electric recently announced that it was pulling out of the portable phonograph business, citing the trend toward sophisticated stereo systems and taped music. Despite sales of about a million units a year (about 50 percent of the market), GE was not able to maintain an adequate profit margin on the portable phonographs due to the increasing costs, heavy price competition and a steady 10-year decline in industry sales. Those firms still making portables were not planning to increase production despite GE's announcement.

a) Stage of product life cycle: ___Sales Mkt decline_____ ✓

b) Explanation: ___Few competitors, declining volume,___ low retail prices, minimum promo - aid, minimal sales.

Question for Discussion

What alternatives should a firm consider when it finds some or all of its products in the market maturity stage of the product life cycle?

Int'l markets, new uses for product, milking of brand

Exercise 10-2
New-product development process

Introduction

The product life cycle shows us that markets and competition are dynamic. Over time old products are replaced with new ones. And as markets mature, firms usually face increasing price competition and erosion of their profit margins. To succeed in spite of these pressures, firms must constantly look for new market opportunities--and that often means identifying and developing new product ideas--and effective strategies to go with them.

While the new-product development process is crucial to the survival and success of most firms, it is also a challenge. Even the best-run companies sometimes miss opportunities that--after the fact--seem obvious. And too often companies go ahead and introduce new products that turn out to be costly failures. Marketing managers can increase the odds of success in this area by really understanding the steps of the new-product development process--and what it takes to generate and screen new product ideas.

This exercise is intended to help develop your skills in this area.

Assignment

The short descriptions that follow provide information about different companies. In each case, there is at least one major problem with the way the company is currently approaching the new-product development process. Read and evaluate each statement carefully, and then explain:

a) your diagnosis of the problem, and

b) your recommendation for what the company should do as a substitute for what is described in the case situation.

1. Beta Medical Supplies Corporation produces a variety of sterile storage containers used in hospital operating rooms. Recently, large companies like Johnson & Johnson have been aggressive in this market, and they seem to have had better success in identifying new-product opportunities. The sales manager at the company recently sent a memo to the firm's salespeople outlining problems related to the firm's weak financial position. He ended the memo with a plea: "To increase our profits in coming years, we must move ahead aggressively with new-product ideas. The president of the company fully backs this thrust. He has established a new-product screening committee with members from different departments of the firm. You are in contact with the customer--and we need for you to submit your ideas. We promise to carry forward with marketing research on every good idea that comes in. Our objective is to really get behind your ideas--and turn them into products."

a) The problem: _____

_____

_____

_____

_____

b) Your recommendation: _____

_____

_____

_____

_____

2. Ethical Drug Company had developed a promising new nonprescription tablet to relieve the symptoms of allergy sufferers. The ideas has successfully passed the screening and idea evaluation stages of the company's new-product development process. The company has also completed concept tests and produced some tablets. Now, the head of the non-product development group has sent the following memo to the marketing department. "Our laboratory tests have satisfied Consumer and Corporate Affairs Canada criteria and we are ready to move ahead with a final test market prior to commercialization. I want you to start thinking about this now. If the product does well in the test market, we will need to develop the rest of the marketing mix. We will want to come up with an attention-getting package design--one that will really stand out on a drugstore shelf. We will also need to decide on the brand name we would use in a national distribution. For now, we will just price the product in test market at the same price as our cold tablets. So final pricing decisions will also need to be made. And, of course, we will need to decide what type of promotion to use--and what message we want to get across to potential customers. I wanted to alert you to these exciting developments so that you could be getting your ideas together. We want to be ready to move quickly into commercialization if the test market is successful."

a) The problem: _____

_____

_____

_____

_____

b) Your recommendation: _____

_____

_____

_____

_____

3. Linkco, Inc. produces and sells special types of wire used in a variety of telecommunication applications. The firm's initial growth came from sales of a new wire that was used by cellular telephone service companies when setting up transmission stations. However, growth in that market has slowed. Moreover, at present, most of the other products offered by the firm are similar to those available from a variety of other suppliers. Cheri Davis, the marketing manager for the company, recently scheduled a meeting with the company president to discuss problems of falling profits. Cheri expressed concern that the company did not have a specific person responsible for identifying new products. The president pointed out that few other firms in their industry had such a position--and generally argues that new-product thinking was the responsibility of everyone in the firm. After further discussion, the president agreed to let Davis send out a memo to all company employees encouraging them to be alert to new product ideas--and to submit any ideas to the research and development department for analysis of their technical feasibility.

   a) The problem: _____

   _____

   _____

   _____

   _____

   b) Your recommendation: _____

   _____

   _____

   _____

   _____

4. Performance, Inc. has been successful in producing and marketing high performance motorcycles. In searching for new product opportunities, the company became interested in small size, three-wheel all-terrain vehicles (ATVs) designed for children in the 10- to 15-year age group. The head design engineer for the company thought that the company's expertise in designing motorcycles would apply directly to this popular new product. In addition, many of the dealers who carry the firm's motorcycles are interested in the idea. However, one of them noted that there have been many accidents involving three-wheel ATVs--and suggested that the company check into product-liability insurance. When this was discussed back at the firm, the engineer said that he did not see a big problem. "After all," he said, "our ATVs will be as safe as others that are available. And in addition the accidents that occur are invariably the fault of the user. We can't be held responsible for user-errors if the product is properly designed and manufactured."

a) The problem: _____

_____

_____

_____

_____

b) Your recommendation: _____

_____

_____

_____

_____

Question for Discussion

The text emphasizes that many of the new products that are developed and introduced prove to be expensive failures. Who pays the cost of these failures? Is it just the owners of the companies that introduced them?

Chapter 11

Place and development of channel systems

What This Chapter Is About

Chapter 11 introduces the strategic decisions in Place--and considers how and why channel systems develop the way they do. These ideas will help you understand the Place-related materials that follow in the next three chapters.

First, the need to adjust discrepancies of quantity and assortment is discussed. This will help you see why channel specialists develop. Later, various types of channel systems are explained--so you will have a better understanding of how channel members work together.

"Ideal" Place objectives are also explained--to emphasize the relevance of potential customers' behavior to Place planning. These ideal Place objectives are related to the product classes introduced in Chapter 9.

At the end of the chapter, the concepts of pushing or pulling within a channel are discussed.

This chapter emphasizes that marketing strategy must consider the whole channel--and that channel management is an ongoing, dynamic process. As you learn about these strategic Place decisions, think about why a channel captain can play such an important role in leading the channel toward a common product-market commitment.

Important Terms

True-False Questions

____ 1. The Place part of the marketing mix is concerned with building channels of distribution and providing the time, place, and possession utilities needed to satisfy target customers.

____ 2. A channel of distribution is any series of firms or individuals who participate in the flow of goods and services from producer to final user or consumer.

____ 3. A marketing manager's decisions on Place have long-range effects and are usually harder to change than Product, Price, and Promotion decisions.

____ 4. Product classes help solve Place problems and in particular how much market exposure will be needed in each geographic area.

____ 5. Discrepancies of quantity exist because producers specialize in making one or a few items--while customers want many items and probably would prefer not to shop at different stores for each item.

____ 6. Because few customers can consume a big part of any producer's output, the large quantities that mass production makes possible generally cause a discrepancy of assortment.

____ 7. Collecting larger quantities of similar products, the accumulating process, creates a discrepancy of quantity but permits economies of scale.

____ 8. Bulk-breaking involves dividing larger quantities into smaller quantities as products get closer to the final market.

____ 9. The sorting process is usually handled by middlemen--when they put together a variety of products to give a target market what it wants.

____ 10. The assorting process means sorting products into the grades and qualities desired by different target markets.

____ 11. Marketing specialists should develop to adjust discrepancies of quantity and assortment only if these discrepancies must be adjusted.

____ 12. Although seldom used, direct-to-user channels are almost always better than channels which use middlemen.

____ 13. In a traditional channel system the various channel members make little or no effort to cooperate with each other.

____ 14. Vertical marketing systems are channel systems in which the whole channel shares a common focus on the same target market at the end of the channel.

____ 15. Corporate channel systems involve corporate ownership all along the channel.

____ 16. In regard to the development of the channel system, vertical integration means acquiring firms which operate at different levels of channel activity.

____ 17. Any administered channel system--by definition--is also a contractual channel system.

____ 18. Because of the importance of Place in a firm's marketing mix, marketing managers should always seek maximum market exposure for their products.

____ 19. Ideal market exposure makes a product widely enough available to satisfy the target customers' needs--but not exceed them.

____ 20. An intensive distribution policy refers to the marketing manager's desire to sell through all responsible and suitable wholesalers and retailers.

____ 21. Since it is not necessary to obtain 100 percent coverage of a market to justify or support national advertising, some firms now using intensive distribution might be wise to switch to selective distribution and use only the better middlemen to distribute and promote their products.

____ 22. Exclusive distribution is likely to be used by a producer--to help control prices and the service offered in a channel.

____ 23. Dual distribution occurs when a manufacturer uses several competing channels to reach the same target market--perhaps using several middlemen in addition to selling directly itself.

____ 24. "Pulling a product through the channel" means using normal promotion effort to help sell the whole marketing mix to possible channel members.

____ 25. Clearly, a producer should always act as "channel captain"--because he is in the best position to help direct the channel as an integrated system of action.

____ 26. A channel system can work well only if its members have accepted a common product-marked commitment and are all strongly market-oriented.

____ 27. The "channels system" concept assumes that all of the functions of marketing must be performed by someone within a channel of distribution--i.e., these functions can be shifted and shared, but not eliminated.

Answers to True-False Questions

1. T, p. 310	10. F, p. 313	19. T. p. 318
2. T, p. 310	11. T, p. 311	20. T, p. 319
3. T, p. 311	12. F, p. 314	21. T, p. 320
4. T, p. 311	13. T, p. 316	22. T, p. 320
5. F, p. 311	14. T, pp. 316-317	23. T, p. 322
6. F, pp. 311-312	15. T, p. 317	24. F, p. 324
7. T, p. 312	16. T, p. 317	25. F, p. 325
8. T, p. 312	17. F, pp. 317-318	26. F, p. 325
9. F, p. 313	18. F, p. 318	27. F, p. 325

Multiple-Choice Questions (Circle the correct response)

1. The "Place" variable deals with the creation of:

    a. time and place utilities only.
    b. time, place, possession, and form utilities.
    c. time utility only.
    d. time, place, and possession utilities.
    e. place and possession utilities only.

2. A channel of distribution:

    a. is any series of firms or individuals who participate in the flow of goods and services from producer to final user or consumer.
    b. must include a middleman.
    c. must have at least three members--a manufacturer, a wholesaler, and a retailer.
    d. All of the above are true statements.

3. Marketing specialists develop to adjust "discrepancies" in the marketplace. Which of the following best explains the concept of "discrepancies"?

    a. There are many more consumers than there are producers.
    b. The assortment and quantity of products wanted by a customer may be different than the assortment and quantity of products normally produced by a manufacturer.
    c. Supply and demand is no longer determined by market forces because "big business" is more powerful than the individual consumer.
    d. Price is not always a reliable measure of a product's quality.
    e. Although most manufacturers claim to be marketing-oriented, most firms would rather produce what they want to sell rather than what customers want to buy.

4. Discrepancies of quantity occur because:

    a. some customers have more money than others.
    b. individual producers tend to specialize while individual consumers want a broad assortment of products.
    c. consumers demand more product variety than producers can make.
    d. to obtain economies of scale, individual producers often make larger quantities of products than individual consumers normally want to buy.
    e. there are many more consumers than producers.

5. If you were a retailer attempting to supply a wide variety of products for the convenience of your customers, which of the following "regrouping activities" would you be *most* involved in?

   a. Sorting
   b. Accumulating
   c. Bulk-breaking
   d. Assorting
   e. Breaking bulk

6. Which of the following statements about channel systems is *true*?

   a. Some administered channel systems have achieved the advantages of vertically integrated systems while retaining more flexibility.
   b. All vertical marketing systems are also contractual channel systems.
   c. The independence of firms in traditional channel systems has led to channel efficiencies because of greater freedom of decision making.
   d. Indirect channel systems seem to be generally more effective than direct channels.
   e. Corporate channel systems are competitively superior to administered channel systems.

7. If Kmart were to purchase the Zenith Radio Corporation, this would be an example of:

   a. vertical integration.
   b. internal expansion.
   c. horizontal integration.
   d. an administered channel system.

8. A manufacturer that tries to sell a product through any *responsible* and *suitable* wholesaler or retailer who will stock and/or sell the product is seeking what degree of market exposure?

   a. Exclusive distribution
   b. Intensive distribution
   c. Selective distribution

9. Which of the following statements about "ideal" market exposure is *true*?

   a. A manufacturer should aim for maximum market exposure.
   b. As a firm moves from intensive to exclusive distribution, it loses more and more control over price and service.
   c. It may be necessary to avoid intensive distribution to avoid dealing with middlemen who buy too little compared to the cost of working with them.
   d. Intensive distribution refers to the desire to sell through any and every retail outlet.
   e. All of the above are true statements.

10. Although some middlemen may resent this approach, a manufacturer may have to use "dual distribution" because:

   a. present channel members are doing a poor job.
   b. the firm desires to reach different target markets.
   c. some customers are widely dispersed geographically.
   d. antitrust regulations prohibit relying on just one channel system.
   e. both a and b above.

177

11. The Boyd Corporation is introducing a new product next month. To prepare for the introduction, the marketing manager is having his sales force call on distributors to explain the unique features of the new product, how the distributors can best promote it, and what sales volume and profit margins they can reasonably expect. In addition, Boyd is budgeting 2 percent of its estimated sales for magazine advertising. This is an example of:

    a. selective distribution.
    b. a "pulling" policy.
    c. exclusive distribution.
    d. a "pushing" policy.
    e. intensive distribution.

12. Ideally, a "channel captain":

    a. has sufficient market power to force his policies on other channel members.
    b. is a manufacturer.
    c. is a strong retailer or wholesaler.
    d. is assigned this role by majority vote among channel system members.
    e. earns his position by effective leadership.

13. When a channel has a "product-market commitment":

    a. all members focus on the same target market at the end of the channel.
    b. its members attempt to share the various marketing functions in appropriate ways.
    c. there is no need for a channel captain to develop.
    d. all of the above.
    e. a and b above--but not c.

Answers to Multiple-Choice Questions

1. d, p. 311	6. a, pp. 317-318	10. a, pp. 322-323
2. a, p. 310	7. a, p. 317	11. d, p. 324
3. b, p. 311	8. b, p. 318	12. e, p. 325
4. d, p. 311	9. c, pp. 318-319	13. e, p. 326
5. d, p. 312		

Exercise 11-1

Evaluating the costs of adjusting discrepancies of quantity and assortment in channel systems

Introduction

If market segmentation were carried to its extreme, every customer would have a set of "tailor-made" goods and services. From an economic standpoint, this normally wouldn't be practical, of course. And fortunately, it isn't necessary--since it's often possible to find reasonably sized groups of consumers having relatively homogeneous needs. This often leads to "economies of scale"--which lower costs to customers.

By their very nature, however, mass production and mass consumption cause discrepancies of quantity and assortment. So, activities for adjusting these discrepancies are needed. The *regrouping activities* are: accumulating, bulk-breaking, sorting, and assorting. These activities can be carried out by the manufacturer or the consumer. Like many activities, however, they are generally performed best by specialists. This is why marketing middlemen develop--and often become important members of channels of distribution.

Assignment

The following case shows the role of marketing middlemen (particularly wholesalers) in creating and adjusting discrepancies of quantity and assortment. Questions appear at various points through the case--to test your understanding of the material. Read the case carefully and answer the questions *as they appear*. It is important that you understand the concepts involved, even though the case has been simplified to aid analysis. So think about the implications for a highly developed economy such as Canada.

FREE MARKET REPUBLIC

The Free Market Republic is a small developing country that recently experienced an industrial revolution. The country's 100 basic commodities are produced by 100 specialized firms, each of which makes only one product. All of the products are in turn sold through a network of 2,000 equal-sized retailers who are scattered all around the country.

The Babbage Company produces widgets (a consumer staple) for the Free Market Republic. Due to large fluctuations in demand, the widgets cannot be manufactured in large quantities--and therefore cost $12.50 each to produce. Each week Babbage's salespeople have to call on all of the retailers to solicit their orders for widgets. This results in a relatively high selling cost of $2.00 per each unit sold. Since orders are generally quite small, order processing costs amount to about 50 cents per unit. Finally, the necessity of shipping many small orders to retailers results in transportation costs of $1.00 per unit. The price Babbage charges for each unit is determined by adding on 50 percent of the *total* unit cost of producing, selling, and delivering the widgets. Each retailer, then, takes a 40 percent markup on the cost they are charged by Babbage.

1. How much do consumers in the Free Market Republic pay for widgets? Show your work (and label your numbers). The retail price of widgets is _____ .

2. What discrepancies of quantity and assortment exist in the Free Market Republic? Be specific.

Consumers in the Free Market Republic complained about the high prices they were being asked to pay for widgets and other commodities. They blamed retailers for the high prices--demanding that the government take some action to reduce the retailers' high markups. However, retailers in turn blamed the high prices on the operating practices of manufacturers. Manufacturers acknowledged inefficiencies in their operations, but contended that such problems were unavoidable given the country's present distribution system.

After thinking over the situation quite carefully, the country's economic advisers concluded that the best solution would be to change the nation's distribution system. They recommended that 10 wholesale establishments be added to facilitate the distribution of manufactured commodities. The welfare minister protested, however, that the addition of more middlemen would only serve to raise prices instead of lowering them. Here, the economists countered with the following list to show the advantages of employing wholesalers in the Free Market Republic:

a. The presence of wholesalers would tend to stabilize demand for manufacturers, allowing them to take advantage of mass production techniques. It was estimated that manufacturing costs could be cut in half by producing products in larger quantities.

b. Since manufacturers would only have to deal with 10 wholesalers who buy in large quantities instead of 2,000 retailers, their unit selling costs would decrease by 60 percent. Furthermore, since each wholesaler would only be required to sell to 200 retailers, the wholesale selling costs would amount to only about 25 cents per unit for most commodities.

c. Order processing costs would decrease 50 percent for manufacturers, because wholesalers would order in large quantities. However, it will still cost wholesalers about 25 cents per unit to process each order from the retailers.

d. By shipping bulk quantities to the wholesalers, the manufacturers could take advantage of carload freight rates, thereby cutting their shipping costs to about 50 cents per unit. Also, since their orders would travel shorter distances, the wholesalers could ship products at a rate of 30 cents per unit.

e. Because they deal in large quantities of merchandise, the wholesalers would operate with only a 20 percent markup on total unit cost. Moreover, retailers could cut their markups down to 25 percent, since they would each be dealing with only one wholesaler rather than with 100 manufacturers--and therefore would have lower costs.

3. Assuming that the economist's estimates are accurate, calculate the new retail price for widgets if Babbage were to distribute them through wholesalers. Show your work (and label your numbers).

The new retail price for widgets would be _____ .

4. Should the Free Market Republic adopt the plan to use wholesalers in its distribution system? ____ Yes ____ No
Why?

5. Explain how the addition of wholesalers would serve to adjust discrepancies of quantity and assortment in the Free Market Republic. Be specific.

Question for Discussion

Which marketing functions were added or eliminated with the addition of wholesalers to the Free Market Republic's macro-marketing system?

Exercise 11-2
Determining market exposure policies

Introduction

Once a producer decides to use middlemen (wholesalers and retailers) to help distribute its products, it must decide what degree of market exposure will be best: *exclusive distribution, selective distribution*, or *intensive distribution*. Contrary to popular opinion, maximum exposure is not always desirable. The ideal market exposure should meet--but not exceed--the needs of target customers. As one moves from exclusive distribution to intensive distribution, the total marketing cost may increase--and the quality of service provided by middlemen may actually decline.

When deciding about the desired market exposure, a marketing manager should consider the functions which middlemen will be asked to perform and the product class for his product. The product classes summarize some of what is known about the product--including what the target customers think of it, their willingness to shop for it, and the amount of personal attention and service they want. The product class often determines the "ideal" market exposure.

Of course, there sometimes is a difference between a firm's *ideal* market exposure and the exposure which it can achieve. Middlemen are not always willing to carry a new product, especially when several similar products are already on the market. The manufacturer must first convince prospective wholesalers and retailers of the product's profit potential. Normally, this is done by using a "pushing" policy. But manufacturers may have to adopt a "pulling" policy to overcome strong channel resistance.

Assignment

This exercise will give you some practice in determining the "ideal" degree of market exposure for a company. Six cases are presented below--with the first serving as an example. Read each case carefully and then indicate (a) the product class which is involved, and (b) the degree of market exposure (intensive, selective, or exclusive) which you think would be "ideal." Then in part (c), explain *why* you think the indicated degree of market exposure would be ideal. State any assumptions which you have made. *Note:* "Ideal" here means the degree of market exposure which will satisfy the target customers' needs (but not exceed them) *and also* will be achievable by the producer. For example, a new producer of "homogeneous" cookies might desire intensive distribution, but agrees to sell to only a few food chains because it knows it will not be able to obtain intensive distribution with its undifferentiated cookies. So its "ideal" is selective distribution and it will adjust the rest of its marketing mix accordingly.

Note: Exhibits 9-4 and 9-5 on pages 256 and 260 of the text may be helpful in completing this exercise.

1. Oriental Designs, Ltd., manufactures decorative items for the home. It recently added beaded bamboo curtains to its product line. Designed for use in open doorways or as room dividers, the curtains are available in several colors and can be mounted easily on curtain rods. They are priced at $20 per set and measure six feet long by three feet wide. Like most of the company's products, the curtains are sold in gift shops, hobby shops, and specialty shops such as "Wicker City" franchise outlets. Initial sales for the curtains have been quite promising. The product seems to have good "eye appeal," according to one shop owner. Apparently, the early customers hadn't planned to buy anything like bamboo curtains, but once they saw them displayed in the store, they couldn't resist buying them.

    a) Product class: <u>Impulse product</u>

    b) "Ideal" market exposure: <u>Intensive distribution</u>

    c) Why? <u>Customers must *see* the product before they will buy it. Therefore, widespread distribution in all suitable outlets including furniture stores, gift shops, etc. would seem essential.</u>

2. Colorwear, Inc. is an English firm that manufactures a high-quality line of fashionable shirts that are popular among young men and teenage boys in Canada. The line is quite expensive--so most customers are from wealthy families. The clothing is sold through specialty shops which handle only this type of wearing apparel (including competing brands). Colorwear will only work with retailers who agree to stock a large variety of sizes and colors of Colorwear fashion. They also must agree to promote the Colorwear line very aggressively. In return, Colorwear agrees not to distribute its line to other retailers within the specialty shop's immediate trading area. Since continuing promotion seems to be necessary in this highly competitive market, advertisements for Colorwear clothes appear regularly in magazines targeted at young men.

    a) Product class: _____

    b) "Ideal" market exposure: _____

    c) Why? _____

    _____

    _____

    _____

    _____

3. A researcher at Enviro Paper Products Co. recently developed a new biodegradable, disposable diaper. Enviro has primarily been an industrial products manufacturer, but had produced diapers for a few large grocery chains to sell as their own dealer brand. The new diaper will be its first attempt at marketing a consumer product under its own brand. So far, results are not encouraging. Only a few wholesalers have taken on the line. Most are very reluctant to handle the diaper, claiming that retail shelves are already overcrowded with other brands of disposable diapers.

    a) Product class: _____

    b) "Ideal" market exposure: _____

    c) Why? _____

        _____

        _____

        _____

        _____

4. International Tractor, Inc. (ITI) manufactures a full line of farm machinery-- including tractors, graders, and materials-handling equipment. ITI farm products are distributed through over 150 independent dealers scattered throughout Canada. Typically, there is only one ITI dealer near any rural community, although there may be several other dealers who sell competing equipment. Many of ITI's dealerships are quite small, and the company lacks adequate dealers in several key market areas. To further complicate matters, price wars between dealerships are becoming common as industry sales continue to decline. In fact, some ITI dealers often find themselves competing directly with other ITI dealers--since many farmers travel 100 miles or more to purchase new equipment.

    a) Product class: _____

    b) "Ideal" market exposure: _____

    c) Why? _____

        _____

        _____

        _____

        _____

5. Lane Furnishings, Inc. manufactures a wide line of bookshelves and entertainment cabinets for sale throughout Canada. The products are distributed through retail outlets. Retailers are supposed to stock a large assortment of the shelves, along with a large inventory of accessory parts (cabinet doors, hinges, shelf supports, etc.). The sets are usually shipped to the retailers unassembled. According to a recent cost study, 30 percent of Lane's retailers account for about 80 percent of the company's sales.

    a) Product class: _____

    b) "Ideal" market exposure: _____

    c) Why? _____

    _____

    _____

    _____

    _____

6. Computer Accessory Equipment, Inc. makes and sells a low-priced line of computer support tables for use in offices. One style of table has casters and a very compact design--so the table, computer, and printer can all be easily moved. Another style is larger and is designed to fit along side a regular desk; it features a pull-out drawer for the keyboard and an electrical outlet to plug in the computer and accessories. The tables are sold directly to large companies, universities, and other institutions--and indirectly through wholesalers to office equipment dealers. The tables sell to final customers (not the middlemen) at prices ranging from about $100 to $360. Most dealers handle several competing brands of computer tables, including some "high quality" brands that sell for as much as $1,000.

    a) Product class: _____

    b) "Ideal" market exposure: _____

    c) Why? _____

    _____

    _____

    _____

    _____

Question for Discussion

How do you think each firm should try to achieve the "ideal" degree of market exposure you discussed above? Are there any legal constraints they should consider?

Chapter 12
Retailing

What This Chapter Is About

Chapter 12 looks at the many changes, sometimes called "scrambled merchandising," which have been taking place in retailing.

Try to understand why and how retailers behave--because retailing probably will continue to change in the future. In particular, try to see why there are so many different types of retailers--and why some seem to be doing well while others have serious problems.

Don't just memorize the definitions of the various types of retailers. Instead, study what each is doing for some group of target customers. A diagram is presented later in the chapter to help organize your thinking.

It is useful to think of retailers from their point of view--rather than only as outlets for manufacturers' products. Most retailers see themselves as buyers for their customers, rather than selling arms of manufacturers. Try to look at retailing the way they do. This should increase your understanding of this vital part of our marketing system.

Important Terms

retailing, p. 331
convenience store, p. 333
shopping stores, p. 333
specialty stores, p. 333
general stores, p. 335
single-line (limited-line) stores, p. 335
specialty shop, p. 336
department stores, p. 336
mass merchandising concept, p. 339
supermarket, p. 339
catalog showroom retailers, p. 340
discount houses, p. 340
mass merchandisers, p. 341
super-stores, p. 341
convenience (food) stores, p. 342

automatic vending, p. 342
telephone and direct mail order, p. 343
door-to-door selling, p. 344
planned shopping centers, p. 345
neighborhood shopping centers, p. 345
community shopping centers, p. 345
regional shopping centers, p. 345
scrambled merchandising, p. 348
wheel of retailing theory, p. 349
corporate chain, p. 352
cooperative chains, p. 352
voluntary chains, p. 352
franchise operation, p. 352

True-False Questions

____ 1. Retailing covers all of the activities involved in the sale of products to final consumers.

____ 2. More than three-fourths of all new retailing ventures fail during the first year.

____ 3. A consumer's choice of a retail store appears to be based almost entirely on emotional needs--economic needs have almost no influence.

____ 4. By definition, a convenience store would not stock shopping products or specialty products.

____ 5. The major attraction of a shopping store would be the width and depth of its merchandise assortment.

____ 6. A specialty store is one that handles an assortment of unusual or exotic merchandise.

____ 7. Single-line stores specialize in a single line of merchandise--such as food--but handle a wide assortment of products within that line.

____ 8. A limited-line store will typically carry a broader assortment than a single-line store.

____ 9. Limited-line stores may carry several lines of merchandise--but with a very limited assortment of products within each line.

____ 10. A specialty shop is a type of limited-line store that usually is small, has a distinct personality, and aims at a carefully defined market segment by offering knowledgeable salespeople, better service, and a unique product assortment.

____ 11. A specialty shop would probably be viewed by most customers as a specialty store that stocks primarily specialty goods.

____ 12. Department stores are becoming less important and they now account for only about 1 percent of retail sales.

____ 13. Conventional retailers believe in a fixed demand for a territory and have a "buy-low and sell-high" philosophy.

____ 14. The mass merchandising concept says that retailers should offer low prices to get faster turnover and greater sales volumes--by appealing to larger markets.

____ 15. A well-managed supermarket can generally count on a net profit level of only about 1 percent of sales.

____ 16. Catalog showroom retailers have become quite successful in Canada using their strategy of stocking little inventory and delivering by mail.

____ 17. While discount selling generally involves price cutting on a limited assortment of products, many modern discount houses are fast-turnover, price-cutting operations that offer full assortments, better locations, and more services and guarantees.

____ 18. The average mass merchandiser has a store that is about the same size as an average supermarket.

____ 19. Super-stores are simply large mass merchandisers that carry more shopping products.

____ 20. Convenience food stores limit their assortment to those "pickup" or "fill-in" items that are needed between major shopping trips to a supermarket, and thus earn smaller profits as a percent of sales.

____ 21. Automatic vending has low operating costs because labor costs are very low.

____ 22. Telephone and mail-order retailing grew for a while but now seems to have leveled off at less than 2 percent of retail sales.

____ 23. Although it's an expensive method of selling--door-to-door retailers may be especially useful for the sale of unsought products.

____ 24. "Scrambled merchandising" is a way of describing the activities of modern retailers who are willing to carry "unconventional" assortments of products--anything they can sell profitably.

____ 25. All major retailing developments can be explained by the "Wheel of Retailing" theory--which describes a recurring retail cycle from low cost and low prices to higher cost and higher prices.

____ 26. Less than 5 percent of all retail stores have annual sales of 2.5 million dollars or more--but these stores account for more than 50 percent of all retail sales.

____ 27. One of the incentives to chain store development is the availability of economies of scale.

____ 28. Voluntary chains are formed by independent retailers in their efforts to compete with corporate chains--while cooperative chains operate similarly except that they are sponsored by wholesalers.

____ 29. The very high failure rate among franchise operations explains why franchises are becoming less popular.

___ 30. By the year 2000 franchise holders will account for one-half of all retail sales.

___ 31. A good example of a planned shopping center is the central business district found in most large cities.

___ 32. Neighborhood shopping centers consist primarily of convenience stores.

___ 33. Although community shopping centers may provide a variety of convenience products--their major emphasis is on shopping products.

___ 34. Regional shopping centers typically serve 40,000 to 150,000 people within a radius of 3-4 miles.

___ 35. In the future, in-home shopping and electronic retailing are both expected to become more popular.

Answers to True-False Questions

1. T, p. 331	13. T, p. 339	25. F, p. 349
2. T, p. 332	14. T, p. 341	26. T, p. 351
3. F, p. 332	15. T, p. 339	27. T, p. 352
4. F, p. 333	16. F, p. 340	28. T, p. 352
5. T, p. 333	17. T, p. 341	29. F, p. 353
6. F, p. 333	18. F, p. 341	30. F, p. 354
7. T, p. 335	19. F, p. 341	31. T, p. 345
8. F, p. 335	20. F, p. 342	32. F, p. 345
9. F, p. 335	21. F, p. 343	33. T, p. 345
10. T, p. 336	22. F, p. 343	34. F, p. 345
11. F, p. 336	23. T, p. 344	35. T, p. 354
12. F, p. 337	24. T, p. 348	

Multiple-Choice Questions (Circle the correct response)

1. Which of the following best describes what "retailing" involves?

   a. The sale of consumer products to wholesalers, retailers, or final consumers.
   b. The performance of all merchandising activities except promotion and pricing.
   c. The sale of both industrial and consumer products.
   d. The sale of products to final consumers.
   e. All of the above describe what retailing involves.

2. Retail stores can be classified as convenience stores, shopping stores, and specialty stores. This classification is based on:

   a. the size of the store.
   b. the customers' image of the store.
   c. the location of the store.
   d. the type of products the store carries.
   e. All of the above.

3. A small privately owned men's clothing store in a university town has stressed personal services (e.g., free 90-day credit) and first-name relationships with student customers. The store carries only expensive, well-known brands of clothing and offers the largest selection of such merchandise in the area. Which of the following classifications is this retailer attempting to achieve?

   a. Specialty store--shopping products
   b. Shopping store--specialty products
   c. Specialty store--convenience products
   d. Shopping store--shopping products
   e. Convenience store--convenience products

4. Which of the following are *not* "conventional retailers" according to the text?

   a. General stores
   b. Single-line stores
   c. Supermarkets
   d. Limited-line retailers
   e. All of the above

5. Which of the following would be considered a *limited-line* retailer?

   a. Supermarket
   b. Gas station
   c. Mass merchandiser
   d. Drugstore
   e. Bakery shop

6. Specialty shops:

   a. generally try to become well known for the distinctiveness of their line and the special services offered.
   b. generally carry complete lines--like department stores.
   c. carry specialty products almost exclusively.
   d. generally achieve specialty store status.
   e. All of the above are true.

7. Department stores:

   a. are often frowned upon by the retailing community because they provide too many customer services.
   b. normally are large stores which emphasize depth and distinctiveness rather than variety in the lines they carry.
   c. achieve specialty store status with some consumers--and thus may be the only way to reach these market segments.
   d. account for less than 1 percent of the total number of retail stores--but over half of total retail sales.
   e. All of the above are true statements.

8. Large departmentalized retail stores that are larger than supermarkets and follow the discount house's philosophy of emphasizing lower margins to achieve faster turnover are called:

    a. department stores.
    b. mass merchandisers.
    c. planned shopping centers.
    d. specialty shops.
    e. box stores.

9. Which of the following statements about supermarkets is *true*?

    a. Supermarkets should be classified as "conventional retailers."
    b. Net profits after taxes in supermarkets usually run about 1 percent of sales--or less.
    c. The minimum annual sales volume for a store to be classified as a supermarket is $500,000.
    d. They typically carry 25,000 product items.
    e. All of the above are true statements.

10. Catalog showroom retailers:

    a. are essentially mail-order sellers.
    b. must charge above-average prices to cover the costs of printing and distributing catalogs to consumers.
    c. stress convenience as their most distinguishing feature.
    d. minimize handling costs by keeping their inventories in backroom warehouses until customer orders are placed.
    e. All of the above are true statements.

11. The "super-store concept":

    a. is just another name for the mass merchandising concept.
    b. essentially refers to large department stores which have adopted supermarket-style operating procedures and methods.
    c. is concerned with providing all of the customer's routine needs at a low price.
    d. probably will not be accepted by mass merchandisers.
    e. All of the above are true.

12. The modern convenience (food) stores are successful because they offer:

    a. wide assortments.
    b. low prices.
    c. expanded customer service.
    d. the right assortment of "fill-in" items.
    e. All of the above.

13. Which of the following statements about telephone and mail-order retailing is *true*?

  a. Most large mail-order houses aim at special-interest target markets.
  b. Mail-order houses tend to have lower operating costs than conventional retailers.
  c. All mail-order houses offer both convenience products and shopping products.
  d. Although mail-order houses have declined in number in North America, they have achieved more than 15 percent of total Canadian retail sales.
  e. Mail-order retailers place their primary emphasis on low-price merchandise.

14. Which of the following concepts is best illustrated by a retail bakery that sells wristwatches?

  a. The "super-store"
  b. Scrambled merchandising
  c. Time-sharing
  d. The "Wheel of Retailing" theory
  e. Mass merchandising

15. The "Wheel of Retailing" theory suggests that:

  a. retail stores do not have life cycles.
  b. retailing profits tend to be cyclical.
  c. only the largest retailers have a chance to survive in a fast-moving economy.
  d. new types of retailers enter as low-price operators and eventually begin to offer more services and charge higher prices.
  e. only discounters can survive in the long run.

16. Census data indicate that:

  a. less than 5 percent of all retail establishments have annual sales of $2.5 million or more.
  b. there are more manufacturers and wholesalers than there are retailers in Canada.
  c. retailing is no longer a field made up mostly of small businesses.
  d. the really large retailers account for a rather small percentage of total retail sales.
  e. all of the above are true.

17. A group of retailers banding together to establish their own wholesaling organization would be known as a:

  a. cooperative chain.
  b. voluntary chain.
  c. consumer cooperative.
  d. corporate chain.
  e. franchise.

18. Franchisers:

    a. are similar to voluntary chain operators.
    b. often provide franchise holders with training.
    c. usually receive fees and commissions from the franchise holder.
    d. reduce their risk of starting a new retailing business.
    e. All of the above are true statements.

19. A new shopping center has been built in an area which allows it to serve about 80,000 people with a five- to six-mile radius. It is composed of a supermarket, drugstore, hardware store, beauty shop, laundry and dry-cleaning store, a gas station, and a small department store. This center would be considered:

    a. a community shopping center.
    b. a neighborhood shopping center.
    c. a central business district.
    d. a regional shopping center.

20. Which of the following is *least likely* to occur in retailing in the future?

    a. Conventional retailers will continue to feel a profit squeeze.
    b. Scrambled merchandising will decline.
    c. There will be more vertical arrangements between producers and retailers.
    d. There may be an increase in in-home shopping.
    e. Stores will continue to make shopping more convenient.

Answers to Multiple-Choice Questions

1. d, p. 331	8. b, p. 339	15. d, p. 349
2. b, p. 333	9. b, p. 339	16. a, p. 351
3. a, p. 333	10. d, p. 340	17. a, p. 352
4. c, p. 335	11. c, p. 341	18. e, p. 352
5. e, p. 335	12. d, p. 342	19. a, p. 345
6. a, p. 336	13. b, p. 343	20. b, p. 353
7. c, p. 336	14. b, p. 348	

Exercise 12-1

Analyzing store-product combinations

Introduction

In Chapter 9, consumer products were classified--as convenience products, shopping products, specialty products, and unsought products--based on how different consumers think about and buy products. But just as the same *product* can mean different things to different people, the same *retail store* may also be seen differently by different target customers. Thus, in Chapter 12--building on the earlier discussion of consumer behavior and product classes--retail stores are classified as convenience stores, shopping stores, and specialty stores.

Because marketing planners should consider both product- and store-related needs, it is helpful to put the products and store classes together to form store-product combinations. (See Exhibit 12-2 on page 334 of the text.)

This exercise illustrates how different customer needs and shopping behavior for basically the same product--in this case, men's shirts--can result in different target customers seeking different store-product combinations. As you do the exercise, try to think about the strategic implications of store-product combinations--both for retailers as well as for manufacturers and wholesalers.

Assignment

The needs and shopping behavior of potential customers for men's shirts are described in the following cases. Assume in each case that the customer being described is representative of a group of customers having similar needs and shopping behavior. Read each case carefully and then: (a) indicate which of the following store-product combinations is most relevant and (b) briefly explain your answer in the space provided. The first case is answered for you as an example.

1. Convenience store selling convenience products
2. Convenience store selling shopping products
3. Convenience store selling specialty products
4. Shopping store selling convenience products
5. Shopping store selling shopping products
6. Shopping store selling specialty products
7. Specialty store selling convenience products
8. Specialty store selling shopping products
9. Specialty store selling specialty products

1. Bob Moore was about to start a new sales job and needed about a dozen new dress shirts--in varying styles and colors--to fill out his wardrobe. He decided to buy all of the shirts at Eaton's Department Store because Eaton's was the only store in town where Bob had a charge account.

    a) Store-product combination: <u>Specialty store selling shopping products</u>

    b) Explanation: <u>He prefers a particular store (Eaton's) because he has a charge account there, but also because he needs an adequate assortment of shirts from which to choose.</u>

2. One Thursday evening, while shopping at Eaton's for a swimsuit for his weekend trip, Phillip Downey remembered that he also needed a casual shirt. After he found a swimsuit, he went over to the sportswear department to see if he could find a casual shirt he would like.

    a) Store-product combination: _____

    b) Explanation: _____

    _____

    _____

    _____

3. Bill Blackmon had been looking for a shirt that would go well with his new suit. As he was looking through Esquire magazine, he saw an ad for an Alexander Julian designer shirt that was just right. The next day, Bill stopped in Eaton's Department Store to buy some shoes that were on sale. On the way out of the store, the men's shirt department caught his eye and he found the exact shirt he wanted. He was pleased that he didn't have to search at a number of other stores.

    a) Store-product combination: _____

    b) Explanation: _____

    _____

    _____

    _____

4. On his way home from work, William Daniels noticed that his felt tip pen had leaked all over the pocket of his white shirt. Will was embarrassed to have to tell his wife that he had ruined another shirt, so he quickly stopped by Eaton's Department Store at the shopping center near his house to replace the stained shirt with another similar shirt.

a) Store-product combination: _____

b) Explanation: _____

_____

_____

_____

5. While getting dressed, Gene Bunn noticed that the collar on his Gant Shirt was looking worn. Gene gave some thought to when he could get to Eaton's Department Store. He always bought his shirts there because they had a "large men's" department that carried extra large sizes in the Gant brand shirts he liked to wear.

a) Store-product combination: _____

b) Explanation: _____

_____

_____

_____

6. After spilling his morning cup of coffee all over his white shirt, bank executive Ronald Smith telephoned all the nearby clothing stores to find one that was willing to deliver a new shirt in time for Ronald to attend an important luncheon meeting. Eaton's Department Store told him they would send a clerk right over with a shirt.

a) Store-product combination: _____

b) Explanation: _____

_____

_____

_____

7. Paden Reeves dislikes white shirts, but has to wear them five days a week in his job as a buyer at Eaton's Department Store. When his white shirts wear out, Paden buys a whole box of Eaton's own brand of shirts at one time--taking advantage of his 20 percent employee discount plus a quantity discount.

    a) Store-product combination: _____

    b) Explanation: _____

_____

_____

_____

8. Jay Klomper decided to buy a colorful sportshirt to wear to his ten-year high school reunion. He didn't have any particular style or color in mind, but he had usually been able to find something he liked at Eaton's Department Store or one of the many men's clothing stores right around Eaton's.

    a) Store-product combination: _____

    b) Explanation: _____

_____

_____

_____

9. When Willa Graham asked her father what he would like for Father's Day, he said that he wanted a white Arrow brand dress shirt to wear with his new gold cuff links. Knowing exactly what she wanted, Willa went from store to store until she found the shirt at Eaton's Department Store.

    a) Store-product combination: _____

    b) Explanation: _____

_____

_____

_____

Question for Discussion

How might a retailer such as Eaton's Department Store use the above store-product combinations in planning its marketing strategies? Are these combinations also relevant for wholesalers and manufacturers?

Exercise 12-2

Identifying and analyzing retail stores

Introduction

Retailing involves the sale of products to final consumers. There are approximately 180,000 retail stores in Canada. However, as discussed in the text, there are many different types of retailers which vary both in size and method of operation. Marketing managers of consumer products at all channel levels must understand retailing--for if the retailing effort is not effective, the products may not be sold and all members of the channel will suffer. Likewise, consumers must be concerned with retailing--because their standard of living is partly dependent on how well retailing is done.

The purpose of this exercise is to focus your attention on the retailers who serve *your* community. What types of stores are there? How do they operate? Who are their target customers? Why might there be different types of retailers selling *basically* the same kind of products?

Assignment

Listed below are several types of retail stores which were discussed in the text. For each type:

a) Give the name and address of a store in your community that illustrates this type.

b) Briefly describe the store in terms of its *width* and *depth* of assortment. Is it a single-line or limited-line store or a "scrambled merchandiser"? Does the store stress high turnover or low turnover products?

c) Briefly describe the store in terms of its price/service blend (is the store price-oriented or service-oriented) and estimate whether the store's gross margin is in the *low range* (below 20 percent), *medium range* (20-35 percent), or *high range* (over 35 percent).

Note: If your community does not have a particular store type, write "none" under part (a) and then answer parts (b) and (c) in terms of how you *think* that type of store would operate.

1. *Limited-Line "Conventional" Retailer*

    a) Store name and address: _____

    b) Assortment: _____

    c) Price/Service blend: _____
    Gross margin range: _____

2. *Department Store*

    a) Store name and address: _____

    b) Assortment: _____

    c) Price/Service blend: _____
    Gross margin range: _____

3. *Supermarket*

    a) Store name and address: _____

    b) Assortment: _____

    c) Price/Service blend: _____
    Gross margin range: _____

4. *Convenience (Food) Store*

    a) Store name and address: _____

    b) Assortment: _____

    c) Price/Service blend: _____
    Gross margin range: _____

5. *Catalog Showroom*

    a) Store name and address: _____

    b) Assortment: _____

    c) Price/Service blend: _____
    Gross margin range: _____

6. *Mass Merchandiser*

   a)   Store name and address: _____

   b)   Assortment: _____

   c)   Price/Service blend: _____

        Gross margin range: _____

7. *Single-line Mass-Merchandiser*

   a)   Store name and address: _____

   b)   Assortment: _____

   c)   Price/Service blend: _____

        Gross margin range: _____

Question for Discussion

Why are there so many different types of retailers in Canada? What implication does this have for marketing strategy planning?

Chapter 13

Wholesaling

What This Chapter Is About

Chapter 13 discusses various kinds of specialized wholesalers who have developed to provide "wholesaling functions"--really just variations of the basic marketing functions. You should become familiar with the various types: what they do, and roughly what they cost.

Wholesalers are not guaranteed a place in channel systems. Some have been eliminated. Others probably will be. And other wholesalers have been making a "comeback" in some lines. Try to understand why.

Like other firms, wholesalers must develop market-oriented strategies. But wholesalers are channel specialists--so think of them as members of channel systems--rather than as isolated firms. This will help you see why wholesalers are very important members of *some* channel systems--while they are not used at all in other channels.

Important Terms

wholesalers, p. 361

merchant wholesalers, p. 364

service wholesalers, p. 365

general merchandise wholesalers, p. 365

single-line (or general-line) wholesalers, p. 365

specialty wholesalers, p. 365

limited-function wholesalers, p. 366

cash-and-carry wholesalers, p. 366

drop-shippers, p. 366

truck wholesalers, p. 367

mail-order wholesalers, p. 367

producers' cooperatives, p. 368

rack jobbers, p. 368

agent middlemen, p. 368

manufacturers' agent, p. 369

brokers, p. 370

commission merchants, p. 370

selling agents, p. 371

auction companies, p. 371

export agents, p. 371

import agents, p. 371

export commission houses, p. 371

import commission houses, p. 371

export brokers, p. 331

import brokers, p. 331

combination export manager, p. 371

manufacturers' sales branches, p. 372

factors, p. 372

field warehouser, p. 372

sales finance companies, p. 373

floor planning, p. 373

True-False Questions

____ 1. A producer who uses a direct channel system normally is also considered a wholesaler--because he must take over the wholesaling functions that an independent wholesaler might provide.

____ 2. All wholesalers perform the following functions for their customers: anticipate needs, regroup products, carry stocks, deliver products, grant credit, provide information and advisory service, provide part of buying function, and own and transfer title to products.

____ 3. A wholesaler might help a producer by reducing the producer's need for working capital.

____ 4. The typical merchant wholesaler's operating expenses amount to about 20 percent of sales.

____ 5. Merchant wholesalers don't necessarily provide all of the wholesaling functions, but they do take title to the products they sell.

____ 6. A general merchandise service wholesaler may represent many different kinds of manufacturers and supply many different kinds of retailers.

____ 7. Drop shippers own the products they sell--but do not actually handle, stock, or deliver them.

____ 8. Service wholesalers provide all of the wholesaling functions--while limited-function wholesalers provide only certain functions.

____ 9. Cash-and-carry wholesalers operate like service wholesalers, except that the customer must pay cash.

____ 10. Truck wholesalers' operating costs are relatively high because they provide a lot of service relative to how much they sell.

____ 11. Mail-order wholesalers should probably be classified as retailers--since they sell out of catalogs.

____ 12. Producers' cooperatives are limited-function wholesalers that specialize in supplying consumer cooperatives at the retail level.

____ 13. Rack jobbers are limited-function wholesalers, with relatively high operating costs, who help retailers offer a more attractive assortment of products--especially nonfood items.

____ 14. A manufacturer who has the capability of operating its own distribution facilities but lacks customer contacts should consider the use of agent middlemen to facilitate the buying and selling functions.

____ 15. The key role of manufacturers' agents is to provide well-established customer contacts for new products--while assuming all the risks of taking title to the products they handle.

___ 16. A broker's "product" is information about what buyers need--and what supplies are available.

___ 17. Probably the most important function of a commission merchant is anticipating the needs of its customers.

___ 18. A small manufacturer with limited financial resources whose only skills are in production should probably consider contracting with a selling agent to act, in effect, as the firm's marketing manager.

___ 19. The primary advantage of auction companies is that they facilitate buying by description.

___ 20. Agent middlemen are less common in international trade than in Canadian markets because merchant wholesalers can both sell products and handle the financing.

___ 21. The fact that many manufacturers have set up their own sales branches suggests that the use of wholesalers usually makes distribution costs unnecessarily high.

___ 22. A small manufacturer of textiles with limited financial resources should probably consider selling its accounts receivable to a factor.

___ 23. A manufacturer who wants to maintain an inventory of goods in a sparsely populated rural area should seek the services of a field warehousing organization.

___ 24. Many appliance dealers do not own outright any of the appliances on their display floor--instead the inventories are financed by sales finance companies as part of an arrangement called "floor planning."

___ 25. Many manufacturers and retailers have realized that wholesaling functions are not always necessary, so wholesalers have been eliminated at an increasing rate in recent years.

___ 26. Most modern wholesalers have become more streamlined in their operations, more computerized in controlling their inventories, and more selective in their distribution policies.

___ 27. Recent trends in wholesaling indicate that wholesaling will survive, even though some wholesalers may disappear.

Answers to True-False Questions

1. F, p. 361	10. T, p. 367	19. F, p. 371
2. F, p. 362	11. T, p. 367	20. F, p. 371
3. T, p. 362	12. F, p. 368	21. F, p. 371
4. F, p. 363	13. T, p. 368	22. T, p. 372
5. T, p. 364	14. T, p. 368	23. F, p. 372
6. T, p. 365	15. F, p. 369	24. T, p. 373
7. T, p. 366	16. T, p. 370	25. F, p. 374
8. T, p. 365	17. F, p. 370	26. T, p. 376
9. T, p. 366	18. T, p. 371	27. T, p. 377

Multiple-Choice Questions (Circle the correct response)

1. Which of the following is *not* a typical wholesaling function?

    a. provide market information to a producer.
    b. grant credit to customers.
    c. supply capital to pay the cost of carrying inventory.
    d. all of the above are typical wholesaling functions.
    e. none of the above is a typical wholesaling function.

2. Which of the following types of wholesalers has the *highest* operating expenses as a percent of sales?

    a. Manufacturers' agents
    b. Manufacturers' sales branches
    c. Brokers
    d. Commission merchants
    e. Merchant wholesalers

3. The two basic types of merchant wholesalers are:

    a. single-line and specialty.
    b. service and limited-function.
    c. service and general merchandise.
    d. single-line and limited-function.
    e. agents and brokers.

4. Which of the following statements about merchant wholesalers is *true*?

    a. The major distinguishing characteristic of merchant wholesalers is that they take title to the products they handle.
    b. Merchant wholesalers are the most numerous type of wholesaling establishment-- but handle only about 25 percent of wholesale sales.
    c. General merchandise wholesalers operating in the consumer products area handle a broad variety of nonperishable items--usually including only convenience products.
    d. A specialty wholesaler generally would limit himself to the industrial products area--as distinguished from the consumer products area.
    e. All of the above statements are true.

5. Which of the following types of wholesalers do *not* carry stocks for their customers?

    a. Cash-and-carry wholesalers.
    b. Rack jobbers.
    c. Truck wholesalers.
    d. Drop-shippers.
    e. Mail-order wholesalers.

6. Which of the following statements about rack jobbers is *true*?

    a. Rack jobbing is a relatively high-cost operation--costing more than the average for merchant wholesaling.
    b. Rack jobbers provide retailers with specialized information about consumer preferences.
    c. Rack jobbers are practically full-service wholesalers--except they usually do not grant credit.
    d. Rack jobbers developed because many grocers did not wish to bother with reordering and maintaining displays of nonfood items.
    e. All of the above are true statements.

7. A type of middleman that does *not* take title to the products is known as:

    a. an agent middleman.
    b. a limited-function wholesaler.
    c. a rack jobber.
    d. a merchant wholesaler.
    e. a drop-shipper.

8. Which of the following statements is *false*?

    a. Agent middlemen generally do not take title to products they sell.
    b. Manufacturers' agents usually do not represent competing manufacturers.
    c. Brokers are often used because of the seasonal nature of production or demand.
    d. Manufacturers' agents generally have more authority over prices and terms of sale than do selling agents.
    e. Agent middlemen are very common in international trade.

9. Turgo, Inc. has just developed a new convenience product for which it wants intensive distribution nationally. It expects a low initial demand and wants to keep selling costs as low as possible while keeping control of marketing. This is Turgo's first product and working capital is small. Which of the following channels would be best?

    a. Turgo's own sales force direct to retailers.
    b. Manufacturers' agents to merchant wholesalers to retailers.
    c. Commission merchants to retailers.
    d. Turgo's own sales force direct to merchant wholesalers to retailers.
    e. Selling agents to merchant wholesalers to retailers.

10. The Jory Co. handles the entire output of several small clothing manufacturers on a national basis. The firm has almost complete control of pricing, selling, and advertising. In addition, Jory often provides working capital to the producers, who have very limited financial resources. In return, Jory is paid a substantial commission on all sales. The Jory Co. is a:

    a. selling agent.
    b. commission merchant.
    c. full-service wholesaler.
    d. manufacturers' agent.
    e. broker.

11. The principal function of a broker is to:

    a. transport acquired products.
    b. facilitate inspection of products.
    c. establish a central market.
    d. bring buyers and sellers together.
    e. distribute grocery products.

12. Manufacturers' sales branches:

    a. have very low sales per branch.
    b. are mainly used in weak market areas, where there is not enough business for other types of wholesalers.
    c. operating costs would be even lower than they are now if manufacturers didn't "charge" them with extra expenses.
    d. handle about a third of all wholesale sales.
    e. serve the same basic needs as do brokers.

13. The Perlman Corp. manufactures and distributes a specialized line of textile products. An opportunity has arisen for Perlman to expand its product line. However, most of Perlman's working capital is tied up due to slow payment of accounts receivable--and management does not wish to take on any additional debt at this time. Perlman should consider employing the services of a:

    a. sales finance company.
    b. field warehouseman.
    c. factor.
    d. floor planner.
    e. any of the above.

14. Which of the following statements is *least relevant* in explaining the "Comeback of the Wholesaler"?

    a. It is due to a natural rise in the need for wholesaling services.
    b. It is caused in part by the fact that wholesalers are now more "retailer-minded."
    c. It has been aided by more selective choice of customers--as many small retailers were clearly unprofitable.
    d. Many wholesalers no longer require each customer to pay for all of the services they provide *some* customers.
    e. Greater emphasis has been placed on training and advising retailer-customers.

Answers to Multiple-Choice Questions

1. d, p. 362	6. e, p. 368	11. d, p. 370
2. e, p. 364	7. a, p. 368	12. d, p. 372
3. b, p. 365	8. d, p. 369	13. c, p. 372
4. a, p. 364	9. b, pp. 369-370	14. a, p. 374
5. d, p. 366	10. a, p. 371	

Exercise 13-1

Choosing the right kind of wholesaler

Introduction

Many years ago, wholesalers dominated marketing in North America. Today, wholesalers have lost much of that market power--but they still play a very important role in our economy. Actually, wholesalers play a variety of roles because no two wholesalers operate exactly alike. Specialization has greatly changed the nature of wholesaling. Selecting a wholesaler is no longer just a problem of finding a good one. It is also a problem of choosing the right *kind* of wholesaler from the many different kinds that are available.

From the standpoint of total dollar sales volume, merchant wholesalers represent the most important class of wholesalers in Canada. Their major distinguishing characteristic is that they take title to the goods they handle. They provide some or all of the major wholesaling functions. Again, however, there are several types of *merchant wholesalers* for the manufacturer to choose from. The basic types are:

a. *Service wholesalers*--including general merchandise, single-line, and specialty wholesalers.

b. *Limited-function wholesalers*--including cash-and-carry wholesalers, drop-shippers, truck wholesalers, mail-order wholesalers, producers' cooperatives, and rack jobbers.

Another important class of wholesalers--*agent middlemen*--do not take title to the goods they sell, and they often provide even fewer functions than limited-function wholesalers. They are marketing specialists whose main task is to facilitate the buying and selling functions. There are several types of agent middlemen--including auction companies, brokers, commission merchants, manufacturers' agents, food brokers, and selling agents.

Marketing managers who decide to use indirect channels of distribution must decide whether to use merchant wholesalers and/or agent middlemen--and what specific type(s). In doing this, they should consider many different things--including their target markets, their financial resources, what wholesaling functions they can and cannot provide for themselves, and how much control they want over their channels of distribution.

Assignment

This exercise will give you some practice in choosing the right kind of wholesaler. Each of the following caselets describes a situation in which a buyer or seller might want to use one or more kinds of merchant wholesalers or agent middlemen. Read each caselet carefully and then indicate which kind(s) of wholesaler(s) would be most appropriate for each situation. Then explain your answer--taking into account the variables mentioned in the Introduction.

The first caselet is answered for you as an example.

1. Jack Miller, a farmer in Manitoba has six truckloads of pumpkins that he wants to sell prior to the approaching Halloween season. Local auction prices have been low, however, and Miller is hoping to sell the pumpkins in Toronto, where greater demand may bring higher prices. Unfortunately, he is too busy with the rest of his fall harvest to transport the pumpkins to Toronto's central market in search of buyers for the best price obtainable.

    a) Type of Wholesaler: <u>Agent middleman--commission merchant</u>

    b) Explanation: <u>The farmer needs a low-cost wholesaler on a temporary basis to represent him in a distant market--providing market contacts, aggressive selling including price negotiation, and transporting. [Note: in the long run, the farmer might be better off joining a producers' cooperative--if one is operating.]</u>

2. Engineer Bill Jeter recently invented a recycling process for diseased trees. Officials from nearby cities--lacking any ecologically acceptable alternatives for disposing of trees that have been cut down have agreed to deliver their trees free of charge to Jeter's manufacturing plant. There, the trees are processed and converted into products such as wood chips for landscaping, bark mulch, railroad ties, patio blocks, and furniture. However, Jeter has little marketing experience and know-how. Usually buyers come to him by way of word of mouth and then he is not sure how to price his products. The firm is in trouble financially and may have to declare bankruptcy unless Jeter can locate a steady and sizeable market for his products. Meanwhile, he has no funds to hire a sales rep or to promote his products. Currently he handles all sales and deliveries himself--often resulting in the plant being shut down while he is away.

    a) Type of Wholesaler: _____

    b) Explanation: _____
    _____
    _____

3. Vancouver Pastries bakes fresh pies and assorted pastries and distributes them daily to restaurants, hospitals, schools, and catering firms. The firm's owners are anxious to expand their operation and seek new profit opportunities. They are considering the possibility of distributing their products to retail food chains in their metropolitan area. However, the owners have no market-contacts in the retail food trade and are not sure any retailer would be interested in stocking their baked goods. Further, while they can handle the physical distribution functions, they need advice concerning pricing, packaging, and advertising.

    a) Type of Wholesaler: _____

    b) Explanation: _____
    _____
    _____

4. Thelma Boyd is marketing manager for Nature's Own, Ltd., a firm that processes and markets premium grade frozen and canned vegetables. In recent years, Thelma has been expanding distribution of the Nature's Own brand. She does not expect more sales growth this year, but large increases are expected over the next few years. The company has planned to expand production capacity as it was needed, but that plan changed when several small vegetable processing plants came on the market. Nature's Own got these processing plants at a very low price because they had not been able to find enough business at profitable prices and were near bankruptcy. Boyd is glad to know that the company now has the capacity to serve expanding market opportunities, but in the meantime she is looking for some way to quickly "get rid of" fairly large quantities of processed peas, corn and other vegetables that were acquired with the processing plants.

a) Type of Wholesaler: _____

b) Explanation: _____

_____

_____

5. Jill Cox has been managing a frame shop that she owned with her husband. That seemed like an in interesting thing to do when she graduated from college, but now she wants to start her own business. She thinks that the growing interest in health food opens up some interesting opportunities. With money borrowed from her father, she made a down payment on a bakery which formerly belonged to a local cookie manufacturer. As her first product, she decided to produce a unique honey and bran muffin. She "discovered" the recipe for this tasty product while traveling in Switzerland, and she is certain that it can be a profitable item if she can distribute it through health food stores and nutrition centers. A number of the health food stores in her area have already expressed interest in carrying the muffins. But Jill knows that she needs to obtain wider distribution--i.e., outside her present area--to be successful. One of the problems with expanding distribution, however, is that the muffins use no preservatives--so they are perishable.

a) Type of Wholesaler: _____

b) Explanation: _____

_____

_____

6. Exide Corporation--a large manufacturer of backup ("uninterruptable") power supplies and battery packs for computer systems--has decided to produce and sell a new line of automobile batteries. The company deliberately avoided the highly competitive consumer replacement market in the past--but now feels that it has a product that is much longer lasting that any battery currently on the market. Exide plans to distribute its new batteries through gasoline service stations, automotive stores, hardware stores, and mass-merchandisers. At the present time, the company has very limited financial resources--due to the cost of expanding its manufacturing facilities to produce the new line of batteries.

a) Type of Wholesaler: _____

b) Explanation: _____

_____

_____

7. Goodco, Inc. makes "Made-Rite" potato chips--the best selling brand of potato chips in the metropolitan Toronto area. The company has grown considerably since it was started during the 1930s. In fact, Made-Rite potato chips have become so popular among customers that the company is now planning to expand its market coverage to the west. New plants will be opened in Calgary and Vancouver. However, company officials doubt that Goodco can afford to operate its own plant-to-retailer delivery service in the new market areas--as it now does in the Toronto area.

   a) Type of Wholesaler: _____

   b) Explanation: _____

   _____

   _____

8. Guertner's Window Co. produces a line of insultated windows that are used for residential and commercial construction and remodeling. It supplies lumberyards, large glass contractors, and home-builders throughout a three-state area. Guertner's uses its own trucks for deliveries within a hundred miles--and ships carload quantities by railroad. Currently, five sales reps call directly on its present customers. The company is faced with large swings in demand, however, and has had difficulty finding new customers.

   a) Type of Wholesaler: _____

   b) Explanation: _____

   _____

   _____

9. The Bolden Supply Company produces a line of building materials including bricks, concrete blocks, cement, and lime. It supplies home builders, industrial contractors, and lumber yards throughout Western Canada. Bolden maintains a fleet of trucks for local deliveries and ships carload quantities by railroad. Currently, Bolden employs three sales reps to call directly on its various customers. The company is faced with large and risky fluctuations in demand, however, and had experienced considerable difficulty in locating new customers.

   a) Type of Wholesaler: _____

   b) Explanation: _____

   _____

   _____

Question for Discussion

Why are there so many different types of wholesalers?

Exercise 13-2

Analyzing channels of distribution

Introduction

A channel of distribution consists of different people performing different functions. They are linked together by a common interest in marketing products that someone needs and wants. At one end of the channel are manufacturers and at the other end are customers, and often there are "middlemen" in between.

Most products are *not* distributed directly from the manufacturer to the consumer or final user. In fact, the variety of middlemen has actually increased over the years. Middlemen exist because they perform some necessary functions--often more efficiently and economically than could either manufacturers or consumers.

This exercise focuses on several important types of middlemen. The objective is to determine what specific functions and activities each middleman performs--and to understand the role each plays in the distribution channel. Further, the exercise illustrates that while one type of middleman can sometimes be substituted for another--in other situations different types of middlemen perform complementary functions. Thus, while one channel may be longer than some others, it may also be faster, more economical, or more effective.

Assignment

The activities of several types of middlemen are described below in five cases. For each middleman described:

A.   Identify the *general type* of middleman (a full-service merchant wholesaler, a limited-function merchant wholesaler, or an agent middleman) *and* the *specific type* of middleman (rack jobber, broker, etc.).

B.   Diagram the channel or *channels* of distribution that are described in the case, using the following symbols.

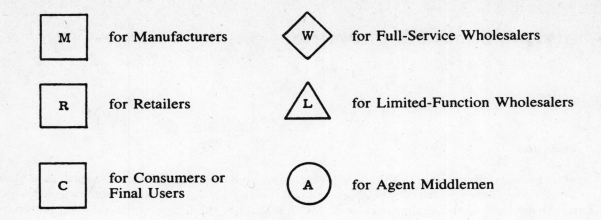

M — for Manufacturers	W — for Full-Service Wholesalers
R — for Retailers	L — for Limited-Function Wholesalers
C — for Consumers or Final Users	A — for Agent Middlemen

The first case has been completed as an example.

1. Ralph Brown sells carload quantities of chemicals for industrial use to several chemical manufacturers. Brown takes title to the products he sells. But he does not take physical possession of them, although he often arranges for transporting the products. One part of his business that is costly is the frequent need to provide credit to the small customers.

   a) General Type: <u>Brown is a limited-function merchant wholesaler</u>.

      Specific Type: <u>drop-shipper</u>

   b) Diagram of the Channel:

2. Sellco, Inc.--in Montreal, Quebec--operates as the "marketing manager" for several manufacturers. For example, it handles the entire output of a small fabric manufacturer whose products are distributed through selected retail outlets in Quebec. While the fabric manufacturer provides transportation for its products, Sellco handles pricing, selling, advertising, billing and collecting, and even product design. This arrangement was made to relieve a strain on the financial and administrative resources of the manufacturer. Sellco earns a large commission on all sales.

a) General Type: _____

Specific Type: _____

b) Diagram of the Channel:

3. Good Valu is a wholesale grocer who sponsors a voluntary chain of independent retailers. In addition to the usual wholesaling functions, Good Valu provides special services for its stores: its own "dealer brand" products at very competitive prices, merchandising assistance, employee training programs, store location and design assistance, and accounting aid. Merchandise economies are achieved through group buying, and a modern distribution center is used to lower operating costs.

Some retailers are too small to benefit from membership in the chain. For these customers, Good Valu operates a subsidiary to provide a smaller assortment of canned goods and other household needs. Perishables are not stocked, and retailers must provide their own transportation. The products are priced attractively-- considering the small order quantities--but no credit is offered.

a) General Type: _____

Specific Type: _____

b) Diagram of the Channel:

4. A number of different food processors, supermarket and restaurant chains, and full-service and limited-function wholesalers turn to Sunshine Coast Produce Company when they want to find a supply for seasonal fruits and vegetables. Sunshine Coast Produce doesn't grow fruits or vegetables itself, nor does it work with any particular farmer on a continuous basis. Instead, farmers who want to find buyers for large quantities of produce that need to be sold quickly turn to Sunshine Coast Produce for help. Sunshine Coast handles the products, negotiates prices, and completes the sale for the producers. Farmers pay Sunshine Coast a commission for its work.

a) General Type: _____

 Specific Type: _____

b) Diagram of the Channel:

5.   Mead, Johnson & Company--a manufacturer of drug products--also produces Pablum, a baby food. Some years ago, Pablum was sold only to wholesale druggists because it was "logical" to send a new product through the company's present distribution channels--even though consumers bought such products mainly in grocery stores. Retail grocers bought the product from wholesale grocers, who in turn bought it from wholesale druggists. Mead wanted to eliminate the problem of Pablum carrying two wholesale margins, but did not want to risk irritating the wholesale druggists by "withdrawing" the product from them. Instead, the company chose to also use the services of people like Donald Tell to help it sell directly to grocery middlemen. Tell works with wholesale and retail grocers in the Toronto area, handling noncompeting lines of several manufacturers. He promotes products very aggressively to earn about a 5 percent commission on sales. In general, Tell does not handle the physical distribution of Pablum.

(Note: Diagram both channels in this case.)

a) General Type: _____

 Specific Type: _____

b) Diagram of the Channel   Diagram of the Channel
   with Wholesale Druggists: with wholesale Grocers:

Question for Discussion

Are salespeople middlemen? Where are salespeople shown in channel diagrams?

Chapter 14
Physical distribution

What This Chapter Is About

Chapter 14 is concerned with the "invisible" part of marketing--the physical movement and storing of products. These activities account for about half the cost of marketing.

This chapter covers some important details on transporting and storing. But the major focus is on integrating transporting and storing into one coordinated effort--to provide the appropriate physical distribution customer service level at the lowest total cost.

The total cost approach to physical distribution, the physical distribution concept, and customer service level are important ideas which have significantly improved some companies' marketing strategy planning. But they are not yet well accepted. Try to see why. Helping to apply these ideas may offer a breakthrough opportunity for you.

Important Terms

physical distribution (PD), p. 384
customer service level, p. 384
transporting, p. 386
ton-mile, p. 388
pool car service, p. 389
diversion in transit, p. 390
lakers, p. 390
containerization, p. 391
piggy-back service, p. 392

freight forwarders, p. 392
storing, p. 393
inventory, p. 393
private warehouses, p. 395
public warehouses, p. 395
distribution center, p. 397
physical distribution (PD) concept, p. 397
total cost approach, p. 398

True-False Questions

____1.   Physical distribution--which is the transporting and storing of goods within individual firms and along channel systems--accounts for nearly half the cost of marketing.

____2.   Customer service level is a measure of how rapidly and dependably a firm can deliver what customers want.

____3.   Marketing managers should be careful to avoid offering customers a level of physical distribution service that might increase storing or transporting costs.

___ 4.   Transporting--which is the marketing function of moving goods--provides time, place, and possession utilities.

___ 5.   The value added to products by moving them should be greater than the cost of the transporting, or there is little reason to ship in the first place.

___ 6.   Based on ton-mile measurements, it is obvious that railroads are the backbone of the Canadian freight transportation system--followed in order of importance by trucks, airways, barges, and oil pipelines.

___ 7.   Railroad pool car service appeals mainly to very large shippers who are transporting to only a few locations.

___ 8.   Railroads offering "diversion-in-transit" enable shippers to ship commodities away from the source, stop them along the way for processing, and then start them moving again, as long as the final destination stays the same.

___ 9.   In contrast to railroads which are best suited for moving heavy and bulky freight over long distances, the flexibility of trucks make them especially suitable for moving small quantities of goods short distances.

___10.   Trucking rates are roughly one-half of airfreight rates.

___11.   An important advantage of using airfreight is that the cost of packing and unpacking goods for sale may be reduced or eliminated.

___12.   Even though freight forwarders usually do not own their own transporting facilities, they can obtain low transporting rates by combining small shipments into more economical quantities.

___13.   The fact that rates on less-than-full carloads or truckloads are often much higher than those on full carloads or truckloads is one reason for the development of wholesalers.

___14.   When a firm's small shipments have to be moved by varied transporters, it probably should consider employing the services of freight forwarders.

___15.   While transporting provides time utility, the storing function provides place utility.

___16.   Inventory means the amount of goods being stored.

___17. The storing function offers several ways to vary a firm's marketing mix--and its channel system--by: (1) adjusting the time goods are held, (2) sharing the storing costs, and (3) delegating the job to a specialized storing facility.

___18. Unless a large volume of goods must be stored regularly, a firm should probably choose public warehouses over private warehouses--even though public warehouses do not provide all the services that could be obtained in the company's own branch warehouses.

___19. The distribution center concept is based on the assumption that--unless storage creates time utility--reducing storage and increasing turnover will lead to bigger profits.

___20. According to the physical distribution concept, a firm might lower its total cost of physical distribution by selecting a higher cost transportation alternative.

___21. The total cost approach to physical distribution involves evaluating each possible physical distribution system--and identifying all of the costs of each alternative.

___22. When a firm decides to minimize total costs of physical distribution, it may also be settling for a lower customer service level and lower sales and profits.

___23. A higher physical distribution service level may mean both higher costs and higher profits.

___24. Improved order processing can sometimes have the same effect on customer service levels as faster, more expensive transportation.

Answers to True-False Questions

1. T, p. 384	9. T, p. 390	17. T, p. 394
2. T, p. 386	10. T, p. 390	18. F, pp. 395-396
3. F, p. 386	11. T, p. 391	19. T, p. 397
4. F, p. 386	12. T, p. 392	20. T, p. 398
5. T, pp. 386-387	13. T, p. 389	21. T, p. 398
6. F, p. 388	14. T, p. 392	22. T, p. 398
7. F, p. 389	15. F. p. 393	23. T, p. 399
8. F, p. 390	16. T, p. 393	24. T, p. 400

Multiple-Choice Questions (Circle the correct response)

1. The physical distribution service level is important because:

    a. it is a measure of how rapidly and dependably a firm delivers what its customers want.
    b. it may result in lost sales if it is too low.
    c. it may result in lower profits if it is too high.
    d. All of the above.
    e. None of the above.

2. Performance of the physical distribution functions provides:

    a. time utility.
    b. place utility.
    c. possession utility.
    d. All of the above.
    e. Only a. and b. above.

3. Transporting costs

    a. are usually more than the value added by shipping, but the products are shipped anyway as there is no choice.
    b. do not vary much as a percentage of the final price of products, since big items are shipped by inexpensive means and small items are shipped by more expensive approaches.
    c. usually do not add much to the final cost of products which are already valuable relative to their size and weight.
    d. usually are not large enough to limit the target market that a marketing manager can serve.
    e. None of the above is true.

4. Based on ton-miles carried, which of the following sets of rankings (from high to low) correctly indicates the relative importance of each mode of intercity freight transportation?

    a. Railways, pipelines, motor vehicles, inland waterways, airways
    b. Motor vehicles, railways, inland waterways, pipelines, airways
    c. Inland waterways, railways, motor vehicles, airways, pipelines
    d. Railways, motor vehicles, inland waterways, pipelines, airways
    e. Motor vehicles, railways, airways, pipelines, inland waterways

5. Which of the following transportation modes is "best" regarding "number of locations served"?

    a. Rail
    b. Water
    c. Truck
    d. Pipeline
    e. Air

6. A railroad shipping process which allows redirection of carloads already in transit is called:

    a. diversion in transit
    b. freight forwarding
    c. transloading privileges
    d. pool car shipping
    e. piggy-back service

7. Berry Bros. wants to ship a somewhat bulky, high-valued commodity a short distance--and it is seeking low-cost and extremely fast service. Berry should use:

    a. airfreight.
    b. railroads.
    c. inland waterways.
    d. trucks.
    e. None of the above.

8. Compared to other forms of transportation, airfreight may result in:

    a. a lower total cost of distribution.
    b. less damage in transit.
    c. higher transportation rates.
    d. lower packing costs.
    e. All of the above.

9. Grouping individual items into an economical shipping quantity and sealing them in protective containers for transit to the final destination is called:

    a. containerization
    b. pool car service
    c. freight forwarding
    d. piggy-back service
    e. all of the above

10. Freight forwarders:

    a. are not very active in international shipping because they are unwilling to handle all the paperwork necessary in overseas shipments.
    b. generally own their own transportation facilities--including pickup and delivery trucks.
    c. can be especially helpful to the marketing manager who ships in larger quantities.
    d. accumulate small shipments from shippers and then reship them in larger quantities to obtain lower transportation rates.
    e. All of the above are true statements.

11. Storing:

    a. is related to Place--but has no effect on Price.
    b. is necessary because production does not always match consumption.
    c. must be performed by all members of a channel system.
    d. facilitates mass production.
    e. All of the above are true statements.

12. A manufacturer having irregular need for regional storage of bicycles should use which one of the following?

    a. A private warehouse to be sure of adequate space.
    b. Public warehouses to provide flexibility and low unit cost.
    c. Merchant wholesalers.
    d. Agent middlemen.
    e. Commission houses.

13. A distribution center is designed to:

   a. stockpile goods for long periods and avoid rising prices.
   b. buy low and sell high.
   c. reduce inventory turnover.
   d. speed the flow of goods and avoid unnecessary storing.
   e. all of the above.

14. According to the "physical distribution concept":

   a. transporting and storing are independent activities.
   b. all transporting and storing activities of a business and a channel system should be thought of as part of one system.
   c. inventories should be based on production requirements.
   d. the production department should be responsible for warehousing and shipping.
   e. the lowest-cost distribution system is the best alternative.

15. The "total cost approach" to physical distribution management:

   a. emphasizes faster delivery service and thus favors the use of airfreight over railroads.
   b. often ignores inventory carrying costs.
   c. might favor a high-cost transportation mode if storage costs are reduced enough to lower total distribution costs.
   d. seeks to reduce the cost of transportation to its minimum.
   e. All of the above are true.

16. Which of the following statements reflects a marketing-oriented approach to physical distribution?

   a. "We should create a position of physical distribution manager and give him authority to integrate all physical distribution activities to minimize the total cost of distribution."
   b. "We should aim to keep our customers fully satisfied 100 percent of the time as this will increase our sales and give us a competitive advantage."
   c. "We should replace our warehouses with distribution centers to speed the flow of products and eliminate all storage."
   d. "We should choose the physical distribution alternative that will minimize the total cost of achieving the level of customer service our target market requires."
   e. All are equally "marketing-oriented."

17. A marketing-oriented physical distribution manager would *insist* that:

   a. the storage function be eliminated to reduce inventory costs.
   b. efficiency in physical distribution can be best achieved by minimizing costs.
   c. emphasis must be on maximizing the customer service level.
   d. both customer service level and total distribution costs be considered.
   e. none of the above.

Answers to Multiple-Choice Questions

1. d, p. 384	7. d, p. 390	13. d, p. 397
2. e, p. 386	8. c, pp. 390-391	14. b, p. 397
3. c, p. 387	9. a, p. 391	15. c, p. 398
4. a, p. 388	10. d, pp. 392-393	16. d, p. 398
5. c, p. 389	11. b, p. 393	17. d, p. 398
6. a, p. 390	12. b, pp. 395-396	

Exercise 14-1

Evaluating physical distribution alternatives

Introduction

Physical distribution costs sometimes make up a large percentage of a product's final selling price. In fact, high distribution costs may block a company from competing effectively in distant markets. On the other hand, a firm may obtain a big competitive advantage if it can keep distribution costs to a minimum. However, it is not easy to pick the lowest cost distribution alternative. One must consider the nature of the products to be shipped, the distances the products will travel, the quantities to be shipped, and the rate structures.

This exercise gets you into the mechanics of selecting the "best" method of distribution when several alternatives are available. Here, the emphasis is on choosing the alternative which minimizes the *total* cost of distribution.

Assignment

Assume that you are physical distribution manager for the ABC Company and that you are considering the following alternative methods of distributing your company's products into a new market. You would like to develop a simple graph to show management that different alternatives may become more economical as the annual quantities shipped change. The estimated costs of the various methods of physical distribution are shown in Table 14-1, on the next page.

Alternative methods of physical distribution:

A. *Rail and local warehouse*--Ship products by railroad to leased warehouse in new territory and use leased trucks to deliver products to customers.

B. *Direct rail*--Store products in plant until ordered and then ship directly to customers by combination of rail and local trucking companies.

C. *Trucks*--Store products in plant until ordered and then ship directly to customers by truck (common carriers).

D. *Airfreight*--Store products in plant until ordered and then ship directly to customers by combination of airfreight and local trucking companies. (Inventories would be smaller due to the speed of airfreight.)

1. To help you plot a graph, calculate the total cost of each alternative for the following annual quantities shipped: (a) zero tons and (b) 50,000 tons.

    Show your answers in Table 14-2. Answers for Alternative A have already been calculated as an example.

    Hint: total cost = fixed cost + (variable cost/ton) x (number of tons shipped)

TABLE 14-1
Costs of Distribution Alternatives

Distribution Alternative	Fixed Cost of Alternative	Variable Cost/Ton of Alternative
A. Rail and Local Warehouse	$3,500,000	$ 50
B. Direct Rail	$1,900,000	$ 80
C. Trucks	$1,600,000	$110
D. Airfreight	$1,000,000	$160

TABLE 14-2
**Total Costs of Physical Distribution Alternatives
for Selected Shipping Quantities**

Distribution Alternative	Total Cost of Quantity Shipped	
	Zero Tons	50,000 Tons
A. Rail and Local Warehouse	$3,500,000	$6,000,000
B. Direct Rail	$_____	$_____
C. Trucks	$_____	$_____
D. Airfreight	$_____	$_____

2. Using Figure 14-1 (on the next page), construct a graph that will show which transportation alternative has the lowest total cost for any annual quantity shipped up to 80,000 tons.

   Hint: For each transportation alternative, plot the two total cost estimates which you calculated in Table 14-2 for quantities of (a) zero units and (b) 50,000 units. Then connect the two points you have plotted with a straight line and extend the line out to a shipping quantity of 80,000 units. Each straight line will then represent the total cost--for a particular alternative--of shipping quantities up to 80,000 units. The total cost of using a particular alternative is represented by a straight line--because the variable shipping cost per unit is constant.

FIGURE 14-1

Total Costs of Physical Distribution for Different Distribution Alternatives

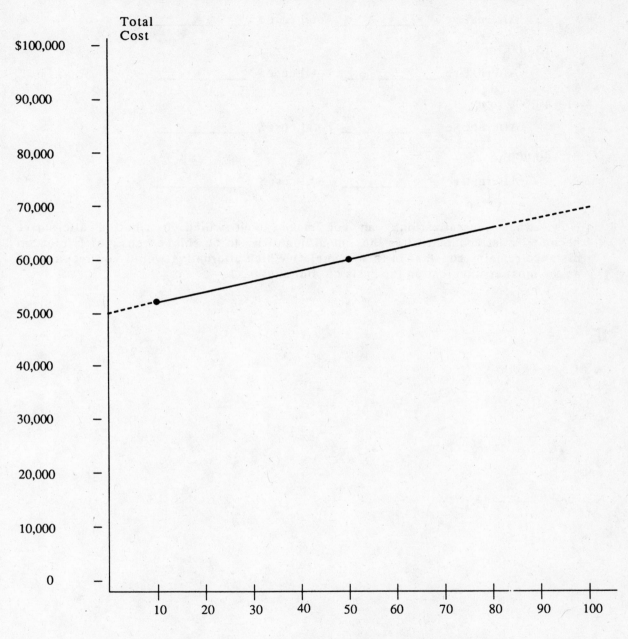

Thousands of Units to be Shipped

3. Reading off of your graph, indicate which distribution alternative offers the *lowest total cost* for each of the following annual quantities shipped and show (estimate) the total cost:

   a) 5,000 tons:

   Alternative _____ Total cost $ _____

   b) 15,000 tons:

   Alternative _____ Total cost $ _____

   c) 40,000 tons:

   Alternative _____ Total cost $ _____

   d) 60,000 tons:

   Alternative _____ Total cost $ _____

4. Now, what generalizations can you make about which distribution alternative becomes most economical as the annual quantities to be shipped change? (Note that distance remains constant in this example.) Which alternative would you recommend as the most economical on the basis of your analysis?

Question for Discussion

Why might the marketing manager for the ABC company object to the use of your graph in selecting a method for distributing the company's products? Should such arguments have any weight in determining what distribution method should actually be employed?

Exercise 14-2

Strategic planning for customer service level

Introduction

Within the framework of marketing strategy planning, physical distribution managers seek to provide the level of customer service that satisfies the needs of the firm's target market. Given some specified level of customer service, it is also the physical distribution manager's job to provide that service at the lowest cost possible. This total cost approach is based on the idea of "tradeoffs" among parts of the distribution system.

For example, a physical distribution manager may be making a tradeoff when he decides to lower his transportation costs, because such a move usually results in larger inventory costs. Following the total cost approach, he would not try to minimize with transportation *or* inventory costs. Instead, he would operate his physical distribution system in a way that would *minimize the total cost of offering the desired customer service level.* The following exercise will illustrate this idea in greater detail.

Assignment

Read the following case and answer the questions that follow.

HILKO COMPANY

The Hilko Company is studying its physical distribution system to see if the system needs to be remodeled. Currently, Hilko's industrial component product is manufactured at the firm's plant in Quebec and then shipped by train to several branch warehouses across Canada. When an order is received at the Quebec plant, the order is relayed to the branch warehouse closest to the customer. The products are then shipped directly to the customer by truck. Hilko tries to maintain a 70 percent customer service level--that is, it tries to deliver 70 percent of its orders to the customer within three days after the orders are received.

Recently, several company managers have expressed dissatisfaction with the present distribution system. Hilko's sales manager feels that the 70 percent service level is inadequate--and should be increased to at least 90 percent by adding more warehouses. The production manager wants to cut the service level to 20 percent, to even out his production schedule--although the traffic manager claims this will increase transportation costs too much. Finally, the finance manager has suggested that the firm try to minimize its total distribution costs by providing whatever level of customer service it can while operating at the lowest possible total cost.

To help resolve this conflicting advice from his top managers, Hilko's president asked his assistant to analyze the relationship between alternative customer service levels and physical distribution costs. The results of this analysis are shown in Figure 14-2.

FIGURE 14-2

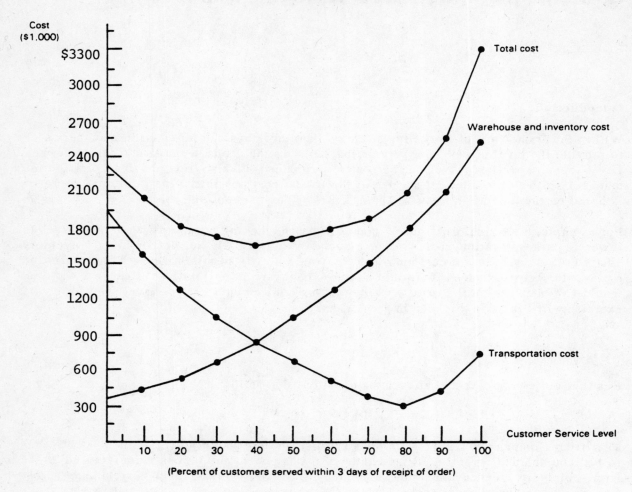

1. According to Figure 14-2, what is Hilko's total cost of physical distribution at its present 70 percent customer service level? $_____

2. What would the total cost be if a 90 percent service level were developed? $_____

3. What would the total cost be if a 20 percent service level were adopted? $_____

4. At what customer service level would the total cost of distribution be *minimized*? What would the minimum total cost be?

   Customer service level _____ % Total cost $_____

5. What would the *total cost* be if Hilko attempted to *minimize* its:

   a) warehouse and inventory costs $_____

   b) transportation costs $_____

6. What would the total cost be if Hilko were to *maximize* its customer service level? $_____

7. Obviously, the optimal customer service level for Hilko would be ___ percent because:

8. As marketing manager for the Hilko Company, what advice would you give the president concerning the customer service level decision?

Question for Discussion

Suppose you were the warehouse manager for the Hilko Company and would have to account for an increase in warehouse and inventory costs of $600,000 if the sales department's plans to increase the service level were implemented. If you were responsible for minimizing warehouse and inventory costs--and this were your only area of responsibility--you would look bad. How would you explain this to your boss? What are the implications of your answer for company organization?

Chapter 15
Promotion--Introduction

What This Chapter Is About

Chapter 15 introduces Promotion--the topic of Chapters 15-17. Be sure to see that Promotion is only one of the four Ps--*not* the whole of marketing. Promotion tries to carry out promotion objectives--just as the other Ps have their own specific objectives.

This chapter looks at promotion objectives and methods from a strategic viewpoint--with emphasis on developing a good promotion blend. Early in the chapter, much attention is given to the communication process and the adoption of new ideas. These theoretical concepts should be studied carefully. They provide a solid base for strategy planning of personal selling (Chapter 16) and advertising (Chapter 17).

Although some of the material appears theoretical, it is important because not all promotion decisions are "just common sense." Poor decisions here could lead to "mass marketing" and the use of a "shotgun" rather than a "rifle" approach to Promotion. This chapter should help you bring a rifle to promotion planning--to practice "target marketing."

Important Terms

promotion, p. 405
personal selling, p. 406
mass selling, p. 406
advertising, p. 407
publicity, p. 407
sales promotion, p. 408
communication process, p. 411
source, p. 411
receiver, p. 412
noise, p. 412
encoding, p. 412
decoding, p. 412
message channel, p. 413
AIDA model, p. 413

adoption curve, p. 415
innovators, p. 415
early adopters, p. 415
early majority, p. 416
late majority, p. 416
laggards, p. 416
nonadopters, p. 416
primary demand, p. 419
selective demand, pp. 419-420
sales managers, p. 425
advertising managers, p. 426
public relations, p. 426
sales promotion managers, p. 426

True-False Questions

___ 1. Promotion is communicating information between seller and potential buyer--to influence attitudes and behavior.

___ 2. Advertising is any form of nonpersonal presentation of ideas, goods, or services.

___ 3. Sales promotion refers to activities such as personal selling, advertising and publicity.

___ 4. All sales promotion is aimed at final consumers or users.

___ 5. Sales promotion aimed at middlemen--sometimes called trade promotion--stresses price-related matters.

___ 6. The overall objective of promotion is to affect behavior.

___ 7. The three basic objectives of promotion are to inform, persuade, and/or remind.

___ 8. Much of what we call promotion is really wasted effort because it does not really communicate.

___ 9. A major advantage of personal selling is that the source can get immediate feedback to help direct subsequent communication efforts.

___ 10. The term "noise" refers only to distorting influences within the message channel which reduce the effectiveness of the communication process.

___ 11. If the right message channel is selected, problems related to encoding and decoding in the communication process will be avoided.

___ 12. The communication process is complicated by the fact that receivers are usually influenced not only by the message but also by the source and the message channel.

___ 13. The AIDA model consists of four promotion jobs: attention, information, desire, and action.

___ 14. The adoption curve focuses on the process by which an individual accepts new ideas.

___ 15. Publicity in technical journals is likely to be a more effective method of promotion than personal selling for reaching extremely innovative business firms.

___ 16. The late majority are influenced more by other late adopters--rather than by advertising.

___ 17. Opinion leaders are often very difficult to identify, especially since different people may be opinion leaders for different products.

_____ 18. Salespeople should usually be expected to do the whole promotion job for industrial products.

_____ 19. Special considerations which may affect the promotion blend are the size of the promotion budget, the stage of the product life cycle, the nature of competition, the target of the promotion, and the nature of the product.

_____ 20. During the market introduction stage of product life cycles, promotion must pioneer acceptance of the product idea--not just the company's own brand--to stimulate primary demand.

_____ 21. In the market growth stage of the product life cycle, promotion emphasis must begin to shift from stimulating selective demand to stimulating primary demand for the company's own brand.

_____ 22. Firms in monopolistic competition may favor mass selling because they have differentiated their marketing mixes somewhat--and have something to talk about.

_____ 23. The large number of potential customers practically forces producers of consumer products and retailers to emphasize mass selling and sales promotion.

_____ 24. Industrial customers are much less numerous than final consumers--and therefore it becomes more practical to emphasize mass selling in the promotion blends aimed at these markets.

_____ 25. One reason personal selling is important in promotion to retailers is that marketing mixes often have to be adjusted from one geographic territory to another.

_____ 26. Promotion to employees is especially important in service-oriented industries where the quality of the employees' efforts is a big part of the product.

_____ 27. In total, personal selling is several times more expensive than advertising.

_____ 28. Typically, manufacturers selling well-branded consumer products through established channels have promotion blends which rely almost exclusively on advertising to consumers.

_____ 29. Planning of promotion blends can be best accomplished by placing specialists in charge of each promotion method; for example, the firm might appoint a sales manager, an advertising manager, and a sales promotion manager to weigh the pros and cons of the various approaches and come up with an effective blend.

_____ 30. To avoid conflicts, it is usually best for sales promotion to be handled by a firm's advertising manager and sales manager--not by a sales promotion specialist.

___ 31. Spending on sales promotion is growing, but in total it is still only about one-third as much as is spent on advertising.

___ 32. Sales promotion aimed at final consumers usually is trying to increase demand and speed up the time of purchase.

Answers to True-False Questions

1. T, p. 405	12. T, p. 413	23. T, p. 421
2. F, p. 407	13. F, p. 413	24. F, p. 421
3. F, p. 408	14. F, p. 415	25. T, p. 422
4. F, p. 408	15. T, p. 422	26. T, p. 423
5. T, p. 408	16. T, p. 416	27. T, p. 425
6. T, p. 409	17. T, p. 416	28. F, p. 425
7. T, p. 409	18. F, p. 421	29. F, p. 425
8. T, p. 411	19. T, pp. 426-27	30. F, p. 426
9. T, p. 412	20. T, p. 419	31. F, p. 427
10. F, p. 412	21. F, p. 419	32. T, p. 428
11. F, p. 413	22. T, p. 420	

Multiple-Choice Questions (Circle the correct response)

1. Promotion does *not* include:

    a. personal selling.
    b. advertising.
    c. publicity.
    d. sales promotion.
    e. Promotion includes all of the above.

2. Personal selling is more appropriate than mass selling when:

    a. the target market is large and scattered.
    b. there are many potential customers and a desire to keep promotion costs low.
    c. flexibility is not important.
    d. immediate feedback is desirable.
    e. All of the above are true.

3. Sales promotion activities:

    a. try to stimulate interest, trial or purchase.
    b. always involve direct face-to-face communication between sellers and potential customers.
    c. usually take a long time to implement.
    d. are usually a good substitute for personal selling and advertising.
    e. All of the above.

4. Sales promotion can be aimed at:

    a. final consumers or users.
    b. middlemen.
    c. the company's own sales force.
    d. all of the above.
    e. only a and b above.

5. Which basic promotion objective should be emphasized by a firm whose product is very similar to those offered by many competitors?

    a. Communicating
    b. Persuading
    c. Reminding
    d. Informing

6. Which of the following is *not* one of the basic elements in the communication process?

    a. Feedback
    b. Receiver
    c. Encoding
    d. Dissonance
    e. Message channel

7. Communication is *most difficult* to achieve when:

    a. the source and the receiver are not in face-to-face contact with each other.
    b. immediate feedback is not provided.
    c. any trace of "noise" remains in the message channel.
    d. the source and the receiver do not have a common frame of reference.
    e. the encoder does not do the decoding.

8. The AIDA model's four promotion jobs are getting:

    a. awareness, interest, demand, action.
    b. attention, interest, desire, action.
    c. action, interest, desire, acceptance.
    d. awareness, interest, decision, acceptance.

9. Mary Jones is strongly influenced by her peer group--and she often adopts a new product only after they have pressured her to try it. She makes little use of mass media and salespeople as sources of information. In terms of the adoption curve, she would be in what category?

    a. Laggard
    b. Late majority
    c. Early adopter
    d. Innovator
    e. Early majority

10. Regarding planning a promotion blend, a good marketing manager knows that:

    a. the job of teaching all the people in a "buying center" is made easier by their low turnover.
    b. there is not much chance of economies of scale in promotion.
    c. it is seldom practical for salespeople to carry the whole promotion load.
    d. salespeople can be very economical since they devote almost all of their time to actual selling activities.
    e. None of the above is true.

11. During the market introduction stage of the product life cycle, the basic objective of promotion is to:

    a. spend more money on promotion than competitors.
    b. remind customers about the firm and its products.
    c. inform the potential customers of the product.
    d. stimulate selective demand.
    e. persuade the early majority to buy the product.

12. Which of the following statements about the *target of promotion* and promotion blends is *true*?

    a. Promotion to wholesalers is very similar to promotion to retailers--except that wholesalers are more numerous and perhaps less aware of demand and cost.
    b. Mass selling is seldom necessary or useful in the industrial products field.
    c. Personal selling is generally quite important for closing the sale in retail stores--regardless of how much mass selling is attempted.
    d. Promotion to retailers is primarily informative--although some persuasion is also needed.
    e. The vast number of potential customers forces consumer products manufacturers and retailers to rely exclusively on mass selling in their promotion blends.

13. Deciding on the appropriate promotion blend is a job for the firm's:

    a. advertising agency.
    b. marketing manager.
    c. advertising manager.
    d. sales manager.
    e. sales promotion manager.

14. Sales promotion:

    a. is currently a weak spot in many firms' marketing strategies.
    b. spending is growing rapidly.
    c. involves a wide variety of activities which often require the use of specialists.
    d. can make the personal selling job easier.
    e. All of the above are true statements.

15. Sales promotion:

    a. to consumers usually is trying to increase demand or speed up the time of purchase.
    b. aimed at middlemen is sometimes called trade promotion.
    c. might include free samples of a product.
    d. aimed at employees is common in service firms.
    e. all of the above.

Answers to Multiple-Choice Questions

1. e, p. 405	6. b, p. 412	11. c, p. 419
2. d, p. 406	7. d, p. 412	12. d, p. 422
3. a, p. 408	8. d, p. 413	13. b, p. 418
4. d, p. 408	9. b, p. 416	14. e, p. 427
5. d, p. 410	10. c, p. 418	15. e, p. 428

Exercise 15-1

The communication process in promotion

Introduction

Promotion must communicate effectively--or it's wasted effort. Yet it is often difficult to achieve effective communication. The communication process can break down in many different ways.

Understanding the whole communication process can improve promotion. As discussed in more detail in the text (see pages 411-13 and Exhibit 15-4), the major elements of the communication process include:

> a source,
> encoding,
> a message channel,
> decoding,
> a receiver,
> feedback, and
> noise.

Each of these different elements can influence the effectiveness of a firm's promotion effort--so marketing managers need to consider each element when planning or modifying their promotion. The whole promotion effort may fail because of a failure in just one element.

This exercise is designed to enhance your understanding of the communication process in promotion planning. The focus here is on specific elements of the process.

Assignment

Listed below are several descriptions of different promotion situations. In each case, there is a problem with the promotion effort. For some reason, communication has not been effective. You may see different elements of the promotion process that may be related to the problem. But, the focus of each situation is on a specific element of the process. So, for each situation, write down *one* element (from the list above) that you think is the major problem. Then, briefly explain why you think that element is a problem, and how the communication process might need to be changed to correct the problem. (Note: your recommendation may include changing one or more elements of the communication process other than the one that you noted as the major problem.)

1. A student newspaper on a college campus wants to increase revenues by attracting more faculty subscriptions. Very few faculty currently subscribe. A study by students in a marketing research course found that many faculty don't subscribe because they think that the price of a subscription is much higher than is actually the case. The subscription manager has placed large ads in the paper that clearly show how little it actually costs to subscribe, but so far faculty response has been very disappointing.

    Problem element of the communication process: _____

    Explanation: _____

    _____

    _____

    _____

    _____

    _____

    _____

    _____

2. A company has been doing advertising for its line of weight-loss diet supplements. The supplements are targeted to overweight, middle-aged men and women. The company's ads appear on TV exercise programs that are viewed by the same target market. In the ad, a trim professional model explains the product and how safely and effectively it works. But the ads do not seem to be effective. Apparently the overweight viewers don't believe that a trim model really knows about the difficulties of losing weight.

    Problem element of the communication process: _____

    Explanation: _____

    _____

    _____

    _____

    _____

    _____

    _____

3. An insurance company has a list of customers whose policies are about to expire. The company has hired sales reps to telephone these customers and ask them if they would like to renew their policies. Research shows that most customers appreciate this service--since it means that there will not be a lapse in their policy. The company has screened and hired sales reps carefully. Each salesperson has been trained concerning the prices for different policies. The company leaves it to each sales rep to decide what to say--so that the presentation will be as natural as possible. But, the inexperienced salespeople have trouble getting the conversation started--and often the customer hangs up before the point of the call is clear.

    Problem element of the communication process: _____

    Explanation: _____

    _____

    _____

    _____

    _____

    _____

    _____

    _____

4. A company that produces expensive leather briefcases for business executives wants to expand its sales in overseas markets. In Canada, the company's ads--placed in business magazines--show a group of well-dressed men and women executives preparing for a meeting. Each executive has a briefcase, and the headline for the ad says "If you want respect, it's as important to look professional as it is to act professional." The company adapted this same copy thrust to a Japanese ad that featured Japanese models. But, the effort was a failure. In Japan, there are still very few women in high executive positions, and for many target customers the ad did not help to create a "prestige" image for the company's products.

    Problem element of the communication process: _____

    Explanation: _____

    _____

    _____

    _____

    _____

    _____

    _____

    _____

Question for Discussion

Does market segmentation make it easier--or more difficult--to develop effective promotion communications? Why?

Exercise 15-2

Using the adoption curve to develop promotion blends

Introduction

We have continually stressed that each of the "four Ps" should be matched with the needs and characteristics of target markets. But marketing mix planning can get more complicated in the promotion area. Even though a target market may have fairly homogeneous needs--*groups of people within this market may differ considerably in their sources of information and how quickly they adopt new products.* Therefore, marketing managers may need to use several promotion blends--over time--to communicate effectively with this target market.

Promotion blend planning should use the adoption curve--which shows when different groups accept ideas. Five adopter groups are commonly used: innovators, early adopters, the early majority, the late majority, and laggards.

As outlined in the text (see pages 414-17), a unique pattern of communication exists within and between each of these adopter groups. Therefore, each may require its own promotion blend.

Assignment

This exercise is designed to show how an understanding of the adoption curve can be helpful when planning promotion blends. Read the following case and then *develop a promotion blend for each adopter group* within the firm's target market. Outline in detail what kind of mass selling, personal selling, and sales promotion you would use, if any, to reach each adopter group. Be specific. For example, if you decide to advertise in magazines, give examples of the magazines you would use. Above all, be creative--it's expected of you!

After you outline your promotion blend for each adopter group, explain *why* you chose that particular blend in the space marked "Comments." Here, you should consider some of the important characteristics of each adopter group--as discussed in the text.

Note that you are only being asked to focus on *promotion to final consumers*. The firm would also have to do some promotion work in the channels--just to obtain distribution--and adoption curve thinking should be applied to middleman adoption, too. But all of this promotion activity should be ignored here--because we want to focus on the way that final consumers would accept the product and its impact on promotion planning.

AUDIOTECH, LTD.

Audiotech, Ltd.--one of the world's largest manufacturers of stereo equipment--has just announced the introduction of a revolutionary new "digital" cassette tape recorder called the Digimax. Aimed primarily at the "serious amateur" market, the Digimax features a new electronic way of recording sound on tape. The sound quality of the Digimax is exceptional. In fact, in the past this quality of sound could only be achieved with prerecorded compact discs. The tape recorder also has an automatic "digital enhancement" system that reduces static and distortion when recording. This means that the user can record collections of records and tapes--and get a higher quality sound than was possible with the original. The recorder does this automatically. Further, the Digimax has *automatic indexing*--so the recorder electronically "marks" the beginning of each new musical selection recorded. This allows the user to easily and quickly skip over a selection and "search" for a particular song. While such features can be found on some other standard cassette recorders, the Digimax is the first digital recorder to offer these features--and it changes to a new selection much more quickly than a standard recorder.

The Digimax also includes several other "firsts." There is a built-in rechargeable lithium battery that powers the unit for several hours after it has been unplugged. With its small case, the unit can be easily moved from one room to another--or taken on trips. In addition, there is a hand-held remote control unit which allows the user to automatically "program" playback of tapes--so that a selection of songs can be played in any order, played any number of times, or even skipped over altogether--without getting up to fuss with the machine.

The Digimax also has a unique "digital dubbing" feature and built-in microphone. This allows the user to simultaneously listen to a selection on the tape and at the same time add additional sounds. For example, users can play an instrumental selection and add in their own voice tracks. In combination, all of these features make the Digimax the world's most sophisticated tape recorder.

The Digimax has a manufacturer's suggested list price of $759--but it is expected to retail for about $520. This price is not out of line when one considers the unique capabilities of the Digimax--but the price is much higher than consumers are used to paying for a cassette recorder--or even a compact disc changer. Therefore, promotion may be critical for the new recorder--which will be distributed through stereo dealers, selected department stores, and electronics equipment mass-merchandisers.

Audiotech, Ltd. managers are not sure what promotion blend to use to introduce this new recorder. One manager has noted that some customers will adopt the Digimax faster than others--and therefore the promotion blend may have to vary over time. So, they are asking you to advise them.

Suggested Promotion Blends for Communicating with Potential
Consumers in Each Adopter Group

1. Innovators

    a) Market characteristics: _____

    _____

    _____

    _____

    b) Promotion blend: _____

_____

_____

_____

    c) Comments: _____

_____

_____

_____

2.   Early adopters

    a) Market characteristics: _____

_____

_____

_____

    b) Promotion blend: _____

_____

_____

_____

    c) Comments: _____

_____

_____

_____

3.   Early majority

    a) Market characteristics: _____

_____

_____

b) Promotion blend: _____
_____
_____
_____

c) Comments: _____
_____
_____
_____

4. Late majority
   a) Market characteristics: _____
   _____
   _____
   _____

   b) Promotion blend: _____
   _____
   _____
   _____

   c) Comments: _____
   _____
   _____
   _____

5. Laggards
   a) Market characteristics: _____
   _____
   _____
   _____

Name: _____ Course & Section:_____

b) Promotion blend: _____
_____
_____
_____

c) Comments: _____
_____
_____
_____

Question for Discussion

Which of the adopter categories is probably the most important from the viewpoint of the marketing strategy planner? That is, which is most crucial in launching a successful new product? Why?

Exercise 15-3

Choosing the right ingredients for the promotion blend

Introduction

Promotion--like all elements of the "marketing mix"--should be planned with the needs and characteristics of the target market in mind. Usually, this will require some combination of personal selling, advertising, and sales promotion. The marketing manager's job is to combine all the possible promotion ingredients into an effective blend which tells target customers that the right product is available at the right place at the right time and at the right price.

But what blend is "best" for a particular situation? One product may need heavy emphasis on personal selling--while another might be sold mainly through advertising and sales promotion. Other products will require a mixture between these two extremes. The particular blend selected depends on a number of factors--including (1) the promotion budget available, (2) the target market, (3) the nature of the product and its stage in the product life cycle, and (4) the competitive environment.

This exercise looks at the ways the various promotion methods can be blended for effective promotion. As you do the exercise, it should become clear that a blend that works well in one situation may be inappropriate for another.

Assignment

The following five cases will help you see why different promotion blends may be needed for different situations. Read each case and then indicate which of the following ratios of advertising to personal selling you would recommend for each situation: 10:1, 5:1, 1:1, 1:5, and 1:10. (For the sake of simplicity, you may ignore sales promotion.) Then explain *why* you chose that ratio and how it would be implemented.

Note: Be sure to study Exhibit 15-8 and the related discussion of the text before starting this exercise.

The first case is answered for you as an example.

1. Poly-Optics, Inc. recently invented a plastic optical fiber--a thin strand of filament that transmits light. It has several industrial uses--ranging from "reading" computer punch cards to monitoring the position of aircraft nose gear through a "fiberscope." For three long years, Poly-Optics tried to sell its fiber instruments to the aerospace, automotive, medical and computer fields--with almost no success. So the company then entered the consumer market with the new "Poly-Optical" lamp--a decorative creation that produced a sort of sunburst of twinkling light. Poly-Optics believed the lamps--which ranged in price from $15 to $300--would become very popular among

homeowners and apartment dwellers. However, since nothing similar existed on the market, the managers were not sure how to promote this new product.

a. Ratio of advertising to personal selling: <u>1:5 (or even 1:10)</u>

b. Explanation: The company probably does not have a large budget for promotion and will have to rely on salespeople (perhaps manufacturer's agents) to set up displays at trade shows and call on prospective wholesalers and retailers. Some consumer advertising in home and apartment magazines may be used to support this personal selling effort, but the newness and distinctiveness of the product suggest that a channel-building "push policy" will be needed in the market introduction stage of the product life cycle. More emphasis may be placed on advertising as the product moves along into the later stages of its life cycle.

2. National Electric Corp.--a leading manufacturer of home appliances--is (finally) introducing its version of a food processor. It will be distributed through its established network of wholesalers and retailers. Food processors cut food preparation time by high-speed cutting, grating, blending, slicing, pureeing, etc. Viewed as an expensive "fad" item when first introduced by Cuisinart, food processors are now well accepted kitchen appliances. As a result, several appliance manufacturers have introduced their own models--and prices have dropped in the face of increased competition. In fact, some companies have already lost money on processors--and one dropped out of the market as industry sales seemed to be leveling off.

Despite its late entry into the market, National expects little channel resistance to its new product--given the popularity of the National brand name among consumers and the above-average profit margins that National producers have tended to provide middlemen. National officials realize that Cuisinart has achieved very strong brand familiarity, but National feels that its product is really the first one to match, or exceed, the quality of the Cuisinart. It also offers consumers a distinct price advantage over the Cuisinart. Nevertheless, an effective promotion blend is seen as critical to the success of National's new food processor.

a. Ratio of advertising to personal selling: _____

b. Explanation:

3. Tom Snyder has just been appointed to manage the major appliance department at Smith's Department Store--which emphasizes nationally advertised refrigerators, freezers, gas and electric ranges, and washing machines and dryers. Smith's has been experiencing a severe drop in sales for these products over the past few years, and Tom's job will be to try to achieve a substantial boost in departmental sales and profits. This is not expected to be easy--given the keen local competition supplied by Eaton's, The Hudson's Bay Company, and a dozen or so smaller appliance dealers. Tom has been told that he may plan to spend about 10 percent of his gross sales to cover promotion expenditures, and he is now trying to determine the best way of allocating his promotion budget to accomplish the desired results.

    a. Ratio of advertising to personal selling: _____

    b. Explanation:

4. PUB, Inc. is a publishing company which was recently formed by a college professor to publish and sell his forthcoming textbook--and perhaps others which he is planning to write. He has high hopes for his new book, because it offers a number of unique topics which are not contained in competing books. In fact, these topics are currently "in" with faculty members. Further, he has developed a more comprehensive test bank--which will make it much easier for instructors to prepare exams.

    This text will normally be used at the junior level, and up to 1,000 colleges and universities offer courses in which the text could be used. Such courses are usually required, and the enrollment tends to be large. The professor estimates that the demand for this kind of text is somewhere between 50 and 80 thousand books a year. But there are already three competitors in this market, so he does not expect to obtain all of this business.

    The professor is now facing the problem of how to handle the promotion effort of his book. Some of the major publishers have large sales forces--which regularly call on professors and arrange to send them complimentary copies when it appears that an adoption is possible. Other publishers rely more on advertisements in trade journals and direct mailings--as well as attendance at teachers' conferences and conventions. The first shipment from the printer is coming to his office shortly--so the professor must soon make a decision about his promotion blend.

    a. Ratio of advertising to personal selling: _____

b. Explanation:

5. Drugco, Ltd.--a large drug wholesaler--is worried about decreasing sales and profits over the past several years. It blames this decline mainly on its independent retailer customers--who are losing much of their business to large retail drug chains. Apparently, the independent druggists tend to be quite inefficient managers--in addition to charging generally higher prices than the chains.

To protect its own position, Drugco has decided to sponsor a voluntary drug chain--aimed at achieving a more effective and economical distribution system for the products it wholesales. This will mean providing additional services to affiliated retailers--including computerized sales and cost analyses, store location and design assistance, help in securing financial resources, merchandising training and assistance, and Drugco's own line of dealer brands. In return, the "independent" druggists will sign contracts specifying common operating procedures-- and the use of a common storefront design, store name, and joint promotion efforts.

Drugco managers expect the proposed voluntary chain to result in economies of scale and more efficient store operation by the independent druggists--thereby achieving the same advantages enjoyed by the drug chains. However, they admit that it will take a strong promotion effort to convince many independents to join--since they will give up some operating freedom and have to pay an annual membership fee.

a. Ratio of advertising to personal selling: _____

b. Explanation:

Question for Discussion

In designing promotion blends, there is a tendency to focus on advertising and personal selling--and ignore sales promotion. How might sales promotion be useful in the cases presented in this exercise?

Chapter 16
Personal selling

What This Chapter Is About

Chapter 16 is concerned with the strategic decisions in the personal selling area.

It is important to see that not all sales jobs are alike. This is why a good understanding of the three basic sales tasks--order getting, order taking, and supporting--is important. The blend of these tasks in a particular sales job has a direct bearing on the selection, training, and compensation of salespeople.

Making an effective sales presentation is an important part of personal selling. Three approaches are explained. Each can be useful--depending on the target market and the products being sold.

Try to see that the strategic personal selling decisions are a part of the whole marketing strategy planning effort. Our earlier discussion of buyer behavior and communication theory is applied here. Be sure to see how materials are being tied together. This chapter continues the strategy planning emphasis which has been running through the text.

Important Terms

basic sales tasks, p. 439

order getters, p. 439

order getting, p. 439

order takers, p. 441

order taking, p. 441

supporting salespeople, p. 444

missionary salespeople, p. 444

technical specialists, p. 444

team selling, p. 445

telemarketing, p. 445

national accounts sales force, p. 445

sales territory, p. 446

job description, p. 447

prospecting, p. 452

sales presentation, p. 453

prepared sales presentation, p. 454

need-satisfaction approach, p. 454

selling formula approach, p. 455

True-False Questions

____ 1. It should be the responsibility of the sales manager--not the marketing manager--to make final decisions about how many and what kind of salespeople are needed.

____ 2. Personal selling has declined in importance to the point that there are now more Americans employed in advertising than in personal selling.

___ 3. Professional salespeople don't just try to sell the customer--they try to help him buy.

___ 4. Some salespeople are expected to act as marketing managers for their own geographic territories and develop their own marketing mixes and strategies.

___ 5. Three basic sales tasks are found in most sales organizations--although in some situations one salesperson might have to do all three tasks.

___ 6. High-calibre order getters are essential in sales of industrial installations and accessory equipment.

___ 7. Sales representatives for progressive merchant wholesalers often serve as advisors to their customers--not just as order takers.

___ 8. Unsought consumer products often require order getters--to convince customers of the product's value.

___ 9. A wholesaler's order takers handle so many items that they usually will not--and probably should not--give special attention to any particular items.

___ 10. A consumer products manufacturer using an indirect channel system has little need to use missionary salespeople.

___ 11. An industrial products manufacturer may benefit considerably by using technical specialists, even though a direct channel of distribution and order getters are used.

___ 12. A national accounts sales force sells directly to very large accounts.

___ 13. A sales territory is a geographic area that is the responsibility of one salesperson or several working together.

___ 14. The first step in deciding how many salespeople are needed is to estimate how much work can be done by one person in some time period.

___ 15. A good job description should not be too specific--since the nature of the sales job is always changing.

___ 16. All new salespeople should receive the same kind of sales training.

___ 17. A written job description can be helpful in setting the level of compensation for salespeople, because it shows whether any special skills or responsibilities are required that will command higher pay levels.

___ 18. A sales manager's control over a salesperson tends to vary directly with what proportion of his compensation is in the form of salary.

___ 19. A combination compensation plan will usually provide the greatest incentive for a salesperson to increase sales.

____20. The most popular compensation method is the straight commission plan.

____21. Many firms set different sales objectives--or quotas--to adjust the compensation plan to differences in potential in each territory.

____22. Basically, prospecting involves following down all the "leads" in the target market--and deciding how much time to spend on which prospects.

____23. Telemarketing is becoming more common because it is an efficient way to find out about a prospect's interest in the company's marketing mix-- and even to make a sales presentation or take an order.

____24. Some kind of priority system is needed to guide sales prospecting--because most salespeople will have too many prospects.

____25. The prepared (canned) sales presentation probably would be appropriate for the majority of retail clerks employed by convenience stores.

____26. An effective office equipment salesperson might use a selling formula sales presentation.

____27. The need-satisfaction approach requires less skill on the part of the salesperson than the prepared approach.

____28. The AIDA sequence is helpful for planning a need-satisfaction sales presentation--but not for a selling formula sales presentation.

Answers to True-False Questions

1. F, p. 434	11. T, p. 444	20. F, p. 450
2. F, p. 435	12. T, p. 445	21. T, p. 450
3. T, p. 435	13. T, p. 446	22. T, p. 452
4. T, p. 437	14. T, p. 446	23. T, p. 445
5. T, p. 439	15. F, p. 447	24. T, p. 453
6. T, p. 439	16. F, p. 448	25. T, p. 454
7. T, p. 440	17. T, p. 447	26. T, p. 455
8. T, p. 440	18. T, p. 449	27. F, p. 455
9. T, p. 442	19. F, p. 450	28. F, p. 456
10. F, p. 444		

Multiple-Choice Questions (Circle the correct response)

1. Which of the following statements about personal selling is *true*?

    a. As a representative of his company, a salesperson's job is to sell the customer rather than to help him buy.
    b. Today's salesperson is really only responsible for "moving products."
    c. The modern salesperson's sole job is to communicate his company's story to customers.
    d. Some sales representatives are expected to be marketing managers in their own geographic territories.
    e. A beginning salesperson could not expect to be responsible for a sales volume as large as that achieved by many retail stores.

2. A salesperson might have to perform three basic sales tasks. Choose the *correct* description of these tasks from the following:

    a. *Supporting:* the routine completion of sales made regularly to the target customers.
    b. *Order getting:* aggressively seeking out potential buyers with a well-organized sales presentation designed to sell a product.
    c. *Order taking:* purpose is to develop goodwill, stimulate demand, explain technical aspects of product, train the middleman's salespeople, and perform other specialized services aimed at obtaining sales in the long run.
    d. All of the above are correct.
    e. None of the above are correct.

3. Order-getting salespeople would be required for which one of the following jobs?

    a. Helping a buyer plan and install a computer system.
    b. Helping drug retailers find new ways to display and promote their products.
    c. Seeking orders from food retailers for a new brand of cake mix which has been added to the company's line.
    d. "Helping" an indecisive supermarket customer select the kind of meat she should buy for dinner.
    e. All of the jobs call for order takers.

4. Chemco, Inc. a three-year-old producer of chemicals, has just hired a manufacturers' agent. The agent:

    a. is probably replacing a company order getter who built up the territory.
    b. should assume that Chemco won't ever hire its own sales force for the territory.
    c. may lose the business when the territory gets to the point where it can be handled by an order taker.
    d. All of the above are equally likely.
    e. None of the above is a good answer.

5. A large appliance manufacturer has adequate wholesale and retail distribution--but is concerned that the middlemen do not push its products aggressively enough--because they also carry competitive lines. The manufacturer should hire some:

    a. missionary salespeople.
    b. order getters.
    c. order takers.
    d. technical specialists.

6. Which of the following statements is *false*?

   a. Team selling involves different specialists--to handle different parts of the selling job.
   b. A national accounts sales force is used to sell to small retailers who are not covered by wholesalers in the channel.
   c. Carefully selected sales territories can reduce the cost of sales calls.
   d. The first step in deciding how many salespeople are needed is to estimate how much work can be done by one person in some time period.

7. With regard to the level of compensation for salespeople, a marketing manager should recognize that:

   a. order takers generally are paid more than order getters.
   b. the appropriate level of compensation should be suggested by the job descriptions.
   c. a good order getter will generally be worth less to a firm than a good technical specialist.
   d. the firm should attempt to pay all its salespeople at least the going market wage for order getters.
   e. salespeople should be the highest-paid employees in the firm.

8. The sales manager of the Bubba Beanbag Corp. wishes to compensate his sales force in a way which will provide some security, incentive, flexibility, and control. The company should offer its sales force:

   a. straight salaries.
   b. straight commissions.
   c. a combination plan.

9. Regardless of the sales volume, the least expensive type of sales force compensation system is always:

   a. straight salary.
   b. straight commission.
   c. a combination plan.
   d. None of the above.

10. Wilma Rogers works as a telephone salesperson for the Catalog Division of Sears, Roebuck. Her primary job is to call customers with Sears charge accounts to inform them about sales items and ask if they would like to order the sales items. Which of the following kinds of sales presentations would be best for Wilma to use?

    a. Prepared sales presentation.
    b. Selling formula approach.
    c. Need-satisfaction approach.

11. Bill White sells life insurance for a large Ontario firm. He locates customers by selecting names out of a telephone directory and calling to arrange an appointment. He begins each presentation by explaining the basic features and merits of his product--eventually bringing the customer into the conversation to clarify the customer's needs. Then he tells how his insurance policy would satisfy the customer's needs and attempts to close the sale. Bill's sales presentation is based on the:

   a. need-satisfaction approach.
   b. selling formula approach.
   c. canned presentation approach.

Answers to Muliple-Choice Questions

1. d, p. 437
2. b, p. 439
3. c, p. 439
4. a, p. 440

5. a, p. 444
6. b, p. 445
7. b, p. 447
8. c, p. 449

9. d, p. 449
10. a, p. 454
11. b, pp. 454-455

Exercise 16-1

Analyzing the nature of the personal selling task

Introduction

Personal selling may involve three basic tasks: (1) *order getting*, (2) *order taking*, and (3) *supporting*. Each task may be done by different individuals--or the same person may do all three. While we use these terms to describe salespeople by referring to their *primary* task, it is important to keep in mind that many salespeople do all of the three tasks to some extent.

Consider, for example, a sales rep for a manufacturer of an established consumer good which is distributed through wholesalers. Since the product is established in the marketplace, the sales rep's primary task would probably be order taking--obtaining routine orders from regular wholesale customers. The same rep may also be expected to do other secondary tasks, however. For example, he may be expected to get orders from new wholesale customers--and so he would also do order getting at times. Further, he might also spend part of his time helping the wholesaler's sales force--by informing retailers about his company's product, building special store displays, and so forth. In this case, the sales rep would be doing a supporting task.

This exercise focuses on the basic differences among the three selling tasks. In some cases, these differences may be rather clear. In other cases, the differences may be quite difficult to see. To determine what kind of sales rep is needed to handle a particular personal selling job, we will try to distinguish between the *primary* and *secondary* selling tasks. *Note: the words "primary" and "secondary" are used in this way in this exercise only--they do not appear in the text.*

Assignment

Six cases are presented below to show how the selling tasks may vary. In some of the cases, the sales rep will perform both primary and secondary selling tasks, while in others only the primary selling task will be discussed. Read each case and then indicate (a) the *primary* selling task *usually required to effectively carry out the specified job* and (b) any secondary selling task(s) which *may also be described in the case*. Then explain your answer in the space marked "Comments." The first case is answered for you as an example.

1. Jane Smith, a sophomore at Dominion University, works part time at the Campus Book Store. During the week, Jane works afternoons waiting on customers at the lunch counter. On weekends, she usually operates the cash register at the candy and cigarette counter--in addition to handling bills for public utilities. According to her boss, Jane is a very good worker.

a) Primary selling task: <u>Order taking</u>

b) Secondary selling task(s): <u>Possibly order getting</u>

c) Comments: <u>No order getting is specifically mentioned, but she may do some occasionally. For example: "Would you like to try some of our fresh strawberry pie today? It's delicious!"</u>

2. Paul Sure is earning most of his own college expenses by selling Fuller Brush personal care products door-to-door. At first, Paul did not like his job, but lately has been enjoying it more--and doing very well. As Paul puts it, "Once you learn the knack of getting your foot in the door, sales come easily and the commissions add up fast. After all, people like our products and the convenience of in-home buying."

a) Primary selling task: _____

b) Secondary selling task(s): _____

c) Comments: _____

_____

_____

3. Jake Woo-lon is a "sales engineer" with Creative Packaging Corporation--which specializes in foam and air "bubble" packaging materials. Producers use these packaging materials to protect their products inside shipping cartons during shipping. Creative Packaging has a line of standard products but also will produce custom packaging materials if that is what a customer needs. The company does advertising in trade magazines, and each ad includes a response card. When a prospect calls to inquire about Creative Packaging products, Woo-lon is sent out to analyze the customer's packaging needs. He determines how much protection is needed and which packaging product would be best. After finishing his work, Woo-lon reports back to his sales manager--who assigns another sales rep to handle the rest of the contacts with the customer.

a) Primary selling task: _____

b) Secondary selling task(s): _____

c) Comments: _____

_____

_____

4. Midwest Power Equipment (MPE) Company is a large merchant wholesaler that distributes chain saws, lawn mowers, and other outdoor power equipment. MPE sells to retailers and also sells direct to large end-users--such as golf courses, and cemeteries. Recently MPE decided to target local government (city and county)

buyers--who purchase equipment to maintain parks, roadside areas, and public schools and hospitals. In the past, these buyers often just purchased equipment from local retailers. Jane Porter, a sales rep for MPE, was assigned responsibility for identifying who influenced these purchase decisions, and for persuading them either to buy from MPE or at least allow MPE to bid on their next order. In addition, Porter has been successful in getting MPE on the provincial government list of approved vendors. That means that various government agencies can select equipment from the MPE catalog and submit a purchase order without a lot of red tape. Porter follows up with the warehouse manager to make certain that these orders are shipped promptly.

a) Primary selling task: _____

b) Secondary selling task(s): _____

c) Comments: _____
_____
_____

5. Pat O'Brien, a marketing major in college, went to work for Campbell's Soup as soon as she graduated. While she hopes to become a brand manager some day, Pat is a district sales representative--calling on supermarkets, grocery stores, and convenience stores. Her job is to build special displays, inform store managers of new products, provide merchandising assistance, review customer complaints, and occasionally to suggest special orders for the stores she visits. Pat is paid a straight salary--plus a bonus when sales in her district are good. (Note: Campbell's uses merchant wholesalers to distribute its products.)

a) Primary selling task: _____

b) Secondary selling task(s): _____

c) Comments: _____
_____
_____

6. For twenty years, Chuck Hayes had been a manufacturer's agent. Based in Vancouver, B.C., he represents a variety of noncompeting manufacturers of parts and components used in the production of recreational vehicles ("vans") and boats. For example, he calls on the many small producers of boats in the British Columbia area and sells them the special water-resistant fabrics and chrome-plated hardware that they need for boat interiors. His customers also include the "conversion shops" that customize vans and RV's, as well as large boatyards that repair and renovate older boats. He also calls on a number of very large boating supply wholesalers. Chuck has worked at getting to know his customers really well. Because of the variety and complexity of the lines he represents, he spends much of this time checking his customers' parts inventories. This gives him continual customer contact--and provides a useful service. He also finds some time to seek new customers--and is always looking for new producers to represent. Recently, however, the producer of one of Chuck's most profitable lines switched to another agent. Apparently, the producer was concerned that Chuck had not been aggressive enough in promoting its

products; the company was especially concerned that a competing European producer represented by another agent was getting an increasing share of the market. Chuck was bitter about losing the account. "I built their B.C. business from scratch--and now they're dropping me cold," he complained. "I handle too many products to devote all of my time to just one manufacturer's offerings."

a) Primary selling task: _____

b) Secondary selling task(s): _____

c) Comments: _____

_____

_____

Question for Discussion

Three different kinds of sales presentations are discussed in the text: the *prepared, need-satisfaction,* and *selling formula* presentations. Which of these three kinds of sales presentations would be most appropriate for each of the sales reps described in Exercise 16-1? Why?

Exercise 16-2

Selecting the appropriate kind of salesperson

Introduction

Promotion involves communicating with potential customers--and personal selling is often the best way to do it. Marketing managers involved in the personal selling function must engage in a number of different activities, including (1) the determination of the number and kind of salespeople needed, (2) the type of sales presentation that should be used, (3) how salespeople should be selected and trained, and finally, (4) how salespeople should be motivated.

Assignment

Table 16-a lists four sales positions and three different types of compensation plans. A brief scenario is presented for seven different companies that are seeking salespeople. Your task is to initially identify the type of sales position each requires and subsequently to choose the most appropriate compensation plan. Be sure to justify your selections. The first one is answered for you as an example.

TABLE 16-a

Sales Position	Compensation Plan
1. Order getter	a. Straight salary
2. Order taker	b. Straight commission
3. Missionary salesperson	c. Combination
4. Technical specialist	

1. Someone is needed to operate an established home-delivered milk route in a suburban area.

   a. Kind of salesperson: <u>Order taker</u>

   b. Method of compensation: <u>Combination</u>

   c. Justification: <u>Since the route has already been established, it is not only important for the salesperson to take orders for existing customers, but potential customers must be pursued. Thus, it is important to motivate the order taker with the combination of straight salary and commission.</u>

2. Fuller brush salesmen are needed to knock on dozens of doors each day, simply asking if the customer needs any brushes.

   a. Type of salesperson: _____

   b. Method of compensation: _____

   c. Justification: _____

   _____

   _____

   _____

3. An aggressive sales representative is needed to attract share of sales of the fast food market for a local restaurant opening up a take-out service.

   a. Type of salesperson: _____

   b. Method of compensation: _____

   c. Justification: _____

   _____

   _____

   _____

4. The designer of a revolutionary recently developed solar system desires to have it specified in architects' and mechanical engineers' plans.

   a. Type of salesperson: _____

   b. Method of compensation: _____

   c. Justification: _____

   _____

   _____

   _____

5. Salesperson representing Bain de Soleil is required to call on various drug store and retail outlets during the summer season. He/she will assist in the setting up of end-of-aisle displays.

   a. Type of salesperson: _____

   b. Method of compensation: _____

   c. Justification: _____

   _____

   _____

   _____

6. A drug wholesaler requires a sales representative to dispense free samples of various products and product information to doctors.

    a.   Type of salesperson: _____

    b.   Method of compensation: _____

    c.   Justification: _____

        _____

        _____

        _____

Question for Discussion

What kind of sales compensation plan--straight salary, straight commission, or a combination plan--would be appropriate in the above situations? Why? What factors must be considered in choosing a sales compensation plan?

Chapter 17
Advertising

What This Chapter Is All About

Chapter 17 focuses on advertising--the main kind of mass selling--and the strategic decisions which must be made.

The importance of specifying advertising objectives is emphasized. Advertisements and advertising campaigns cannot be effective unless we know what we want done.

Next, the kinds of advertising which can be used to reach the objectives are explained. Then, how to deliver the message--via the "best" medium, and what is to be communicated--the copy thrust--is discussed.

Advertising agencies are treated also. They often handle the advertising details for advertisers--under the direction of the firm's advertising manager. Avoiding deceptive advertising is also treated. Increasingly, this has strategic importance-- because of further government regulation.

Try to see how advertising would fit into a promotion blend--and be a part of a whole marketing strategy. Advertising is not an isolated topic. It can be a vital ingredient in a marketing strategy.

Important Terms

product advertising, p. 463
institutional advertising, p. 463
pioneer advertising, p. 463
primary demand, p. 463
competitive advertising, p. 463
selective demand, p. 463
direct type, p. 464
indirect type, p. 464

comparative advertising, p. 464
reminder advertising, p. 465
advertising allowances, p. 466
cooperative advertising, p. 466
direct mail advertising, p. 470
copy thrust, p. 472
advertising agencies, p. 476

True-False Questions

____ 1. Although it is the most expensive form of promotion on a per-contact basis, advertising does permit communication to large numbers of potential customers at the same time.

____ 2. Canadian corporations spend an average of 20 percent of their sales on advertising--with the largest share of this going to television.

___ 3. Advertising objectives should be very specific--much more so than personal selling objectives.

___ 4. A firm whose objective is to help buyers make their purchasing decision should use institutional advertising.

___ 5. Pioneering advertising should be used in the market introduction stage of the product life cycle to develop selective demand for a specific brand.

___ 6. The objective of competitive advertising is to develop selective demand--demand for a specific brand.

___ 7. Direct competitive advertising involves making product comparisons with competitive brands, while indirect competitive advertising focuses solely on the advertiser's products.

___ 8. Because comparative advertising involves specific brand comparisons--using actual product names--it has been banned by Consumer and Corporate Affairs Canada.

___ 9. Reminder advertising probably should not be used unless the firm has achieved brand preference or brand insistence for its products.

___ 10. Advertising allowances are price reductions to firms further along in the channel to encourage them to advertise or otherwise promote the firm's products locally.

___ 11. The main reason cooperative advertising is used is that large manufacturers usually can get lower media rates than local retailers.

___ 12. Regardless of a firm's objectives, television advertising is generally more effective than newspaper or magazine advertising.

___ 13. A major limitation of using audience data which has been collected by the various media to aid in media selection is that the data seldom contain the market dimensions which a particular advertiser may feel are most important.

___ 14. A firm that wants to send a specific message to a clearly identified target market probably should seriously consider using direct-mail advertising.

___ 15. Copy thrust means what is to be communicated by written copy and illustration.

___ 16. The first job in message planning is determine how to get attention.

___ 17. Advertising agencies are specialists in planning and handling mass selling details for advertisers.

___ 18. Normally, media have two prices: one for national advertisers and a lower rate for local advertisers.

___ 19. Advertising effectiveness can be measured quite simply and accurately just by analyzing increases or decreases in sales.

____ 20. Unfortunately, no effort at self-regulation by advertisers has ever been successful in either shaping advertising guidelines or in stopping problem ads.

____ 21. Consumer and Corporate Affairs Canada has the power to control deceptive or false advertising.

Answers to True-False Questions

1. F, p. 459	8. F, p. 464	15. T, p. 472
2. F, p. 481	9. T, p. 465	16. T, p. 473
3. T, p. 460	10. T, p. 466	17. T, p. 476
4. F, p. 463	11. F, p. 466	18. T, p. 478
5. F, p. 463	12. F, p. 467	19. F, p. 479
6. T, pp. 463-464	13. T, p. 469	20. F, p. 483
7. F, p. 464	14. T, p. 470	21. T, p. 483

Multiple-Choice Questions (Circle the correct response)

1. The largest share of total advertising expenditures in Canada goes for:

   a. newspaper advertising
   b. television advertising
   c. magazine advertising
   d. direct-mail advertising
   e. radio advertising

2. Regarding "good" advertising objectives:

   a. Given no clearly specified objectives, advertising agencies may plan campaigns that will be of little benefit to advertisers.
   b. Advertising objectives often are not stated specifically enough to guide implementation.
   c. Advertising objectives should be more specific than personal selling objectives.
   d. The objectives should suggest which kinds of advertising are needed.
   e. All of the above are true.

3. Which of the following statements about advertising objectives is *false*?

   a. They should be as specific as possible.
   b. They should be more specific than personal selling objectives.
   c. They usually are quite clear from the nature and appearance of an advertisement.
   d. They should flow from the overall marketing strategy.
   e. They should set the framework for an advertising campaign.

4. Bill Smith developed an innovative machine to make a more effective and less expensive bottle cap. He found a backer, produced a model, photographed it, and placed an advertisement in a food canners magazine explaining how caps could be made as needed--right in the canner's plant. Much of the ad copy tried to sell the convenience and inventory cost-saving features of in-plant production as needed rather than purchasing large quantities. Smith's advertising was trying to develop:

   a. selective demand.
   b. primary demand.
   c. derived demand.
   d. elastic demand.

267

5. The message "Drink milk every day," is an example of which type of advertising?

   a. Pioneering
   b. Competitive
   c. Indirect action
   d. Reminder
   e. Direct action

6. "Better things for better living through chemistry," is an example of:

   a. pioneering advertising.
   b. reminder advertising.
   c. competitive advertising.
   d. institutional advertising.
   e. cooperative advertising.

7. "Cooperative" advertising refers to the practice of:

   a. manufacturers and middlemen sharing in the cost of advertising which is done by the manufacturer.
   b. manufacturers doing some advertising and expecting their middlemen to cooperate by providing the rest of the promotion blend.
   c. the manufacturer paying for all of the advertising which is done by its middlemen.
   d. local retailers doing advertising which is partially paid for by a manufacturer.
   e. middlemen picking up the promotion theme of the manufacturer and carrying it through.

8. The choice of the "best" advertising medium depends upon:

   a. the promotion objectives.
   b. the budget available.
   c. the target markets.
   d. the characteristics of each medium.
   e. all of the above.

9. To communicate a very specific message to a very select, well-identified group of consumers--one probably should use:

   a. magazines aimed at special-interest groups.
   b. newspapers.
   c. television.
   d. direct mail.
   e. radio.

10. Which of the following statements about advertising agencies and compensation methods is true?

    a.   The 15 percent commission system is no longer required--and some advertisers have obtained discounts or fee increases.

    b.   Some agencies were quite dissatisfied with the traditional compensation arrangements between advertisers and agencies because their costs were rising--and some advertisers were demanding more services than could be provided profitably.

    c.   Some advertisers--especially industrial goods manufacturers--were quite satisfied with the traditional compensation arrangements whereby the agency did the advertiser's advertising work in return for the normal discount allowed by the media.

    d.   The agencies earn commission from media only when time or space is purchased at the national rate (as opposed to local rates).

    e.   All of the above are true statements.

11. Which of the following statements about measuring advertising effectiveness is *false*?

    a.   The most reliable approach is to check the size and composition of media audiences.

    b.   Some progressive advertisers are now demanding laboratory or market tests to evaluate the effectiveness of advertisements.

    c.   No single technique or approach has proven most effective.

    d.   When specific advertising objectives are set, then marketing research may be able to provide feedback on the effectiveness of the advertising.

    e.   Ideally, management should pretest advertising before it is run rather than relying solely on the judgment of creative people or advertising "experts."

Answers to Multiple-Choice Questions

1. a, p. 481	5. a, p. 463	9. d, p. 470
2. e, p. 463	6. d, p. 463	10. e, p. 478
3. c, p. 460	7. d, p. 466	11. a, pp. 479-80
4. b, p. 463	8. e, p. 467	

Exercise 17-1

Identifying different kinds of advertising

Introduction

Perhaps because of the high cost of advertising, some companies try to use multi-purpose ads to reach several promotion objectives at the same time. Studies have shown, however, that such ads often fail to produce *any* of the desired effects. On the contrary, several special-purpose ads are much more likely to stimulate positive responses than a single multi-purpose ad. Thus, a marketing manager usually should use different kinds of advertising to accomplish different promotion objectives.

This exercise is designed to show the different kinds of advertising which can be used--and to show the various objectives an advertisement might have. While doing the assignment, you should see that promotion objectives may be only indirectly concerned with increasing sales--and that a firm may have other reasons for advertising. Try to guess what these "other reasons" are--and how they might relate to a company's overall marketing mix.

Assignment

Using recent magazines and newspapers, find advertisements to *final customers* which illustrate the following kinds of advertising (as defined in the text):

> A. Institutional
> B. Pioneering
> C. Direct competitive
> D. Indirect competitive
> E. Comparative
> F. Reminder

Clip out the ads--and for each ad attach a separate sheet of paper indicating:

a) what kind of advertising the ad illustrates.
b) what target market, if any, the ad appears to be aimed at.
c) the general and specific objectives of each ad--e.g., to inform consumers (general) about three new product improvements (specific).
d) the name of the magazine or newspaper in which the ad appeared.

Question for Discussion

When one overall objective of a company's marketing activities must be to sell its products, why would advertisements have objectives such as those you indicated for your examples?

Exercise 17-2

Determining advertising objectives and the appropriate kind of advertising

Introduction

About 1910 George Washington Hill--president of the American Tobacco Company--is said to have made this now-famous quote: "I am convinced that 50 percent of our advertising is sheer waste, but I can never find out which half." Today, there are many business executives who would probably share Mr. Hill's feelings. Billions of dollars are spent each year creating clever--and sometimes annoying--ads which often appear to be poorly designed and largely ineffective.

Actually, it is extremely difficult to measure the effectiveness of advertising--because companies often lack clearly defined advertising objectives. In hopes of remaining competitive, advertisers often budget some fixed percent of their sales dollars to advertising without any specific objectives in mind--other than to just "promote the product."

Like all business expenditures, however, there is no reason for making advertising expenditures unless the company has some specific purpose in mind. Since the advertising objectives selected will largely determine the kind of advertising that is needed, companies should set specific advertising objectives which are tied to their overall marketing strategies.

Assignment

This exercise will give you some practice determining the kind of advertising that may be needed to obtain some specific advertising objectives. Described below are several situations in which some kind of advertising may be necessary or desirable. For each situation: (a) indicate what *general* (i.e., inform, persuade, and/or remind) and *specific* objectives the advertising probably would be meant to achieve; and (b) indicate which of the following kinds of advertising would be *most* appropriate to accomplish that objective.

      A. Pioneering advertising
      B. Direct competitive advertising
      C. Indirect competitive advertising
      D. Reminder advertising
      E. Institutional advertising

The first situation is answered for you as an example.

1. The Harper Life Insurance company is planning to place ads in college newspapers to tell students about the importance of owning a well-planned life insurance program--and. to explain how its agents are trained to help plan an insurance program that fits their needs.

   a) Advertising objectives: <u>To INFORM prospects about the company's name and the merits of its products, and to "open the door" for the company's sales reps.</u>

   b) Kind of advertising: <u>Indirect competitive</u>

2. CompuAdd, a company that got its start selling computers and computer accessories by mail order, recently opened a chain of retail stores. CompuAdd has an outstanding reputation among corporate buyers for reliable computers and after the sale service--all at a low cost. But, marketing research reveals that many individual computer buyers don't know about the company and think that buying a CompuAdd brand computer would be risky. Managers of the firm's new retail stores complain that many consumers never even consider CompuAdd brand computers.

   a. Advertising objectives: _____

   _____

   _____

   b: Kind of advertising: _____

3. A large department store chain decides to drop its "full-service" approach and switch to a discount selling operation with "low everyday prices."

   a. Advertising objectives: _____

   _____

   _____

   b: Kind of advertising: _____

4. After a below-normal Christmas season--due to a major snow storm which reduced travel to the downtown area--the Altman Department Store is planning a half-price inventory clearance sale on "everything."

   a. Advertising objectives: _____

   _____

   _____

   b: Kind of advertising: _____

5. Qualitas, Ltd. is one of the leading producers of stereo speakers in Canada. Unlike the technological advances in other types of stereo components, there has been little change in speakers in the last 30 years. However, Qualitas has just patented a revolutionary new way to reproduce sound through a speaker. The new Qualitas speaker produces music that is significantly better. Some industry sources predict that by the year 2000 the new technology will capture 40 to 50 percent of the stereo speaker market.

    a. Advertising objectives: _____

    _____

    _____

    b: Kind of advertising: _____

6. The Alyeska Pipeline-Service Company, which constructed a highly controversial crude oil pipeline across Alaska, wishes to tell concerned citizens about the steps it is taking to preserve and protect the fragile Arctic environment.

    a. Advertising objectives: _____

    _____

    _____

    b: Kind of advertising: _____

7. The Association of Soy Oil Producers wants to increase sales by getting more food producers to use cholesterol-free soy oil--rather than other types of oils--as an ingredient in their products. At a meeting with association leaders, an advertising agency executive suggested several possible approaches. But, the association leaders decided to go with a campaign that targeted ads directly at health conscious "baby boomers"--to encourage them to purchase products made with soy oil. As one association leader put it, the objective would be "to help stimulate demand for products made with soy oil, and thus to increase per capita consumption of soy oil."

    a. Advertising objectives: _____

    _____

    _____

    b: Kind of advertising: _____

8. Oberlin's Clothing Store has lost its lease after 20 successful years in the same location. Susan Oberlin has found a new store in a shopping center that is just being built. She is going to have a sale to reduce her inventory before the move--and she worries about whether her customers will "follow her" to her new location.

a. Advertising objectives: _____

_____

_____

b: Kind of advertising: _____

9. International Juice Corporation received much bad publicity when a lawsuit by a competitor revealed that a number of International's "all natural" fruit juices contained artificial ingredients. The problem arose because one of International's key suppliers had secretly substituted artificial juices for the natural products International had specified. Alarmed by the new reports, many customers stopped buying International's products. The firm's president held a press conference at which he promised to rebuild faith in the firm and its many fine products.

a. Advertising objectives: _____

_____

_____

b: Kind of advertising: _____

Question for Discussion

Would there be difficulties in evaluating the effectiveness of ads for the situations mentioned in Exercise 17-2? Why?

Chapter 18
Pricing objectives and policies

What This Chapter Is About

Chapter 18 talks about the strategic decisions in the Price area. You should see that there is much more to Price than accepting the "equilibrium price" set by the interaction of supply and demand forces (as discussed in Appendix A). The actual price paid by customers depends on many factors. Some of these are discussed in the chapter. They include the trade, quantity, and cash discounts offered; trade-ins; who pays the transportation costs; and what actually is included in the marketing area.

The chapter begins with a discussion of possible pricing objectives--which should guide price setting. Then, the marketing manager's decisions about price flexibility and price level over the product life cycle are discussed.

The marketing manager must also set prices which are legal. The chapter discusses what can and cannot be done legally.

Clearly, there is much more to pricing than the simple economic analysis which we used earlier to understand the nature of competition. Chapter 18 is an important chapter--and deserves very careful study.

Important Terms

True-False Questions

_____ 1. Any business transaction in our modern economy can be thought of as an exchange of money--the money being the Price--for something of greater value.

_____ 2. The "something" that Price buys is different for consumers or users than it is for channel members.

_____ 3. A target return objective is often used in a large company with several divisions for administrative convenience.

_____ 4. Profit maximization objectives are undesirable from a social viewpoint, because profit maximization necessarily leads to high prices.

_____ 5. Instead of setting profit-oriented objectives, a marketing manager should follow sales-oriented objectives because--in the long run--sales growth leads to big profits.

_____ 6. Market share objectives provide a measurable objective--but an increase in market share does not always lead to higher profits.

_____ 7. Status quo pricing objectives make it virtually impossible for a firm to implement an effective marketing strategy because of the non-price competition.

_____ 8. Instead of letting daily market forces determine their prices, most firms (including all of those in monopolistic competition) set their own administered prices--sometimes holding them steady for long periods of time.

_____ 9. A one-price policy means offering the same price to all customers who purchase goods under essentially the same conditions and in the same quantities.

_____ 10. Flexible pricing is seldom used any more in Canada because it does not aid selling--and because flexible prices are generally illegal under Canadian legislation.

_____ 11. A skimming pricing policy is especially desirable when economies of scale reduce costs greatly as volume expands--or when the firm expects strong competition very soon after introducing its new product.

_____ 12. A penetration pricing policy might be indicated where there is no "elite" market--that is, where the whole demand curve is fairly elastic--even in the early stages of the product's life cycle.

_____ 13. Introductory price dealing means the same thing as using a penetration pricing policy.

_____ 14. A firm involved in an oligopoly situation should not engage in "conscious parallel action" because such conspiracies are illegal.

____ 15. Sellers who may appear to emphasize below-the-market prices in their marketing mixes may really be using different marketing strategies--not different price levels.

____ 16. Basic list prices are the prices final consumers (or industrial consumers) are normally asked to pay for products.

____ 17. Discounts from the list price may be granted by the seller to a buyer who either gives up some marketing function or provides the function for himself.

____ 18. Quantity discounts may help the seller to get more of a buyer's business or to reduce the seller's shipping and selling cost--but they usually also shift some of the storing function from the buyer back to the seller.

____ 19. Cumulative quantity discounts tend to encourage larger single orders than do noncumulative quantity discounts.

____ 20. The following is an example of a seasonal discount. A local supermarket gives a free half gallon of milk with every order of $10.00 or more, provided the purchases are made on either Monday, Tuesday, or Wednesday--which normally are slow days in the food business.

____ 21. Cash discounts are used to encourage buyers to pay their bills quickly--meaning they are granted to buyers who pay their bills by the due date.

____ 22. The following terms of sale appear on an invoice: 1/10, net 30. A buyer who fails to take advantage of this cash discount offer is--in effect--borrowing at an annual rate of 18 percent a year.

____ 23. A mass merchandiser that allows government employees to purchase goods at 10 percent below the store's normal selling prices is using a trade or functional discount.

____ 24. Allowances are typically given only to channel members who provide some service--such as additional selling effort.

____ 25. Trade-in allowances are price reductions given for used goods when similar new goods are bought.

____ 26. PMs or "spiffs" are given to retailers by manufacturers or wholesalers to pass on to their salespeople in return for aggressively selling particular items or lines.

____ 27. F.O.B. pricing simplifies a seller's pricing--but may narrow his target market because a customer located farther from the seller must pay more for his goods and might be inclined to buy from nearby suppliers.

____ 28. With zone pricing, an average freight charge is made to all buyers within certain geographic areas, thus lowering the chance of price competition in the channel and simplifying the figuring of transportation charges.

____29. Uniform delivered pricing--which is used when the seller wishes to sell his products in all geographic areas at one price--is most often used when transportation costs are relatively high.

____30. Freight absorption pricing means absorbing freight costs so that a firm's delivered price will meet the nearest competitor's.

Answers to True-False Questions

1. F, p. 488
2. T, p. 488
3. T, p. 490
4. F, p. 491
5. F, p. 491
6. T, pp. 491-492
7. F, p. 492
8. T, p. 492
9. T, p. 493
10. F, p. 493

11. F, p. 494
12. T, p. 495
13. F, p. 496
14. F, pp. 496-497
15. T, p. 497
16. T, p. 498
17. T, p. 498
18. F, p. 498
19. F, p. 498
20. T, p. 499

21. F, p. 499
22. T, p. 499
23. F, p. 500
24. F, p. 501
25. T, p. 502
26. T, p. 502
27. T, p. 504
28. T, p. 504
29. F, p. 504
30. T, p. 505

Multiple-Choice Questions (Circle the correct response)

1. Which of the following would be least *likely* to be included in the "something" part of the "price equation" for channel members?

   a. Quantity discounts
   b. Repair facilities
   c. Price-level guarantees
   d. Sufficient margin to allow chance for profit
   e. Convenient packaging for handling

2. Which of the following price objectives would a marketing manager for a public utility be most likely to pursue?

   a. Status quo
   b. Market share
   c. Target return
   d. Profit maximization
   e. Sales growth

3. With respect to pricing objectives, a marketing manager should be aware that:

   a. profit maximization objectives generally result in high prices.
   b. status quo pricing objectives can be part of an extremely aggressive marketing strategy.
   c. target return objectives usually guarantee a substantial profit.
   d. sales-oriented objectives generally result in high profits.
   e. All of the above are true statements.

4. Prices are called "administered" when:

   a. they are determined through negotiations between buyers and sellers.
   b. they fall below the "suggested list price."
   c. a marketing manager has to change his strategy every time a customer asks about the price.
   d. government intervenes to ensure that prices fluctuate freely in response to market force.
   e. firms set their own prices for some period of time--rather than letting daily market forces determine their prices.

5. In contrast to flexible pricing, a one-price policy:

   a. means that the same price is offered to all customers who purchase goods under the same conditions.
   b. involves setting the price at the "right" level from the start-- and holding it there.
   c. generally results in rigid prices which change very infrequently.
   d. means that delivered prices will be the same to all customers.
   e. All of the above.

6. Which of the following factors would be *least favorable* to a skimming price policy?

   a. The firm is a monopoly.
   b. The whole demand curve is fairly elastic.
   c. The product is in the market introduction stage of its life cycle.
   d. The firm follows a multiple target market approach.
   e. The firm has a unique, patented product.

7. The Gill Corp. is introducing a new "me-too" brand of shampoo in market maturity. To speed its entry into the market--without encouraging price competition with other shampoo manufacturers--Gill should consider using:

   a. a penetration pricing policy.
   b. a flexible-price policy.
   c. a skimming pricing policy.
   d. introductory price dealing.
   e. an above-the-market price-level policy.

8. The Stark Corporation purchases large quantities of iron castings from a well known producer. Stark receives a discount which increases as the total amount ordered during the year increases. What type of discount is involved here?

   a. Seasonal discount
   b. Cumulative quantity discount
   c. Brokerage allowance
   d. Noncumulative quantity discount
   e. Cash discount

9. The terms "3/20, net 60" mean that:

    a. in effect--the buyer will pay a 27 percent interest rate if he takes 60 days to pay the invoice.
    b. the buyer must make a 3 percent down payment--with the balance due in 20 to 60 days.
    c. a 3 percent discount off the face value of the value of the invoice is permitted if the bill is paid within 60 days-- otherwise, the full face value is due within 20 days.
    d. the invoice is dated March 20 and must be paid within 60 days.
    e. None of the above is a true statement.

10. The Bowman Co., a manufacturer of sports equipment, gives its retailers a 2 percent price reduction on all goods with the expectation that the dealers will advertise the goods locally. Apparently, Bowman believes that local promotion will be more effective and economical than national promotion. This is an example of:

    a. "push" money.
    b. a brokerage allowance.
    c. a cash discount.
    d. a trade discount.
    e. an advertising allowance.

11. Some producers give _____ to retailers to pass on to the retailers' salesclerks in return for aggressively selling particular items or lines.

    a. brokerage commissions
    b. advertising allowances
    c. trade discounts
    d. "push money"
    e. cash discounts

12. A producer in Quebec sold some furniture to a firm in Toronto. If the seller wanted title to the goods to pass immediately--but still wanted to pay the freight bill--the invoice would read:

    a. F.O.B. delivered.
    b. F.O.B. seller's factory--freight prepaid.
    c. F.O.B. Toronto.
    d. F.O.B. seller's factory.
    e. F.O.B. buyer's warehouse.

13. If a buyer purchases a shipment of products from a seller in another city and the invoice reads "F.O.B. shipping point,"

    a. the seller pays the freight bill and keeps title to the products until they are delivered.
    b. the seller pays the freight bill but title to the products passes to the buyer at the point of loading.
    c. the buyer pays the freight but the seller keeps title to the products until delivery.
    d. the buyer pays the freight and gets title to the products at the point of loading.
    e. Both a and c.

14. Which of the following statements about geographic pricing policies is true?

    a.   Zone pricing penalizes buyers closest to the factory.

    b.   Uniform delivered pricing is more practical when transportation costs are relatively low.

    c.   Freight absorption pricing may increase the size of a firm's market territories.

    d.   F.O.B. pricing tends to reduce the size of market territories.

    e.   All of the above are true statements.

Answers to Multiple-Choice Questions

1. b, p. 488	6. b, p. 494	11. d, p. 502
2. c, p. 489	7. d, p. 496	12. b, p. 504
3. b, p. 492	8. b, pp. 498-499	13. d, p. 504
4. e, p. 492	9. a, p. 499	14. e, pp. 504-505
5. a, p. 493	10. e, p. 501	

Exercise 18-1

Using discounts and allowances to improve the marketing mix

Introduction

Most price structures have a basic list price from which various discounts and allowances are subtracted. *Discounts* (not to be confused with discount selling) are reductions from list price that are given by a seller to a buyer who either gives up some marketing function or provides the function himself. Several types of discounts are commonly used, including:

    a) Cumulative quantity discounts
    b) Noncumulative quantity discounts
    c) Seasonal discounts
    d) Cash discounts
    e) Trade (functional) discounts. These are legal in the U.S. but illegal in Canada.

Allowances are similar to discounts. They are given to final consumers, customers or channel members for doing "something" or accepting less of "something." Different types of allowances include:

    a) Trade-in allowances
    b) Advertising allowances
    c) Push money or prize money allowances

While many firms give discounts and allowances as a matter of custom, they should be viewed as highly useful tools for marketing strategy planning. As outlined in the text, each type is designed for a specific purpose. Thus, some firms offer buyers a choice of several discounts and allowances.

The purpose of this exercise is to illustrate how discounts and allowances can be used in marketing strategy planning. The emphasis will be on recognizing opportunities to improve a firm's marketing mix. In Exercise 18-2, we will discuss various legal restrictions which may affect a firm's policies regarding discounts and allowances.

Assignment

Presented below are five cases describing situations in which a firm *might* want to add or change some discount or allowance--as part of its marketing mix. Read each case carefully and then answer the questions which follow.

1. Athletic Footwear Company produces a high-quality line of Lightfoot brand men's and women's running shoes. Lightfoot shoes are distributed nationally through a network of carefully selected sporting stores and runners' stores. When jogging first became popular, Lightfoot sales grew rapidly--in part because of its ongoing advertising in national magazines. Now, however, sales are flat--and in some areas falling. Most retailers now carry several competing brands of shoes--and the company is concerned about what it considers "a lack of adequate promotion support at the retail level."

    Could Athletic Footwear Company use discounts or allowances to obtain additional promotion support at the retail level? Why? If so, what type would you recommend? Why?

2. Richmond Auto Supply sells a wide assortment of products to gas stations and auto service centers in the Richmond British Columbia area. Richmond's line includes almost everything its customers might need--ranging from tune-up parts, mufflers, batteries, tires, brake repair items, automobile paint, hand cleaner, and a wide variety of mechanic's tools and equipment. In addition, like most other auto parts wholesalers in the area, Richmond offers free delivery. Despite Richmond's efforts to promote itself as "the most economical source for all your needs," most of its customers split their business among a number of different auto supply wholesalers. When Richmond's owner complained about this, one of his counter clerks offered an explanation: "The garage owners don't care what parts house gets the business--so the different mechanics just call whoever comes to mind first."

    Could discounts or allowances be useful to Richmond Auto Supply? Why? If so, what type would be best? Explain.

3. Southag, Ltd. manufactures a large assortment of fertilizers, weed killers, plant nutrients, and insecticides. Southag's products are sold across Canada through merchant wholesalers (distributors) who supply not only farmers but also plant nurseries, landscaping services, hardware stores, and lumberyards. Southag's production manager recently complained to the firm's marketing manager that "the sales force needs to do a better job of smoothing out sales. In the fall and winter--when there is little planting activity--we have extra capacity. Then, in the spring all of the orders come in at once--and we have to pay overtime to get everything produced. It's not just a matter of putting items in our warehouse. We need to get the orders. We have bills to pay."

Could Southag's problem be due in part to a lack of appropriate discounts of allowances? Why? If so, what type might be best for the company to adopt? Explain.

4. The Trend-Setters Dress Shop has just purchased $10,000 worth of women's dresses from Fashion Manufacturing Company. The invoice for the dresses included the terms "4/10, net 60."

   a) What do the terms 4/10, net 60 mean?

   b) Suppose Trend-Setters pays the invoice 10 days after receipt. What amount should it pay Fashion Manufacturing?

c) If Trend-Setters does not pay the invoice until 60 days after receipt, it will in effect be borrowing money at a fairly high interest rate. Calculate what the effective interest rate would be in this case. (Assume a 360 day year.)

d) What conditions would make it sensible for Fashion Manufacturing to offer these terms?

Question for Discussion

Do discounts and allowances really offer marketing managers a great deal of flexibility in varying their marketing mixes? Explain.

Exercise 18-2
Pricing decisions

Introduction

Price is one of the four major variables within the control of the marketing manager. Pricing decisions are very important as they have the potential to affect both the firm's sales and profits. Guided by the firm's various objectives, these marketing managers must develop a set of specific pricing objectives and policies.

Numerous conditions in the marketplace affect the price of products. It is difficult for marketing managers to single out these variables and subsequently react to them as separate entities.

Assignment

Assume that you are a marketer of dishwashing liquid and the following factors hold true for your present situation:

    a.   the competition sells their product for the same price of $1.35
    b.   each event listed in the table below is dealt with in isolation

Look at each of these five possible competitive actions (free samples, etc.) and then indicate how you would respond to each such action if your pricing objective were maximization of sales, if it were ROI, etc. Use the following symbols to indicate your choice of course of action.

        S   = similar action

        R   = raise your price

        L   = lower your price

        M   = maintain current price (no other action)

        C   = counteraction--specify

        N   = non-price competitive response

Competition	Maximization of Sales	Target ROI	Status Quo: Competitive Action is Minimized	Market Share
1. Free samples of dishwashing liquid via mail (door to door)				
2. Complimentary set of rubber gloves with each purchase				
3. Price reduction: Buy one bottle and the second bottle can be purchased for $0.95				
4. Increased costs in production causes a price increase of $0.09				
5. Offer coupons worth $0.20 in local newspapers				

290

Exercise 18-3

How legislation affects pricing policies

Introduction

Pricing legislation is a very complex field and often even legal counsel cannot assure their clients of clear-cut advice in pricing matters. This is due in part to the vague and ambiguous way in which many laws have been phrased by legislators and in part to the fact that no two situations are ever exactly alike. It is up to the courts and administrative bodies to interpret pricing legislation, and their interpretation of laws has tended to vary considerably, depending on the political and social environment.

Nevertheless, a marketing manager should try to understand the legal environment and know how to work within it. Legislation and legal cases often tend to focus on pricing matters because prices are tangible and highly visible elements of the marketing mix. Businessmen have considerable freedom to charge whatever prices they choose, subject to the forces of competition, of course. But they must be aware of, and adhere to, the restrictions which do exist. Ignorance of the law is no excuse, and the penalty for violating pricing laws can be quite severe.

This exercise is designed to enhance your understanding of the Competition Act provisions which pertain to pricing matters. Here, the intent is not to make you a legal expert but rather to examine in detail the kinds of pricing activities which *might* be viewed as illegal in certain situations. A review of pages 114-18 of Chapter 4 would be in order before you proceed.

Assignment

Described below are several situations involving pricing activities which might be judged illegal in certain circumstances. Study each situation carefully and then answer the questions which follow.

1. Jumping Jeans Ltd., a retail sportswear chain, has four locations in Toronto and plans to open its first store in Montreal next month. The Quebec sales manager has proposed a "two for the price of one" sale for the first week of Montreal operations. However, his proposal has run into some opposition from the president of Jeans who thinks that, since the same offer isn't being made in Toronto, the proposed sale may be illegal. The president is also afraid of being accused of "predatory pricing." The sales manager has assured him that such a sale would be legal, but the president refuses to give his blessing until he consults his lawyer.

    Do you think the sales manager or the president is correct in this case? Why? Do you think a "one-shot" deal of this nature should be subject to restrictive legislation? Why or why not?

2. Lazy Laundry Ltd. is a highly successful coin-operated laundry chain in Quebec. For several years it was the only laundry in Povungnituk but now another firm has opened up. At this location Lazy charges ten cents less per load for washing and five cents less for drying than is charged at its other Quebec outlets. Last week a complaint alleging "predatory pricing" was sent to the Restrictive Trade Practices Commission by the new competitor in Povungnituk. As far as the company is concerned, it maintains that lower prices are being charged at Povungnituk because the prospective customers are relatively poor. Also, the costs of operation are lower in this far northern community than in it is other locations.

    You have been asked to assist in preparing the defense to the predatory pricing complaint. Do you think the company can successfully defend its pricing policy for Povungnituk? Why or why not?

3. You have recently been hired as marketing consultant to a major U.S. cake mix company which wants to enter the Canadian market. It estimates that its start-up costs for Canada will be substantial, e.g., new packaging, national advertising campaign, etc. To help defray some of these expenses, it plans initially to limit its discounts to the following three types:

    a. A quantity discount of 10 percent but only on sales of more than ten cases.
    b. A 10 percent discount, over and above any quantity discount, on all sales to wholesalers, and
    c. An additional 5 percent cumulative quantity discount of all sales to retailers in a given year of over 100 cases.

    For Canadian purposes, you are asked to comment on the legality or illegality of each type of discount under the Competition Act as described in your text. Also, comment on whether you think functional, quantity and cumulative quantity discounts ought to be legal.

4. As marketing manager for Carefree Carpet Retailers Ltd., you have been asked to approve the following copy for next week's newspaper ad:

Carefree Carpets Ltd. Charme Sales
Top Quality Broadloom $10.95 per yd.
Normally $15.95 per yd or more
Hurry! Limited quantity

You immediately telephone the sales manager for further details about the proposed sale stock. He advises you that over 75 yards are available for the sale. In addition, he has a substantial stock of similar broadloom which is regularly priced at $11.95 per yard. As well, the sales manager tells you that the broadloom to be advertised was priced at $16.95 per yard when it was first introduced four years ago. The $15.95 price applied as recently as last year when this broadloom was discontinued due to manufacturing irregularities.

Do you see any ethical or moral reason for not approving this advertisement? If you approve it, will Carefree be vulnerable to prosecution for false or deceptive advertising? Why or why not?

5. Gleam and Sheen is a new hair product which provides long-lasting highlights. It has been extremely successful since it was introduced into the market two months ago. This success is largely due to a national TV advertising campaign which began at the time of launch and has created a high degree of consumer awareness of this unique new product. Orders have temporarily exceeded supply, and the Montreal distributor learned today that a refusal to supply complaint has been filed against it with the Restrictive Trade Practice Commission. The complaint was filed by a Montreal discount drugstore which was one of the first firms to place its order for Gleam and Sheen. This order was placed within the first week of the TV campaign, and it has yet to be filled while other orders have been filled. The complaint alleges that sales of approximately $300 have been lost to date.

You are an investigator for the Restrictive Trade Practices commission and must determine whether or not remedial action is required in this matter. Do you have sufficient information to make the determination? If so, do you think remedial action is required? If you do not have sufficient information, what additional data is required?

6.   The Better Business Bureau of Yourtown, Canada, recently received a telephone call from an irate customer who wished to voice a complaint about "Honest Sam's," a mass merchandiser with several stores in the surrounding area. It seems the customer had gone to "Honest Sam's" to take advantage of some bargain items that were featured in an "inventory clearance sale" advertisement. The first item on his shopping list was a compact stereo marked down from $150 to $99.95. Upon arrival at the store, he found only one of the featured stereos in stock--a floor model in very poor condition. The salesclerk apologized and suggested that he consider buying one of the store's other models at "regular everyday low pricing," ranging from $199 on up. The customer then went over to the clothing department to check on some men's blazers which, according to the ad, were "regularly priced from $50-$90" and "now reduced to only $39.99." He found a large array of cheap blazers, many of them out-of-style by several seasons, which were hardly worth the sale price let alone the prices quoted in the ad. An official from BBB sympathized with the customer and admitted that his agency had received many similar complaints about "Honest Sam's." He went on to say, however, that there was very little anyone could do about such merchandising tactics, other than to avoid shopping at such stores.

Comment on the Better Business Bureau's analysis of the above situation. Are "Honest Sam's" merchandising practices deceptive? Was the customer really deceived? Can anything be done in such situations?

Questions for Discussion

According to one point of view, the Competition Act benefits consumers by prohibiting pricing practices which may tend to injure competition. Another point of view, however, holds that the Act only serves to protect inefficient competitors and thus may actually be harmful to consumers. Which view to you agree with? Why? How can we determine which view is "right"?

Appendix C
Marketing arithmetic

What This Chapter Is About

Appendix C provides a brief introduction (or review) of some important accounting terms which are useful in analyzing marketing problems.

The content of an operating statement (profit-and-loss statement) is reviewed first. Accounting terms are used in a technical sense--rather than a layman's sense--and should be studied with this in mind. Accountants try to use words precisely--and usually try to place the same kinds of data in the same places in their statements. So try to capture the "model" which they are using. Basically, it is: sales minus costs equals profit.

It also is useful to be able to calculate stockturn rates, operating ratios, markups, markdowns, and ROI and ROA--to fully understand some of the concepts in the text chapters.

This material should be "easy review" for those who have had some accounting. But regardless of your background, it probably will be helpful to study this material--to deepen your understanding of accounting statements and tools. Familiarity with these ideas is assumed in the text!

Important Terms

operating statement, p. 511
gross sales, p. 513
return, p. 514
allowance, p. 514
net sales, p. 514
cost of goods sold, p. 514
gross margin, p. 514
expenses, p. 514
net profit, p. 514

purchase discount, p. 515
stockturn rate, p. 516
operating ratios, p. 517
markup, p. 518
markdown ratio, p. 519
markdown, p. 520
return on investment (RO1), p. 520
balance sheet, p. 520
return on assets (ROA), p. 521

True-False Questions

_____ 1.   An operating statement is a simple summary of the financial results of a company's operation over a specified period of time.

_____ 2.   The three basic components of an operating statement are sales, costs, and return on investment.

____ 3. Net sales equal gross sales minus returns and allowances.

____ 4. The "cost of goods sold" is the total value (at cost) of all the goods sold during the operating period.

____ 5. Gross margin (or gross profit) equals net sales minus operating expenses.

____ 6. Net profit equals net sales minus the cost of sales minus operating expenses.

____ 7. To calculate the net profit accurately, purchase discounts and freight charges should be added to the cost of sales.

____ 8. Expenses do not include the cost of sales.

____ 9. The stockturn rate is a measure of how long it takes a certain inventory of goods to be sold.

____ 10. Stockturn rate may be calculated as the "cost of goods sold" divided by the average inventory at cost.

____ 11. The various components of an operating statement should always be expressed in absolute numbers rather than in percentages.

____ 12. If a store takes a 50-cent markup on a certain product, then its net profit for that item is also 50 cents.

____ 13. A 25 percent markup on cost equals a 20 percent markup on selling price.

____ 14. A markdown ratio equals dollar markdowns divided by net sales; returns and allowances are not included.

____ 15. Markdowns are generally shown on a firm's operating statement.

____ 16. Return on investment is not shown on the firm's operating statement.

____ 17. To increase return on investment, a firm *must* increase sales.

____ 18. Although return on investment is calculated in the same way as return on assets, the two ratios are trying to show different things about the company's use of resources.

Answers to True-False Questions

1. T, p. 511	7. F, p. 515	13. T, p. 519
2. F, p. 512	8. T, p. 516	14. F, pp. 519-520
3. T, p. 514	9. F, pp. 516-517	15. F, p. 520
4. T, pp. 514-515	10. T, p. 517	16. T, p. 520
5. F, p. 514	11. F, p. 518	17. F, p. 521
6. T, p. 514	12. F, p. 519	18. F, p. 521

Multiple-Choice Questions (Circle the correct response)

1. The primary purpose of the operating statement is:

   a. to determine which products or customers are most profitable.
   b. to determine the net profit figure for the company.
   c. to present data to support the net profit figure.
   d. to indicate the source of the firm's assets.
   e. both b and c above.

2. The essential components of an operating statement are:

   a. gross sales, gross margin, and net profit.
   b. net sales, cost of sales, and profit or loss.
   c. sales, costs, and profit or loss.
   d. gross sales, gross margin, expenses, and net profit.
   e. sales, markdowns, and ROI.

3. Which of the following statements is *true*?

   a. "Gross sales" is equal to revenue actually received and kept.
   b. "Cost of goods sold" means the cost value of goods on hand at any given time.
   c. Expenses are included in the "Cost of goods sold" section of the operating statement.
   d. "Gross margin" less the "Cost of goods sold" equals "Net profit."
   e. None of the above statements are true.

4. Given the following data for the XYZ Company for the year 199X, calculate XYZ's net profit.

Gross sales	$157,000
Returns	3,000
Allowances	4,000
Purchases	60,000
Beginning inventory	50,000
Freight-in	3,000
"Cost of goods sold"	100,000
Expenses	30,000

   a. $10,000
   b. $12,000
   c. $17,000
   d. $20,000
   e. $27,000

5. Which of the following statements is *false*?

   a. Stockturn rate equals cost of sales divided by average inventory at cost.
   b. Stockturn rate equals gross sales divided by average inventory at selling price.
   c. Stockturn rate equals net sales minus gross margin divided by average inventory at cost.
   d. Stockturn rate equals sales in units divided by average inventory in units.
   e. Stockturn rate equals net sales divided by average inventory at selling price.

Use the following data to answer questions 6 and 7.

Gross sales	$1,020,000	
Markdowns	50,000	
"Cost of goods sold"		50%
Beginning inventory	150,000	
Returns and allowances	20,000	
Expenses		30%
Purchases	400,000	

6. Calculate the net profit (or loss) for the firm described above.

   a. $150,000
   b. $190,000
   c. $204,000
   d. $200,000
   e. Cannot be determined without more information.

7. Assume that the average stockturn rate for this industry is 4. How does this firm compare to its competitors?

   a. The firm has an above-average turnover rate.
   b. The firm has a below-average turnover rate.
   c. The firm has an average turnover rate.
   d. Cannot be determined.

Use the following data from a company's last accounting period to answer questions 8-10.

Gross sales	$300,000	
Sales returns	10,000	
Sales allowances	15,000	
Expenses	75,000	25%
Closing inventory at cost	50,000	
Markdowns	45,000	
Freight-in	5,000	
Purchases	150,000	
Net profit	30,000	10%

8. The "cost of goods sold":

   a. $225,000
   b. $105,000
   c. $145,000
   d. $195,000
   e. $ 75,000

9. The stockturn rate is:

   a. 6.0
   b. 3.9
   c. 4.3
   d. 2.8
   e. 1.5

10. The markdown ratio is:

    a. 20 percent
    b. 11 2/3 percent
    c. 18 1/3 percent
    d. 10 percent
    e. 15 percent

11. Joe's Shoe Store uses a traditional markup of 25 percent for all of its shoes. If a pair of shoes costs him $6, what should Joe *add* to this cost to determine his selling price?

    a. $1.50
    b. 33 1/3 percent of $6.00
    c. 125 percent of $6.00
    d. $3.00
    e. 25 percent of $6.00

12. Knowledge of departmental markdown ratios for a given period would be useful in:

    a. preparing an operating statement for that period.
    b. determining the value of goods on hand.
    c. measuring the efficiency of the various retail departments.
    d. computing the stockturn rate for that period.
    e. All of the above.

13. To increase its return on investment (ROI), a firm could:

    a. increase its profit margin.
    b. increase its sales.
    c. decrease its investment.
    d. increase its leveraging.
    e. All of the above.

14. *Given the following information, calculate the ABC Company's ROI.*

Net sales	$1,000,000
Gross margin	200,000
Markdowns	200,000
Assets	300,000
Net profit (after taxes)	10,000
Owner's investment	100,000

    a. 3.3 percent
    b. 1,000.0 percent
    c. 10.0 percent
    d. 2.5 percent
    e. 5.0 percent

15. In Question 14, the ABC Company's ROA was:

   a. 3.3 percent.
   b. 2.5 percent.
   c. 30.0 percent.
   d. 150.0 percent.
   e. Some negative number--because the assets were larger than the owners' investment.

Answers to Multiple-Choice Questions

1. e, p. 511
2. c, p. 512
3. e, pp. 513-514
4. d, p. 514
5. b, p. 517

6. d, p. 514
7. a, p. 517
8. d, pp. 514-515
9. d, pp. 516-517
10. a, pp. 519-520

11. b, p. 519
12. c, pp. 519-520
13. e, p. 520
14. c, pp. 520-521
15. a, p. 521

Exercise C-1
Marketing arithmetic

Introduction

A firm's financial records contain much useful information for a marketing manager. An effective marketing manager will make regular use of them in his planning. This exercise is designed to improve your understanding of the operating statement and the information it contains.

Assignment

Answer each of the following questions about the financial records of ABC Corporation.

1.   Complete ABC's operating statement.

ABC Corporation
Operating Statement
For the Year Ending December 31, 199X

Gross sales			$62,000
Less: Returns and allowances			a)_____
Net sales			58,000
Cost of sales			
Beginning inventory at cost		$12,000	
Purchases at billed cost	$26,000		
Less: Purchase discounts	3,000		
Purchases at net cost	b)_____		
Plus freight-in	3,000		
Net cost of delivered purchases		c)____	
Cost of goods available for sale		d)____	
Less: Ending inventory at cost		8000	
Cost of sales			e)____
Gross margin (gross profit)			f)____
Expenses			
Selling expense			
Sales salaries	7,000		
Advertising expense	2,200		
Delivery expense	3,300		
Total selling expenses		g)____	

Administrative expense		
Office salaries	$3,800	
Office supplies	900	
Miscellaneous	1,300	
Total admin. expense		h)___
General expense		
Rent expense	1,100	
Miscellaneous	100	
Total general expense		i)___
Total expense		j)___
Net profit from operation		k)___

2. Calculate the stockturn rate (using cost figures).

3. Calculate the following operating ratios. (Round each answer to one decimal place.)

a) Net sales   100%

b) Cost of sales   _____

c) Gross margin   _____

d) Expenses   _____

e) Net profit   _____

Question for Discussion

What additional financial information would help the marketing manager of ABC Corporation to improve his operation?

Chapter 19

Price setting in the real world

What This Chapter Is About

Price setting is challenging--but deciding on the right price is crucial to the success of the whole marketing mix.

Chapter 19 treats cost-oriented pricing in detail--because it is commonly used and makes sense for some firms. But cost-oriented pricing doesn't always work well. You should study this approach carefully, so you can better understand its advantages and disadvantages.

Pay special attention to the relationships of the various cost curves. Notice how costs vary at different levels of operation.

Some business managers have recognized the problems with average-cost pricing and have tried to bring demand into their price-setting. Demand-oriented pricing requires some estimate of demand--and ideally a whole demand curve. But demand curves are not easy to estimate. This is one reason why demand-oriented pricing has not been widely used. But it is possible to *estimate* demand curves. And it is probably better to try to estimate a demand curve than ignore it. Some examples of how this is being done are presented at the end of the chapter.

By estimating demand, it is possible to estimate the likely profit of various quantities--and find the most profitable price and quantity. Although this approach is not as widely used as cost-oriented pricing, it deserves careful study. Demand must be considered when setting price--unless you are willing to leave making a profit to chance. Demand-oriented pricing can be done--and can be very useful in helping to carry out the marketing concept--that is, satisfying customers *at a profit*.

Important Terms

markup, p. 526
markup (percent), p. 526
markup chain, p. 527
stockturn rate, p. 528
average-cost pricing, p. 530
total fixed cost, p. 531
total variable cost, p. 532
total cost, p. 532
average cost, p. 532
average fixed cost, p. 532
average variable cost, p. 532
experience curve pricing, p. 534
target return pricing, p. 534
long-run target return pricing, p. 535
break-even analysis, p. 535
break-even point (BEP), p. 535
fixed-cost (FC) contribution per
unit, p. 536

marginal analysis, p. 538
marginal revenue, p. 538
marginal cost, p. 539
rule for maximizing profit, p. 541
marginal profit, p. 543
price leader, p. 545
value in use pricing, p. 547
leader pricing, p. 547
bait pricing, p. 548
psychological pricing, p. 548
odd-even pricing, p. 548
prestige pricing, p. 548
price lining, p. 549
demand-backward pricing, p. 550
full-line pricing, p. 550
complementary product pricing, p. 551
bid pricing, p. 551
negotiated price, p. 552

True-False Questions

_____ 1. Markup (dollars) means the dollar amount added to cost of products to get the selling price--or markup (percent) means a percentage of the selling price which is added to the cost to get the selling price.

_____ 2. Considering the large number of items the average retailer or wholesaler carries--and the small sales volume of any one item--a markup approach to pricing makes sense.

_____ 3. According to the definition of markup given in the text, a product which a retailer buys for $2.00 would be priced at $3.20 if the retailer applied a markup of 60 percent.

_____ 4. A producer--whose product sells for $24--distributes its product through wholesalers and retailers who traditionally use a "markup chain" of 20 percent and 40 percent, respectively. Therefore, the retail selling price of this product is $50.

_____ 5. A wholesaler or retailer concerned with increasing profits should consider using a smaller markup as a way of achieving a substantial increase in turnover.

_____ 6. "Stockturn rate" means the number of times a firm's beginning inventory is sold in a year.

_____ 7. Producers commonly use a cost-oriented pricing approach--adding a standard markup to obtain their selling price.

_____ 8.   Because average-cost pricing consists of adding a "reasonable" markup to the average cost of a product, it assures the producer of earning a profit at any level of output.

_____ 9.   Total fixed cost is the sum of those costs that are fixed in total--no matter how much is produced.

_____ 10. Total variable cost would include items such as wages paid to workers, sales commissions, and salaries paid to top executives.

_____ 11. The rate of growth of total cost as output increases is not affected by total fixed cost.

_____ 12. Average cost is obtained by dividing total cost by the related total quantity.

_____ 13. Average fixed cost increases as the total quantity produced increases.

_____ 14. Average variable cost is obtained by dividing total variable cost by the number of units produced.

_____ 15. Because of economies of scale, all average and total costs tend to decline as the quantity produced increases.

_____ 16. Average-cost pricing works best when demand conditions are changing rapidly and substantially.

_____ 17. Experience curve pricing is like average-cost pricing--except that prices are based on an estimate of future average costs.

_____ 18. Unlike the average-cost curve approach, target return pricing assures that the target return is achieved--even if the quantity that is actually sold is less than the quantity used in setting the price.

_____ 19. Those who use long-run target return pricing assume that short-run losses and above-normal profits will average out in the long run--thus allowing the firm to achieve its long-run target return objectives.

_____ 20. Break-even analysis suggests that once a firm reaches its break-even point, profit will keep increasing with every additional unit sold.

_____ 21. Although break-even analysis considers the relationship of total revenue and total cost, it may not solve the firm's pricing problem because the assumed price may not be tied to realistic demand estimates.

_____ 22. The traditional goal of economic analysis--to maximize profits--is a reasonable one because if you know how to make the biggest profit, you can always adjust your price to pursue other objectives--while knowing how much profit you are giving up.

_____ 23.   Marginal analysis helps the marketing manager make the best pricing decision by focusing on the last unit which would be sold--to determine how total revenue and total cost would be affected.

_____ 24.   Since marginal revenue is the change in total revenue which results from the sale of one additional unit of a product--and since this extra unit will be sold while charging a positive price for all items--marginal revenue can never be negative.

_____ 25.   The marginal revenue curve is the same as the demand curve when the demand curve is down-sloping.

_____ 26.   Marginal cost--which is the change in total cost that results from producing one more unit--might also be defined as the change in total variable cost that results from producing one more unit.

_____ 27.   If an average-cost curve first drops and then rises, the related marginal cost curve would also start rising--but at a greater level of output.

_____ 28.   To maximize profit--the firm should produce that output where the difference between marginal revenue and marginal cost is the greatest.

_____ 29.   When using a graph to determine the most profitable output and price for a firm, the best price is obtained by going from the MR-MC intersection over to the price axis.

_____ 30.   Marginal analysis indicates that--to maximize profits--a firm should be willing to increase the quantity it will sell until the marginal profit of the last unit is at--or near--zero.

_____ 31.   If marginal costs can be covered in the short run--even though all fixed costs cannot--the firm should remain in operation.

_____ 32.   A firm in an oligopoly situation cannot use marginal analysis to maximize its profits because of the "kinked" demand curve facing the firm.

_____ 33.   A price leader in an oligopoly situation should have a very good understanding of its own and its competitors' cost structures--as well as an estimate of the industry demand curve.

_____ 34.   Value in use pricing is setting prices which will capture some of what customers will save by substituting the firm's product for the one currently being used.

_____ 35.   Leader pricing is most common in oligopoly situations--where most firms will raise or lower their price only after the industry leader raises or lowers its price.

_____ 36.   Items featured in "bait pricing" are real bargains priced low to get customers into the store to buy these and other items.

___ 37. Psychological pricing assumes that some price changes will not affect the quantity sold.

___ 38. Retailers who use "odd-even pricing" seem to assume that they face a rather jagged demand curve--that slightly higher prices will substantially reduce the quantity demanded.

___ 39. Prestige pricing is possible when target customers think that high prices mean high quality or high status--and the demand curve for this market slopes down for a while and then bends back to the left again.

___ 40. Although price lining may result in higher sales, faster turnover, and simplified buying--it also increases the retailer's total inventory requirements and often leads to greater markdowns.

___ 41. Henry Ford's decision to build a car for the "masses"--setting "a price so low as to force everybody to the highest point of efficiency"--is an example of demand-backward pricing.

___ 42. A manufacturer that offers a complete line (or assortment) of products should not be overly concerned about full-line pricing if it is aiming at different target markets for each of its products.

___ 43. Complementary product pricing is setting prices on several products as a group.

___ 44. The major job in bid pricing is assembling all of the costs--including the variable and fixed costs--that should apply to each job.

___ 45. Bargaining may involve the whole marketing mix, not just the price level in arriving at a negotiated price.

Answers to True-False Questions

1. T, p. 526	16. F, p. 533	31. T, p. 544
2. T, p. 527	17. T, p. 534	32. F, pp. 544-545
3. F, p. 527	18. F, p. 535	33. T, p. 545
4. T, p. 527	19. T, p. 535	34. T, p. 547
5. T, p. 528	20. T, p. 535	35. F, pp. 547-548
6. F, p. 528	21. T, p. 536	36. F, p. 548
7. T, p. 529	22. T, p. 537	37. T, p. 548
8. F, p. 530	23. T, p. 538	38. T, p. 548
9. T, p. 531	24. F, pp. 538-539	39. T, p. 548
10. F, p. 532	25. F, p. 539	40. F, p. 549
11. T, p. 532	26. T, p. 539	41. T, p. 550
12. T, p. 532	27. F, p. 540	42. T, p. 550
13. F, p. 532	28. F, p. 541	43. T, p. 551
14. T, p. 532	29. F, p. 543	44. T, p. 551
15. F, p. 533	30. T, p. 543	45. T, p. 552

Multiple-Choice Questions (Circle the correct response)

1. A certain product retails for $100. How much does this product cost the retailer if his markup is 33 1/3 percent?

    a. $25.00
    b. $33.00
    c. $50.00
    d. $75.00
    e. $66.67

2. A certain item is sold at retail for $50. The retailer's markup is 25 percent *on cost*. The wholesaler's markup is 25 percent. What is the manufacturer's selling price?

    a. $30.00
    b. $32.00
    c. $28.10
    d. $35.11
    e. $25.00

3. With respect to markups and turnover, a marketing manager should be aware that:

    a. although supermarket operating expenses run 16-20 percent of sales, items sold at lower markups (i.e., less than 12 percent) still may be very profitable.
    b. depending on the industry, a stockturn rate of 1 or 2 may be quite profitable.
    c. high markups don't always mean big profits.
    d. speeding turnover often increases profits because the firm's operating costs are a function of time and the volume of goods sold.
    e. All of the above are true statements.

4. Which of the following statements about average-cost pricing is *true*?

    a. The chief merit of this approach is that it is based on well-researched pricing formulas.
    b. It consists of adding a "reasonable" markup to the average cost of a product.
    c. This method takes into consideration cost variations at different levels of output.
    d. It assumes that the average cost for the next period will be different from that of the last period.
    e. All of the above are true statements.

5. Total cost usually:

    a. is zero at zero quantity.
    b. grows at a rate determined by increases in total variable cost.
    c. is the sum of total fixed and total marginal costs.
    d. grows at a rate determined by increases in total fixed cost.
    e. None of the above is a true statement.

6. The *major* weakness of average-cost pricing is that:

   a. it always leads to losses instead of profits.
   b. costs decline and rise at different levels of output.
   c. demand is ignored.
   d. average fixed cost increases as the quantity increases.
   e. All of the above.

7. Average cost pricing will result in *larger* than expected profit:

   a. most of the time.
   b. if the average fixed cost estimate is based on a quantity that is smaller than the actual quantity sold.
   c. if the average total cost is higher than expected.
   d. only if the manager makes arithmetic errors in computing average variable cost.
   e. None of the above is correct.

8. Trying to find the *most profitable* price and quantity to produce:

   a. requires average-cost pricing.
   b. requires an estimate of the firm's demand curve.
   c. is easy once the average fixed cost is known.
   d. is only sensible if demand estimates are exact.
   e. All of the above are true.

9. When a firm seeks to obtain some specific percentage return on its investment (or a specific total dollar return), it is using:

   a. break-even pricing.
   b. experience curve pricing.
   c. "what the traffic will bear" pricing.
   d. target return pricing.
   e. average-cost pricing.

10. A manufacturer who uses "target return" pricing sold 1,000 units of his product last year. He wants to earn a profit of at least $20,000 in the coming year. If his fixed costs are $40,000 and his variable costs equal $20 per unit, what price would he charge (assuming that he could still sell 1,000 units)?

    a. $60
    b. $40
    c. $80
    d. $120
    e. Cannot be determined with information given.

11. Break-even analysis assumes that:

    a. variable cost is constant per unit but varies in total.
    b. average fixed costs increases as quantity increases.
    c. the demand curve slopes downward and to the right.
    d. average variable cost first decreases and then increases as quantity increases.
    e. All of the above.

12. Assume that a producer's fixed costs amount to $240,000, its variable costs are $30 per unit, and it intends to sell its portable washer to wholesalers for $50. Given this information, the break-even point is:

    a. 8,000 units.
    b. 12,000 units.
    c. 14,000 units.
    d. 20,000 units.
    e. almost 50,000 units.

13. Given the following data, compute the BEP *in dollars*:

    Selling price = $1.25
    Variable cost = $ .75
    Fixed cost   = $45,000

    a. $36,000
    b. $60,000
    c. $90,000
    d. $112,500
    e. None of the above.

14. Break-even analysis can be used for:

    a. relating prices to potential demand.
    b. comparing various assumed pricing alternatives.
    c. finding the most profitable price.
    d. estimating future sales.
    e. All of the above.

15. A monopolistic competitor's "marginal revenue":

    a. is always positive.
    b. is always shown above the corresponding down-sloping demand curve on a graph.
    c. is the change in total revenue that results from the sale of one more unit of a product.
    d. All of the above are true statements.
    e. Only a and c above are true statements.

16. The change in total cost that results from producing one more unit is called:

    a. average variable cost.
    b. marginal cost.
    c. average fixed cost.
    d. total variable cost.
    e. average total cost.

17. To maximize profit, a firm should:

    a. produce that output where marginal revenue is at a maximum.
    b. produce that output where marginal cost is just less than or equal to marginal revenue.
    c. produce that output where marginal cost is greater than marginal revenue.
    d. try to maximize the difference between marginal revenue and marginal cost.
    e. produce that output where marginal profit is at a maximum.

18. A marketing manager should be aware that the most profitable level of output:

   a. is where total revenue equals total cost.
   b. is where the difference between marginal revenue and marginal cost is the greatest.
   c. is where the vertical difference between total revenue and total cost is the greatest.
   d. is where marginal revenue is at a maximum.
   e. Both b and c are correct.

Use the following figure to answer questions 19-21.

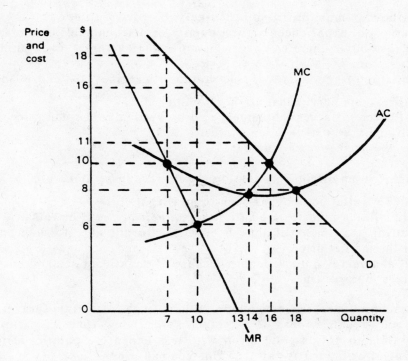

19. The most profitable quantity to sell would be:

   a. 7
   b. 10
   c. 13
   d. 14
   e. 18

20. The most profitable price would be:

   a. $6
   b. $8
   c. $10
   d. $16
   e. $18

21. The break-even point is:

    a. 10 units
    b. 13 units
    c. 14 units
    d. 16 units
    e. 18 units

22. In applying traditional economic analysis, a firm has discovered *two* break-even points--rather than a single break-even point. This means that:

    a. the firm's demand curve cannot be down-sloping.
    b. there is a profitable operating range which surrounds the point of maximum profit.
    c. seeking the maximum profit point is likely to prove fruitless.
    d. the firm has not experienced any economies or diseconomies of scale.
    e. None of the above--there can never be more than one break-even point.

23. Profit-maximizing oligopolists will find that their marginal cost curves intersect:

    a. marginal revenue curves that are horizontal.
    b. marginal revenue curves that appear to drop vertically at some prices.
    c. down-sloping marginal revenue curves.
    d. negative marginal revenue curves.

24. A "price leader" in an oligopoly situation should recognize that:

    a. "conscious parallel action" has been ruled illegal.
    b. other firms in the industry are sure to raise their prices if he raises his first.
    c. price cutting may occur if the "followers" are not able to make a reasonable profit at the market price.
    d. marginal analysis is not applicable because of the kinked demand curve.
    e. All of the above are true.

25. An equipment producer is introducing a new type of paint sprayer to sell to automobile body-repair shops. The sprayer saves labor time in painting the car, makes it possible to get as good a job with less expensive paint, and requires less work polishing after the car is painted. This company should use:

    a. leader pricing.
    b. bait pricing.
    c. complementary product pricing.
    d. odd-even pricing.
    e. value in use pricing.

26. Setting relatively high prices on products with perceived high status is known as:

    a. price lining.
    b. odd-even pricing.
    c. leader pricing.
    d. prestige pricing.
    e. bait pricing.

27. The manager of Green's Dress Shop has concluded that her customers find certain prices very appealing. Between these prices are whole ranges where prices are apparently seen as roughly equal--and price cuts in these ranges generally do not increase the quantity sold (i.e., the demand curve tends to drop vertically within these price ranges). Therefore, the manager has decided to price her dresses as close as possible to the top of each price range. This is known as:

a. prestige pricing.
b. bait pricing.
c. leader pricing.
d. psychological pricing.
e. odd-even pricing.

28. The practice of setting different price levels for different quality classes of merchandise--with no prices between the classes--is called:

a. full-line pricing.
b. prestige pricing.
c. price lining.
d. odd-even pricing.
e. psychological pricing.

29. "Demand-backward" pricing:

a. is like leader pricing.
b. has been called "market-minus" pricing.
c. requires no demand estimates.
d. is usually performed by retailers.
e. All of the above are true statements.

30. Which of the following statements about "full-line pricing" is *true*?

a. A marketing manager usually attempts to price products in the line so that the prices will seem logically related and make sense to potential customers.
b. Most customers seem to feel that prices in a product line should be somewhat related to cost.
c. The marketing manager must try to recover all his costs on the whole product line.
d. Not all companies that produce a variety of products must use full-line pricing.
e. All of the above are true statements.

31. With regard to bid pricing, a marketing manager should be aware that:

    a.   the customer is always required to accept the lowest bid.

    b.   since it costs very little to submit a bid, most firms try to bid for as many jobs as possible.

    c.   the same overhead charges and profit rates usually apply to all bids.

    d.   the major task is assembling all the costs--including the variable and fixed costs that apply to a particular job.

    e.   All of the above are true statements.

Answers to Multiple-Choice Questions

1. e, p. 526	12. b, p. 536	22. b, p. 544
2. a, p. 527	13. c, pp. 536-537	23. b, p. 545
3. e, pp. 527-528	14. b, p. 537	24. c, p. 546
4. b, p. 530	15. c, p. 538	25. e, p. 547
5. b, p. 532	16. b, p. 539	26. d, p. 548
6. c, p. 533	17. b, p. 541	27. d, p. 548
7. b, p. 533	18. c, p. 542	28. c, p. 549
8. b, p. 534	19. b, p. 543	29. b, p. 550
9. d, pp. 534-535	20. d, p. 543	30. e, p. 550
10. c, pp. 534-535	21. e, p. 544	31. d, p. 551
11. a, p. 535		

Exercise 19-1
Elements of cost-oriented price setting

Introduction

This exercise is designed to familiarize you with the arithmetic of cost-oriented pricing. Because most firms use cost-oriented methods to set prices, it is important that you understand these methods. Retailers and wholesalers, for example, use traditional markups that they feel will yield a reasonable rate of profit. You should be aware of how markups are figured. And you should know how stock turnover is calculated. Further, you should understand how the various types of costs differ, how they relate to each other, and how they affect profits as the sales volume varies.

Note: It is highly recommended that you review Appendix C: Marketing Arithmetic on pages 511-22 of the text before starting this exercise.

Assignment

Answer the following set of problems. Show your work in the space provided.

1.   The usual retail price of an item is $200.00. The manufacturer's cost to produce the item is $80.00. Retailers take a 40 percent markup and wholesalers take a 10 percent markup. (Note: markup is calculated on selling price, unless otherwise indicated.)

a)   What is the retailer's markup in dollars? _____ ~~$53.33~~ _____

see pg 530.- chpt 19

$40\% \ of \ ^\$200$

$^\$120.-$

b)   What is the wholesale price? ~~$88.88~~ _____

c)   What is the manufacturer's price? _____ $108.- _____

d) What is the manufacturer's markup percentage? _~~25·8%~~ ~~25~~ ~~8 35%~~_

e) What is the manufacturer's markup percentage *on cost*? _~~$~~ ~~25~~ $35%_

2. The Headen Manufacturing Company is trying to set its price on an item that will sell at retail for $60.00.

   a) For retailers to earn a markup of 25 percent, what should the wholesale price be?

   _$~~85~~.-_

   b) For the wholesalers in 2a to earn a markup of 10 percent, what should the manufacturer's price be? _~~66.66~~_

   _40.50_

3. Complete the following table by filling in the blanks. *Hint:* start with the first column and work to the right, column by column.

Item	Quantity produced				
	0	1	2	3	4
Total cost	$40	$60	$80	100	$120
Total fixed cost	$40	$40	$40	$40	$40
Total variable cost	$0	$20	$40	60	80
Average cost	n/a*	$60	$40	$33.3	30
Average fixed cost	n/a*	$40	$20	$13.33	$10.00
Average variable cost	n/a*	$20	$20	20	20

Note: n/a means not applicable (because at zero output there is not an average cost per unit).

4. a) Using the data from Question 3, plot the total cost, total fixed cost, and total variable cost curves on the following graph.

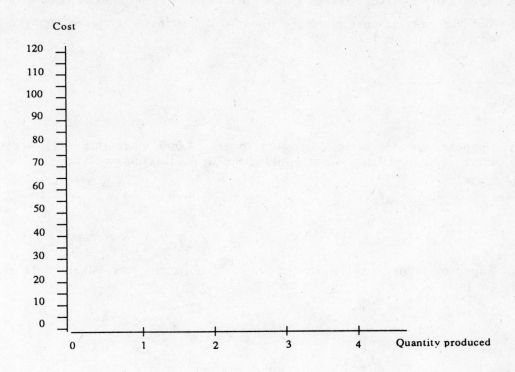

b) Using the data from Question 3, plot the average cost, average fixed cost, and average variable cost curves on the following graph.

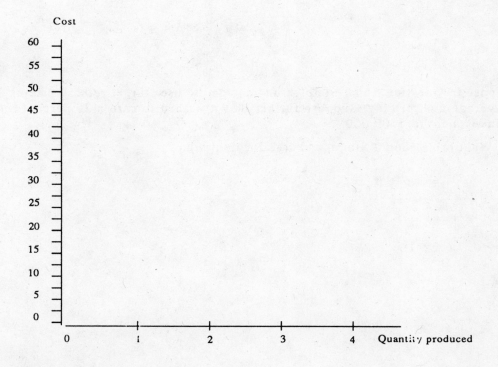

5. Simplex Corp. has fixed costs of $2,000,000 and average variable costs of $100 per unit at all levels of output. It wishes to earn a profit of $300,000 this year--which is an increase of 10 percent over last year when Simplex sold 5,000 units of its product.

a) Use the average-cost pricing method to determine what price Simplex should charge for its product.

$$\#560.- \quad \text{Total Cost } 2,000 + [5,000 \times 100] = 2,500,000$$
$$\text{Profit} = 300,000$$
$$2,800,000 \div 5,000 = \$560/\text{unit}$$

b) Suppose Simplex were only able to sell 4,000 units this year because of increased competition. What would its profit (or loss) be?

$$\text{TRev. } 4,000 \times 560. = 2,240,000$$
$$\text{TC } 2,000,000 + (4,000 \times 100) = 2,400,000$$
$$(\$ - 160,000)$$

c) Suppose Simplex's sales increased to 7,000 units this year. What would its profit (or loss) be?

$$\text{TR } 7,000 \times 560 = 3,920,000,$$
$$\text{TC } 2,000,000 + [7000 \times 100] = 2,700,000$$
$$1,220,000$$

d) Based on your answers to parts a, b, and c, what do you conclude about the effectiveness of average-cost pricing?

6. Suppose in Question 5 that Simplex had decided to use "target return" pricing instead of average-cost pricing. Suppose further that it wished to earn a 20 percent return on its investment of $500,000.

a) What price should Simplex charge for its product?

$$20\% \text{ of } 500,000 = 100,000. \text{ Profit}$$

$$\text{TFC } 2,000,000$$
$$\text{V/C } 500,000 \checkmark$$
$$\frac{100,000 \checkmark}{2,600,000} \div 5000 = \$520$$

318

b) What would Simplex's return on investment be if it were only able to sell 4,000 units?

$$4,000 \times 520 = 2,080,000$$

$$2,000,000 + [4,000 \times 100] = 2,400,000$$
Profit $(320,000)$

Rol $\dfrac{320,000}{500,000} \times 100 = 64\%$

c) What would Simplex's return on investment be if its sales increased to 7,000 units?

$$7,000 \times 520 = 3,640,000$$

$$+ (\qquad) =$$

Profit

Rol $\times 100 =$

Question for Discussion

Why do so many firms use cost-oriented pricing methods when such methods have so many obvious shortcomings?

Exercise 19-2

Using break-even analysis to evaluate alternative prices

Introduction

Break-even analysis can be a very useful tool for evaluating alternative prices--especially when the prices being considered are fairly realistic from a demand point of view. Break-even analysis shows how many units would have to be sold--or how much dollar volume would have to be achieved--to just cover the firm's costs at alternative prices. A realistic appraisal of the likelihood of achieving the break-even point associated with each alternative price might show that some prices are clearly unacceptable--that is, there would be no way that the firm could even reach the break-even point, let alone make a profit.

The mechanics of break-even analysis are relatively simple--once you understand the concepts and assumptions of break-even analysis. This exercise reviews these ideas and then has you apply them to a fairly common decision-making situation.

Assignment

Read each of the following problems carefully--and fill in the blanks as you come to them. Where calculations are required, make them in the space provided--and show your calculations to aid review.

1. Study the break-even chart in Figure 19-2a and answer the following questions:

    a) According to Figure 19-2a, at what quantity, total revenue, and price will the firm break even?

    Quantity _6 units_ Total Revenue _$120.00_ Price _~~$720.00~~_ ? _$20.00_

    b) The firm's total fixed cost in this situation is: 60.00

    c) The firm's average variable cost (AVC) is: $10.00 (slope of line)

    d) Using the information in Figure 19-2a, plot the firm's *demand curve* (D), *average fixed cost curve* (AFC), and *average variable cost curve* (AVC) in Figure 19-2b. Label each curve and both axes.

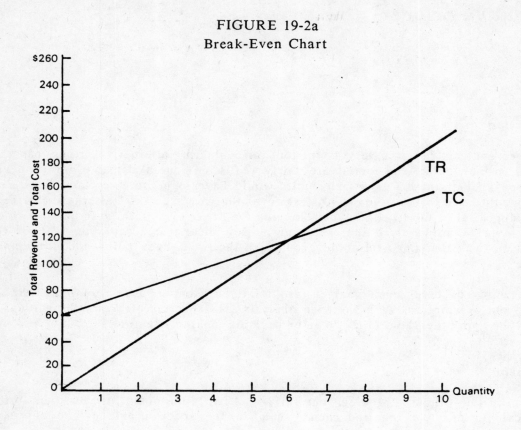

FIGURE 19-2a
Break-Even Chart

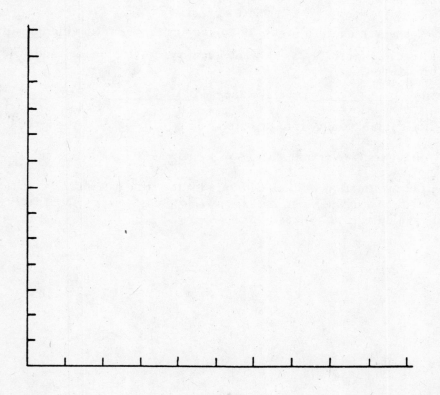

e) Using Figure 19-2a, draw the total revenue curve which would be relevant if the firm were considering a price of $50 per unit. Given this price of $50 per unit, at what quantity and total revenue would the firm break even?

Quantity _____ Total Revenue _____

f) What price should the firm charge to <u>maximize</u> profits--the price you calculated in (a) or $50? <u>Why</u>?

2. a) Suppose you were considering going into the car-washing business and investing in a new kind of car-washing unit which is more mechanized than the usual ones--but also has higher fixed costs. Calculate the break-even point in dollars and units if the usual price of $5.00 per car were charged. The variable cost per car is estimated at $2.50. The total fixed cost per year (including depreciation, interest, taxes, fixed labor costs, and other fixed costs) is estimated at $425,000.

BEP in $ _850,000_ BEP in units _170,000_ ✓

units × S/P

b) There is some possibility that there will be price cutting in your proposed market in the near future. Calculate the BEPs for the situation in (a) if the retail price drops to $4.50 per car.

BEP in $ _956,250_ BEP in units _212,500_ ✓

units × S/P

c) There is also a possibility that the new washing unit will deliver a better job for which some people will be willing to pay more. Calculate the new BEPs if it were possible to raise the retail price to $5.50.

BEP in $ _779,169_ BEP in units $ _141,667_ ✓

units × sp

d) Should you go into the car-washing business in *any* of the above situations? Explain.

Question for Discussion

Looking at Figures 19-2a and 19-2b, what does break-even analysis assume about the nature of demand and about the competitive environment? Is break-even analysis relevant for monopolistic competition?

Exercise 19-3

Setting the most profitable price and quantity to produce

Introduction

Demand must be considered when setting prices. Ignoring demand curves does not make them go away. Usually, a market will buy more at lower prices--so total revenue *may* increase if prices are lowered. But this probably won't continue as the price gets closer to zero. Further, total cost--and perhaps average costs--will increase as greater quantities are sold.

So, if a firm is at all interested in making a profit (or avoiding losses), it should consider demand and cost curves *together*. This exercise shows how this can be done--and emphasizes that not all prices will be profitable.

Assignment

Figure 19-3 shows the XYZ Manufacturing Company's estimated total revenue and total cost curves for the coming year. Study this figure carefully and answer the questions which follow.

FIGURE 19-3

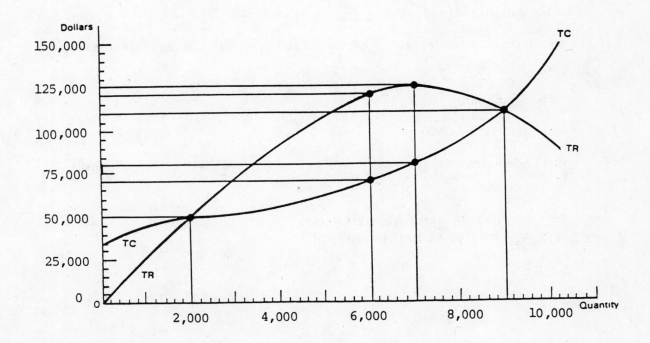

1. Complete the following chart by referring to Figure 19-3-the graph of XYZ's total costs and revenues.

Quantity	Total Cost	Average Cost	Total Revenue	Price*	Total Profit (loss)
1,000	_____	_____	_____	_____	_____
3,000	_____	_____	_____	_____	_____
3,500	_____	_____	_____	_____	_____
4,500	_____	_____	_____	_____	_____

*Remember: Total Revenue = Price X Quantity
Total Profit = Total Revenue - Total Cost

Using the information from Question 1, and Figure 19-3, answer Questions 2-11.

2. Given that Total Revenue = Price X Quantity, what should XYZ's price be if it wants to get the most total revenue it can and plans to sell:

   a. 1,000 units: _____
   b. 3,000 units: _____
   c. 3,500 units: _____
   d. 4,500 units: _____

3. What would XYZ's average cost per unit be at:

   a. 1,000 units: _____
   b. 3,000 units: _____
   c. 3,500 units: _____
   d. 4,500 units: _____

4. XYZ has total fixed costs of: $ _____

5. To maximize its *total revenue*, XYZ should sell (check the correct response):

   ____ a. 1,000 units.
   ____ b. 3,000 units.
   ____ c. 3,500 units.
   ____ d. 4,500 units.
   ____ e. more than 4,500 units.

6. Figure 19-3 indicates that XYZ's demand curve is (check the correct response):

   ____ a. horizontal.
   ____ b. vertical.
   ____ c. downward-sloping from left to right.
   ____ d. upward-sloping from left to right.

7. XYZ's demand curve is (check the correct response):

    ____ a.   elastic.
    ____ b.   inelastic.
    ____ c.   unitary elastic.
    ____ d.   elastic up to 3,500 units and inelastic beyond 3,500 units.
    ____ e.   inelastic up to 3,500 units and elastic beyond 3,500 units.

8. XYZ's *average* cost curve is (check the correct response):

    ____ a.   horizontal.
    ____ b.   U-shaped.
    ____ c.   vertical.
    ____ d.   upward-sloping from left to right.

9. XYZ will *lose money* if it sells (check the correct response):

    ____ a.   less than 1,000 units.
    ____ b.   less than 4,500 units.
    ____ c.   more than 3,500 units.
    ____ d.   more than 4,500 units.
    ____ e.   both a and d are correct.

10. XYZ will *break even* if it sells (check the correct response):

    ____ a.   1,000 units.
    ____ b.   3,000 units.
    ____ c.   3,500 units.
    ____ d.   4,500 units.
    ____ e.   both a and d are correct.

11. To *maximize profit*, XYZ should sell (check the correct response):

    ____ a.   1,000 units.
    ____ b.   3,000 units.
    ____ c.   3,500 units.
    ____ d.   4,500 units.
    ____ e.   more than 4,500 units.

12. The maximum amount of profit XYZ can earn is: $ _____

Question for Discussion

Should a firm in monopolistic competition try to sell as many units as it can produce? Why or why not? State your assumptions.

Exercise 19-4

Using marginal analysis to set the most profitable price and quantity to produce

Introduction

Too many firms seem to ignore demand--depending almost blindly on cost-oriented pricing. A firm might operate quite profitably using cost-oriented pricing--but could it earn larger profits by charging a different price? The firm has no way of answering this question unless it also takes demand into consideration. When both costs and demand are known (or estimated), marginal analysis can be used to determine the most profitable price and the most profitable quantity to produce. Of course, in the short run the firm's objective may *not* be to maximize profit. In this case, marginal analysis can be used to show how much profit is "lost" when the firm pursues some other objective--such as maximizing sales.

This exercise uses the graphic approach to marginal analysis. You are asked to interpret--from a graph--the relationships among demand, price, quantity, average cost, marginal cost, and marginal revenue. (See page 542 in the text.)

Assignment

Use Figure 19-4 on the next page to answer the following questions:

1. At what price would 130 units be sold? _____

2. How many units would be sold if the firm priced its product at $40?
    _____

3. At what output (quantity) _____ and price _____ would the average cost per unit be *minimized*?

4. At what output _____ and price _____ would the firm break even?

5. At what output _____ and price _____ would the firm maximize its *total revenue*?

6. At what output _____ and price _____ would the firm maximize its *total profit*?

7.   What will the average profit per unit be when the firm maximizes its total profit?
_____

8.   What is the maximum amount of profit this firm can earn? _____

FIGURE 19-4

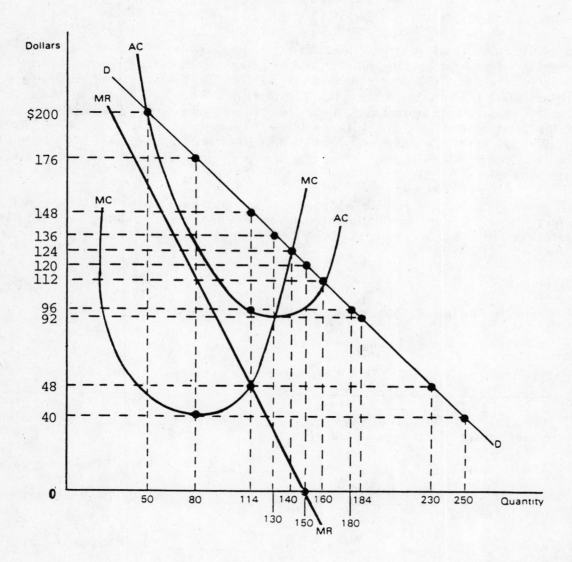

Question for Discussion

Why do so few firms use demand-oriented pricing? Is it an impossible task?

Chapter 20

Planning and implementing marketing programs

What This Chapter Is About

Chapter 20 emphasizes that marketing strategy planning requires creative *blending* of all the ingredients of the marketing mix. And, eventually, a marketing manager must develop a time-related *plan* that spells out the implementation details for a strategy. Then, since most companies have more than one strategy, marketing managers should develop a whole marketing *program* which integrates the various plans.

You need an estimate of potential sales to know if a marketing plan will be profitable. So this chapter explains different methods for forecasting sales. You should become familiar with the different methods and their likely accuracy--because each has advantages *and* disadvantages. Some firms make several forecasts on the way to developing one final estimate of future sales.

Sales forecasting must consider not only market potential but also the firm's (and competitors') marketing plans--and how customers might respond to those plans. The concept of a response function is introduced to show the kind of thinking that applies here. Unfortunately, the shapes of response functions must be estimated in each particular situation. But just as with demand curves, which do not go away if they are ignored, response functions *should* be considered in strategy planning--because they show the potential effectiveness of alternative strategies. Even crude estimates of response functions are better than none.

Since Chapter 9, we have been discussing various aspects of the four Ps. The product classes and the product life cycle are integrating themes which have been running through these chapters. This chapter highlights these ideas. A product's class and stage in the life cycle can suggest some "typical" marketing mixes. In addition, some special factors are discussed which should help you understand why and when typical mixes might be suitable--and when it would be desirable to modify the typical to develop the firm's own unique marketing strategy.

Following selection of a firm's marketing program, implementation efforts may be helped by some flow-charting techniques, which are explained toward the end of the chapter.

Important Terms

market potential, p. 558

sales forecast, p. 558

trend extension, p. 560

factor method, p. 562

factor, p. 562

time series, p. 566

leading series, p. 566

indices, p. 567

jury of executive opinion, p. 567

response function, p. 571

threshold expenditure level, p. 574

saturation level, p. 574

spreadsheet analysis, p. 575

task method, p. 589

True-False Questions

____ 1. A marketing strategy is a "big picture" of what a firm will do in some target market--while a marketing plan includes the time-related details for that strategy--and a marketing program is a combination of the firm's marketing plans.

____ 2. Market potential is an estimate of how much a whole market segment might buy.

____ 3. A major limitation of trend extension is that it assumes that conditions in the past will continue unchanged into the future.

____ 4. National economic forecasts available in business and government publications are often of limited value in forecasting the potential of a specific market segment.

____ 5. The factor method of sales forecasting tries to find a relation between a company's sales and data on some other factor which is readily available.

____ 6. A factor is a variable which shows the relation of some other variable to the item being forecasted.

____ 7. A leading series is a time series which, for some reason, changes in the opposite direction but ahead of the series to be forecasted.

____ 8. Indices are statistical combinations of several time series.

____ 9. "Trend-projecting" forecasting techniques should probably be supplemented by a "jury of executive opinion" or some other type of judgmental approach.

____ 10. Instead of relying heavily on salespeople to estimate customers' intentions, it may be desirable for a firm to use marketing research techniques such as surveys, panels, and market tests.

____ 11. Annual forecasts of national totals such as GNP are likely to be more accurate than industry sales forecasts--and in turn industry sales forecasts will almost always be more accurate than estimates for individual companies and individual products.

_____ 12. When marketers fully understand the needs and attitudes of their target markets, they may be able to develop marketing mixes which are obviously superior to "competitive" mixes.

_____ 13. A response function shows (mathematically or graphically) how a firm should respond to changing customer needs and attitudes.

_____ 14. The response functions for each of the four Ps tend to have the same shapes for all firms--regardless of the target market.

_____ 15. The typical general marketing effort response function shows that there is a straight-line relationship between marketing expenditures and sales.

_____ 16. Usually there is some threshold expenditure level which is needed just to be in a market--and therefore that expenditure level may be necessary to get any sales at all.

_____ 17. Typical marketing mixes are a good starting point for developing possible marketing mixes--and estimating their response functions.

_____ 18. Even if you don't know as much as you would like about potential customers' needs and attitudes, knowing how they would classify your product--in terms of the product classes--can give you a starting point in developing a marketing mix.

_____ 19. A spreadsheet analysis is a useful tool for demonstrating how rules and profits change over a range of prices.

_____ 20. Even low-priced items such as newspapers may be distributed directly if they are purchased frequently and the total volume is large.

_____ 21. Some products--because of their technical nature, perishability, or bulkiness--require more direct distribution than is implied by their product class.

_____ 22. Aggressive, market-oriented middlemen usually are readily available and eager to handle the distribution of any new products.

_____ 23. Distribution through national middlemen will generally guarantee a new producer fairly uniform coverage in all geographic markets.

_____ 24. Some wholesalers enter a channel of distribution mainly because they can give financial assistance to other channel members.

_____ 25. A company's own size affects its place in a channel system--because size affects discrepancies of quantity and assortment.

_____ 26. Typically, marketing variables should change during a product's life cycle.

_____ 27. Finding the best marketing program requires some juggling among the various plans--comparing profitability versus resources needed and available.

___ 28. Budgeting for marketing expenditures as a percentage of either past or forecasted sales leads to larger marketing expenditures when business is good and sales are rising--and to reduced spending when business is poor.

___ 29. The most sensible approach to budgeting marketing expenditures is the "task method."

___ 30. Marketing program implementation efforts can be greatly aided by use of PERT--which stands for Product Evaluation and Rating Techniques.

Answers to True-False Questions

1. T, p. 558	11. T, p. 568	21. T, p. 579
2. T, p. 558	12. T, p. 569	22. F, p. 580
3. T, p. 560	13. T, p. 571	23. F, p. 580
4. T, p. 562	14. F, p. 571	24. T, p. 580
5. T, p. 562	15. F, pp. 573-574	25. T, p. 580
6. T, p. 562	16. F, p. 574	26. T, pp. 581-582
7. F, pp. 566-567	17. T, p. 577	27. T, p. 589
8. F, p. 567	18. T, p. 577	28. T, pp. 589-590
9. T, p. 567	19. T, p. 578	29. T, p. 589
10. T, pp. 567-568	20. T, p. 579	30. T, p. 591

Multiple-Choice Questions (Circle the correct response)

1. The main difference between a "strategy" and a "marketing plan" is:

    a. that a plan does not consider the firm's target market.
    b. that a plan includes several strategies.
    c. that time-related details are included in a plan.
    d. that resource commitments are made more clear in a strategy.
    e. There is no difference.

2. As defined in the text, market potential is:

    a. what a market segment might buy (from all suppliers).
    b. how much a firm can hope to sell to a market segment.
    c. how much the firm sold to a market segment in the last year.
    d. the size of national income for the coming year.

3. A good marketing manager knows that:

    a. market potential is an estimate of how much a firm can hope to sell to a particular market segment.
    b. sales forecast should be developed BEFORE marketing strategies are planned.
    c. a firm's sales forecast probably will be less than the estimated market potential.
    d. sales forecasts are estimates of what a whole market segment might buy.
    e. All of the above are true.

4. The trend-extension method often can be useful for forecasting annual sales, but it depends upon the assumption that:

    a. the forecast is for a new product.
    b. sales during the coming period will be about the same as the previous period.
    c. there will be big changes in market conditions.
    d. the general growth (or decline) which has been seen in the past will continue in the future.
    e. the firm will continue to improve its marketing mixes.

5. You have been asked to develop a sales forecast for one of your company's major products. What would be the most logical *starting point*?

    a. Determine why the company's sales fluctuate the way they do.
    b. Consider the prospects for the economy as a whole.
    c. Determine your industry's prospects for the near future.
    d. Analyze regional sales for this product for last year.
    e. Perform marketing research into consumer buying habits.

6. *Sales & Marketing Management* magazine's "Buying Power Index" is based on:

    a. each market's share of the total Canadian population.
    b. each market's share of the total income in Canada.
    c. each market's share of the total retail sales in Canada.
    d. All of the above.
    e. Only a and b above.

7. Given the complexity of buyer behavior, sales forecasts for established products are likely to prove more accurate if based on:

    a. market tests.
    b. trend extension.
    c. a single factor.
    d. several factors.

8. Sales forecasters often try to find business indicators which change before sales and thus will help predict future sales. These indicators are called:

    a. correlation coefficients.
    b. time series.
    c. leading series.
    d. trend extenders.
    e. input-output measures.

9. Q.R. Smith Specialist, Inc., has developed a new product about which it is quite excited. Which of the following sales forecasting methods would be *least appropriate*?

    a. Market tests
    b. Sales force estimates
    c. Trend extension
    d. Jury of executive opinion
    e. A survey of customers

10. Which of the following sales forecasting techniques would be most useful for the marketing manager of an industrial products manufacturer facing intense competition?

    a. Sales force estimates
    b. Jury of executive opinion
    c. Use of a national economic forecast
    d. Trend extension of past sales
    e. Multiple-factor method

11. A company which wants to *objectively* estimate the reaction of customers to possible changes in its marketing mix should use:

    a. trend extension.
    b. jury of executive opinion.
    c. sales force estimates.
    d. surveys, panels, and market tests.
    e. None of the above.

12. Generally, the *largest* percentage error in a forecast should be expected when forecasting:

    a. sales for well-established products.
    b. industry sales.
    c. sales for a new product for a company.
    d. a company's total sales.
    e. national economic forecasts.

13. Developing a "marketing plan":

    a. means selecting a target market and developing a marketing mix.
    b. involves nothing more than assembling the four Ps better than your competitors.
    c. is easy--and profits are virtually guaranteed--provided that a firm fully understands the needs and attitudes of its target market.
    d. All of the above are true statements.
    e. None of the above is a true statement.

14. A "response function":

    a. shows how target customers are expected to react to changes in marketing variables.
    b. measures the firm's performance in responding to customer needs.
    c. generally focuses on the whole marketing mix--not each of the four Ps.
    d. is usually shown on a graph in the form of a U-shaped curve.
    e. All of the above are true statements.

15. The following response function for product quality indicates that:

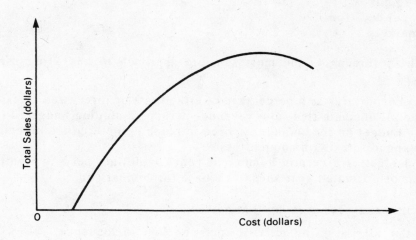

a. consumers want as much product quality as it is possible to provide.
b. product quality is the most important element in a firm's marketing mix.
c. the ideal level of expenditure for product quality is at the point where sales are at a maximum.
d. expenditures to increase product quality can produce diminishing or negative returns.
e. there is no "threshold expenditure level" for product quality.

16. Marketing strategy planners should keep in mind that:

a. there will be different response functions for different target markets.
b. different response functions for alternative marketing mixes can be compared to select the "best" mix.
c. response functions for each of the four Ps are useful--but the firm also needs a general marketing effort response function.
d. there usually is not a straight-line relationship between marketing expenditures and sales.
e. All of the above are true statements.

17. A manufacturer of a consumer product is trying to establish brand recognition and preference in monopolistic competition. The firm places considerable emphasis on channel development and is becoming somewhat less selective in its choice of middlemen. Promotion is both informative and persuasive--as the firm is seeking to increase both primary and selective demand. Prices in the industry are competitive--but there has been little price-cutting to date. What stage of the product life cycle is this firm's situation characteristic of?

a. Market introduction
b. Market growth
c. Market maturity
d. Sales decline

18. A marketing program can be best described as consisting of several:

    a. marketing plans.
    b. advertising campaigns.
    c. marketing mixes.
    d. operational decisions.
    e. target markets.

19. Which of the following is the most sensible approach to budgeting for marketing programs?

    a. Budget expenditures as a percentage of either past or forecasted sales.
    b. Set aside all uncommitted sales revenue--perhaps including budgeted profits.
    c. Base the budget on the amount required to reach predetermined objectives.
    d. Match expenditures with competitors.
    e. Set the budget at a certain number of cents or dollars per sales unit--using the past year or estimated year ahead as a base for comparison.

20. Flow-charting techniques such as CPM and PERT:

    a. require that all marketing activities must be done in sequence.
    b. do not indicate how long a project will actually take to complete.
    c. identify the tasks which must be performed to achieve predetermined objectives.
    d. require complex mathematical tools and analysis.

Answers to Multiple-Choice Questions

1. c, p. 558	8. c, pp. 566-567	15. d, p. 572
2. a, p. 558	9. c, p. 560	16. e, pp. 571-574
3. c, p. 558	10. a, p. 567	17. b, pp. 581-582
4. d, p. 560	11. d, pp. 567-568	18. a, p. 583
5. b, p. 562	12. c, p. 568	19. c, pp. 588-589
6. d, p. 563	13. c, pp. 568-569	20. c, p. 591
7. c, p. 562	14. a, p. 571	

Exercise 20-1

Using the "Survey of Buying Power" to estimate market and sales potential

Introduction

All marketers are faced with the ongoing problem of forecasting market and sales potentials. Forecasting is as much an art as it is a science, and there are many different forecasting methods that can be used. Regardless of which method is used, the forecast should be based on data that is accurate, reliable, and up to date.

Many forecasters rely very heavily on market data published in *Sales and Marketing Management's* annual "Survey of Buying Power." The "Survey" provides data on three important market characteristics--population, "Effective Buying Income," and retail sales. Both total and household population are given. "Effective Buying Income" (comparable to disposable income) is broken down into five income groups, and retail sales are shown for nine categories. Further, the data is broken down geographically according to Census Metropolitan Areas, counties, and cities.

While there is usually a lengthy time lag in the publication of Canadian census data, the "Survey of Buying Power" is carefully updated and published each year. Moreover, "Survey" data has been shown to correlate very highly with the census data on which it is based. A disadvantage, however, is that "Survey" data, like all published data, may not be available in the exact form a particular firm desires--and thus may not be directly applicable. Most firms find it necessary to modify the data, or supplement it with other data--before making their forecasts.

Probably the most widely used aspect of the "Survey" is the "Buying Power Index" (BPI), a weighted index of three variables--population, Effective Buying Income, and retail sales--which measures a market's ability to buy and expresses it as a percentage of the total Canadian potential. The BPI is calculated by giving a weight of 5 to the market's percent of the Canadian Effective Buying Income, a weight of 3 to its percent of Canadian retail sales, and a weight of 2 to its percent of the Canadian population. The sum of those weighted percents is then divided by 10 to arrive at the BPI.

For example, suppose Anytown, Canada, had about 5 percent of the total Canadian Effective Buying Income, about 4 percent of Canadian retail sales, and about 1 percent of the Canadian population. Then the BPI for Anytown would be:

$$\frac{5(5) + 3(4) + 2(1)}{19} = 3.9$$

Thus Anytown's market potential, relative to the Canadian, in total, would be 3.9 percent. So if Canadians were expected to buy $10,000,000 worth of "widgets" during the coming year, the population of Anytown might be expected to buy 3.9 percent x $10,000,000 or $390,000 worth of widgets.

FIGURE 20-1 Sample Tables from <u>Sales and Marketing Management</u>'s "Survey of Buying Power"

Ont. (cont.)
S&MM ESTIMATES

County / City	Metro Area Code	Total Pop (thousands)	% Of Canada	Households (thousands)	% Of Canada	Total Retail Sales ($000)	% Of Canada	Food ($000)	Eating & Drinking Places ($000)	General Mdse ($000)	Apparel & Acces- sories ($000)	Furniture/ Furnish/ Appliance ($000)	Auto- motive ($000)	Gas Stations ($000)	Hard- ware ($000)	Drug ($000)	Sales Activity	Buying Power	Quality
Essex	.536	308.1	1.2316	113.8	1.2335	1,818,458	1.4067	398,634	159,510	202,832	85,691	82,528	309,033	112,765	8,424	62,326	114	1.2862	104
▲Windsor		193.4	.7731	69.6	.7544	1,339,481	1.1642	333,551	137,754	191,516	77,537	70,083	241,050	89,676	4,711	50,853	151	.8814	114
Frontenac	.510	111.2	.4446	43.2	.4482	665,437	.5957	164,795	47,583	101,645	35,431	28,669	119,484	63,773	2,116	24,881	134	.5285	119
△Kingston		51.1	.2043	21.6	.2341	382,803	.3327	94,889	40,291	42,745	31,962	20,704	53,198	25,338	1,402	15,137	163	.2868	140
Glengarry		19.7	.0787	6.7	.0726	63,889	.0555	14,873	7,596	2,759	2,638	1,421	16,407	7,272	814	539	71	.0818	104
Grenville		26.5	.1060	9.5	.1030	71,924	.0625	18,465	6,578	5,981	2,667	4,062	13,903	8,557	835	2,341	59	.0713	67
Grey		76.8	.3070	29.8	.3143	420,709	.3657	100,497	28,492	44,992	19,964	21,699	92,645	38,627	6,466	17,374	119	.3195	104
Haldimand-Norfolk Reg.																			
Mun.		91.6	.3661	33.8	.3577	509,998	.4432	128,135	38,544	30,792	21,902	22,081	141,078	39,016	6,021	16,521	121	.3974	109
Haliburton		11.4	.0456	4.7	.0509	82,748	.0720	19,394	1,044	11,404	2,318	2,478	15,083	11,182	362	4,246	158	.0604	132
Halton Reg. Mun.	.532	269.3	1.0764	92.5	1.0026	1,579,365	1.3726	362,643	130,369	145,276	75,429	54,025	407,479	126,010	8,742	79,113	127	1.4708	137
Burlington		118.5	.4737	41.7	.4520	791,540	.6879	194,872	57,568	103,667	42,142	23,223	189,115	57,708	3,639	38,677	145	.6768	143
Halton Hills		36.9	.1475	13.0	.1409	193,208	.1679	41,129	22,640	9,454	8,491	8,083	56,534	11,754	1,315	9,229	114	.1954	132
Milton		30.3	.1211	9.9	.1073	103,654	.0901	20,520	10,332	1,965	4,455	1,694	33,417	10,074	299	4,468	74	.1435	118
Oakville		82.5	.3298	27.9	.3024	490,963	.4267	106,122	39,829	30,190	20,341	21,025	128,413	46,474	3,489	26,739	129	.4542	138
Hamilton-Wentworth																			
Reg. Mun.	.507	424.3	1.6962	162.1	1.7569	1,942,490	1.6883	527,029	159,894	316,676	83,515	85,713	285,936	145,322	10,099	73,117	100	1.6874	99
▲Hamilton		301.9	1.2069	117.5	1.2735	1,672,003	1.4532	410,702	134,431	297,368	76,920	79,405	261,643	120,711	7,984	59,563	120	1.2547	104
Stoney Creek		37.6	.1503	12.3	.1333	120,543	.1048	44,764	17,802	2,201	2,163	2,140	24,030	10,871	335	4,210	70	.1251	83
Hastings		111.4	.4453	41.8	.4531	474,035	.4120	111,036	16,638	52,532	20,292	17,290	115,539	38,634	2,781	16,444	93	.4003	90
Belleville		36.2	.1447	13.6	.1474	194,722	.1692	44,086	14,393	21,236	11,251	10,645	46,094	9,574	1,043	7,776	117	.1378	95
Huron		57.8	.2311	20.7	.2243	331,083	.2877	72,300	21,013	35,235	12,416	12,514	97,952	20,233	4,334	9,198	124	.2464	107
Kenora Terr. Dist.		63.6	.2542	22.0	.2383	213,616	.1856	20,406	13,511	28,884	6,179	4,542	26,686	18,350	1,645	4,643	73	.2281	94
Kent		105.9	.4233	39.1	.4238	520,110	.4520	123,909	40,547	51,971	24,963	28,252	109,644	48,508	3,157	29,794	107	.4510	107
Chatham		41.9	.1675	13.4	.1452	273,038	.2373	64,822	27,103	41,736	17,061	15,276	50,684	16,494	1,040	16,276	142	.1851	111
Lambton	.525	134.2	.5365	50.0	.5419	390,969	.3398	95,196	33,441	56,187	18,551	15,544	77,519	25,903	2,299	13,435	63	.4740	88
△Sarnia		34.5	.1379	21.1	.2287	239,356	.2080	57,717	16,638	36,299	12,937	12,208	54,360	9,971	933	6,335	95	.2208	101
Lanark		50.6	.2023	18.6	.2016	144,131	.1253	28,723	8,399	13,960	5,925	4,160	37,188	12,475	1,738	4,787	62	.1244	67
Leeds		53.7	.2147	20.6	.2233	172,201	.1497	33,291	14,900	17,180	5,389	5,964	38,042	17,816	1,629	6,275	70	.1685	78
Lennox & Addington		19.6	.0784	7.6	.0824	91,094	.0792	24,259	7,546	8,097	3,713	2,995	18,299	14,549	932	3,576	61	.1340	99
Manitoulin Terr. Dist.		11.0	.0440	4.8	.0433	59,712	.0519	9,186	2,441	12,153	629	1,743	12,454	6,685	1,316	2,915	118	.0420	95
Middlesex	.512	326.0	1.3032	130.1	1.4101	2,084,090	1.8114	517,271	198,894	303,893	100,620	77,270	381,133	146,023	8,716	55,130	139	1.7211	137
△London		264.7	1.0582	104.6	1.1554	1,902,999	1.6539	476,505	190,174	287,330	97,164	71,471	341,365	130,745	6,593	46,525	156	1.4552	138
Muskoka Dist. Mun.		40.3	.1607	15.7	.1702	339,605	.2953	94,034	33,571	25,482	12,520	10,079	84,475	40,012	3,728	13,234	184	.2195	137
Niagara Reg. Mun.	.522	370.2	1.4799	138.9	1.5055	1,451,716	1.2617	374,984	152,510	173,902	74,486	57,704	262,435	102,019	6,758	49,903	83	1.3996	95
Fort Erie		25.1	.1003	11.7	.1268	75,903	.0660	20,404	14,153	3,329	2,063	3,468	12,788	4,953	458	3,753	66	.0980	98
△Niagara Falls		72.6	.2902	25.7	.2786	321,949	.2798	81,151	55,735	28,485	12,939	12,384	50,294	21,576	1,229	15,076	96	.2617	90
Port Colborne		19.6	.0784	7.4	.0792	94,751	.0824	30,622	7,196	8,087	4,247	3,172	16,364	6,409	438	3,447	101	.0760	97
△St. Catharines		127.1	.5081	47.4	.5137	631,832	.5491	162,426	44,322	112,818	42,258	23,891	111,330	41,873	2,694	13,065	108	.5267	104
Welland		47.8	.1911	16.5	.1788	224,399	.1950	57,613	15,671	15,102	11,376	11,054	50,373	19,851	372	8,685	102	.1673	88
Nipissing Terr. Dist.	.515	80.0	.3198	28.9	.3132	403,489	.3507	97,419	41,019	56,252	17,203	15,003	76,199	36,731	2,526	10,272	110	.3110	97
△North Bay		50.9	.2035	16.5	.1788	292,358	.2541	72,235	25,737	46,624	12,328	12,079	54,176	23,922	1,849	7,356	125	.1987	96
Northumberland		67.6	.2702	24.3	.2648	349,402	.3037	90,192	29,764	27,656	12,925	14,737	60,666	50,739	3,565	7,825	112	.3282	121

POPULATION 12/31/83 · **RETAIL SALES BY STORE GROUP—1983** · **SALES/ADVERTISING INDEXES**

FIGURE 20-1 (concluded)

Ottawa-Carleton Reg.																			
Mun. 517	570.1	2.2791	236.4	2.4772	2,816,896	2.4482	687,128	275,594	500,906	137,177	104,451	435,737	148,777	19,330	87,298	107	2.8948	127
△Ottawa	301.0	1.2033	126.5	1.3711	2,272,756	1.9753	511,759	237,034	411,687	132,715	88,993	371,711	88,213	8,790	64,370	164	1.4924	124
Oxford	88.2	.3526	31.2	.3382	444,936	.3867	98,615	32,197	40,696	18,077	21,104	126,007	42,351	3,648	10,961	110	.3493	108
Woodstock	26.0	.1039	8.9	.0965	218,878	.1902	56,725	14,441	24,941	10,665	8,797	57,245	15,698	1,376	6,026	183	.1408	136
Parry Sound Terr. Dist.	34.6	.1383	13.1	.1419	134,140	.1166	32,799	9,298	8,470	2,920	3,713	28,518	19,929	1,818	3,237	84	.1051	76
Peel Reg. Mun. ...532	535.7	2.1415	172.6	1.8708	2,381,200	2.0696	642,093	240,534	148,527	79,997	84,895	516,868	242,406	13,135	110,550	97	2.2751	106
Brampton	171.4	.6852	53.4	.5788	784,796	.6821	213,018	49,388	57,286	31,374	27,169	182,158	86,029	4,013	36,896	100	.7489	109
Caledon	34.9	.1395	10.1	.1095	120,431	.1047	37,922	9,855	6,319	2,642	3,292	23,603	10,692	443	7,753	75	.1236	89
Mississauga	328.9	1.3148	109.1	1.1825	1,475,973	1.2828	391,153	181,293	84,922	45,981	58,434	311,107	145,685	8,679	65,901	98	1.4022	107
Perth	64.7	.2746	25.9	.2709	284,001	.2468	85,325	24,196	33,239	16,549	13,737	15,292	34,725	2,437	9,934	90	.2426	84
Stratford	28.3	.1131	10.5	.1138	184,904	.1607	57,569	16,240	26,761	10,518	7,623	8,475	18,537	1,206	7,000	142	.1252	111
Peterborough ...518	104.7	.4186	40.6	.4401	694,043	.6032	173,517	57,736	98,159	31,483	31,405	123,642	50,641	3,369	19,725	144	.5054	121
△Peterborough	61.4	.2455	23.2	.2515	555,573	.4829	145,917	34,376	91,320	30,115	26,694	97,438	27,116	3,019	16,031	197	.3401	139
Prescott	30.3	.1211	10.4	.1127	128,195	.1114	29,099	14,104	14,637	8,654	5,118	23,238	13,329	1,694	1,761	92	.1196	99
Prince Edward	22.7	.0908	8.4	.0911	84,489	.0735	24,014	4,680	4,983	2,836	2,010	23,981	8,879	810	1,971	81	.0827	91
Rainy River Terr. Dist.	23.6	.0943	8.7	.0943	76,555	.0666	20,940	5,909	6,302	3,620	3,403	15,295	6,228	515	2,576	7?	.0904	1--
Renfrew	89.5	.3578	32.0	.3468	544,638	.4751	141,861	22,844	50,324	27,196	18,367	137,018	51,247	4,194	22,600	13:	.4163	116
Russell 517	23.7	.0947	7.5	.0813	90,533	.0787	19,944	7,292	13,288	2,138	5,249	27,627	5,247	401	844	8--	.0718	76
Simcoe	233.7	.9343	83.8	.8996	1,336,863	1.1618	322,903	126,896	146,437	44,369	54,311	281,021	108,541	16,759	49,659	121	1.0412	111
Barrie	41.1	.1643	13.7	.1485	460,161	.3999	101,248	29,649	54,793	16,051	19,398	128,126	28,146	3,255	15,302	213	.2431	148
Orillia	25.1	.1003	8.8	.0954	226,136	.1965	60,811	19,290	34,296	9,471	11,015	41,696	14,488	1,840	9,284	1?0	.1320	132
Stormont	63.8	.2550	23.6	.2558	339,233	.2948	86,664	28,267	41,448	16,029	15,804	60,335	27,495	849	11,181	116	.2509	9?
Cornwall	47.0	.1879	16.0	.1734	307,871	.2676	75,472	24,798	40,008	15,912	14,680	54,939	22,714	700	10,724	141	.1950	164
Sudbury Reg. Mun. ...529	160.4	.6412	56.4	.6113	643,400	.5940	192,341	57,956	76,888	26,840	27,356	129,437	48,724	3,610	17,568	93	.5832	91
△Sudbury	91.2	.3646	32.8	.3555	580,376	.5044	163,295	45,005	73,744	33,863	22,705	111,073	36,089	2,626	14,063	1?8	.3966	139
Sudbury Terr. Dist.	26.4	.1054	9.8	.0975	64,058	.0557	20,844	4,650	9,323	1,613	1,090	4,282	10,127	753	1,959	?3	.0697	64
Thunder Bay Terr.																		
Dist. 531	154.5	.6254	57.7	.6254	763,600	.6636	199,611	61,974	119,482	26,324	20,827	128,520	63,520	3,129	32,325	106	.6300	101
△Thunder Bay	113.3	.4529	42.3	.4585	613,654	.5333	172,702	41,332	96,412	23,545	17,072	104,812	39,896	2,638	28,920	?18	.4913	108
Timiskaming Terr. Dist.	42.1	.1683	15.7	.1702	177,065	.1539	54,119	14,700	13,478	9,610	5,633	33,451	16,843	1,094	5,820	91	.1356	81
Toronto Met. Mun. ...532	2,127.9	8.5065	835.4	9.0545	9,595,167	8.3394	2,318,126	1,114,123	1,286,961	539,651	375,277	1,814,436	590,679	40,434	389,545	98	8.7261	103
△Toronto	586.3	2.3438	238.9	2.5893	3,857,154	3.352	857,195	600,366	655,855	279,771	180,927	567,063	142,202	16,598	135,748	143	2.8306	121
Victoria	50.2	.2007	19.3	.2092	347,723	.3022	98,090	26,191	22,164	12,292	17,195	67,301	28,994	4,440	12,058	151	.2482	124
Waterloo Reg. Mun. ...511	321.1	1.2844	118.3	1.2822	2,029,174	1.7627	438,500	162,904	220,790	99,971	87,973	464,235	160,873	9,223	49,238	137	1.4612	129
△Cambridge	80.8	.3230	28.0	.3033	437,437	.3802	108,814	44,037	23,529	18,163	18,205	112,404	32,071	2,073	13,113	118	.376?	117
△Kitchener	149.2	.5964	56.0	.6070	1,087,930	.9455	200,743	77,116	229,443	67,177	51,303	235,127	78,919	2,575	26,884	159	.8257	130
Waterloo	49.0	.1959	20.6	.2233	332,891	.2893	94,049	28,946	47,548	11,874	11,509	65,957	21,353	2,033	8,250	148	.2779	132
Wellington 540	136.7	.5465	49.6	.5376	626,606	.5447	142,409	50,367	75,181	32,136	27,139	137,505	66,591	3,692	29,316	100	.5888	102
△Guelph	78.5	.3138	28.3	.3067	462,174	.4017	118,390	32,606	59,305	28,973	21,629	98,734	32,367	1,184	20,909	120	.3569	114

It should be noted that there is nothing sacred or necessarily valid about the weights used to calculate the BPI. Many firms tailor the index to their own needs by applying a different set of weights or adding additional variables to the index based on their past experience. A manufacturer of snowmobiles, for example, might add a weather variable, such as average inches of snowfall, to the BPI. Another pitfall in applying the BPI is that because it is broadly based, the BPI is said to be most useful for "mass products sold at popular prices." Thus, for more expensive products, the BPI may need to be modified by taking additional buying factors into account.

Assignment

The purpose of this exercise is to familiarize you with the Buying Power Index and show you its use in forecasting market and sales potentials. Answer each of the following questions and show your work in the space provided.

1. Suppose that Yourtown, Canada, accounts for 5 percent of the Canadian population, 6 percent of the nation's Effective Buying Income, and 3 percent of Canadian retail sales. Calculate Yourtown's "Buying Power Index."

2. Reading from Figure 9-3, what is the Buying Power Index for:

   a. the city of Toronto: _____

   b. Toronto Metropolitan Area: _____

3. a. About 700,000 electric toasters are sold in Canada each year. Based on the Buying Power Index, estimate the number of toasters that are sold in the Toronto metropolitan area each year.

   b. Assume that your firm has captured a 20 percent share of the electric toaster market. About how many electric toasters should your firm sell in the Toronto metropolitan area?

   c. Suppose your firm sold 1,000 electric toasters last year in the Toronto metropolitan area. Considering your answer to part (b) above, what does this fact indicate?

4. Assume that a firm with annual sales of $2,000,000 sells its products only in the Toronto metro area. In order to allocate its sales force to different cities within the Toronto metro area, the firm's sales manager wants to know what volume of sales the firm can expect in each city. Use the BPI to estimate the firm's sales volume in dollars for the city of Toronto only. (Hint: Although the percentages reflected in the BPI are relevant for all of Canada--not just the Toronto area--the relative positions of the different cities within this area remain the same.) Explain your answer.

5. Suppose a national manufacturer of expensive mink coats wanted to estimate its sales potential in the Toronto metropolitan area. Would the BPI be useful for this purpose? Why or why not?

Question for Discussion

Would the "Survey of Buying Power," data be more useful to "mass marketers" or "target marketers"? Why?

Exercise 20-2

Using response functions to help plan marketing mixes

Introduction

A "response function" shows (mathematically and/or graphically) how a firm's target market is expected to respond to changes in marketing variables. This concept may seem rather "academic"--but it is not. Marketing managers must make judgments about the likely responses of their potential customers to alternative marketing mix variables. Whether they actually attempt to draw such curves--or only have "gut feelings"--is not important. What *is* important is that they must have *some* feeling for how marketing expenditures affect sales or profits if they are to have any hope of making effective use of the firm's resources. Just as demand curves do not "go away" if they are ignored--response functions will not "go away" either.

At the same time, it is only fair to say that estimating response functions is not easy. A lot of information and judgment is needed--and even then the results are only "guesstimates." For this reason, most marketers have not done much with response functions. However, most do try to make rough estimates of how sales would increase if a few more salespeople were added, or an additional $50 thousand was allocated to advertising, and so on. Basically, they are attempting to estimate one or a few points on the relevant response function. This is all they feel they need--so they do not bother to estimate the whole function. This may be a practical approach--but it also may cause the marketing manager to under- or overuse some variables--perhaps missing their most productive range, where sales rise sharply with small increases in marketing effort.

This exercise seeks to deepen your understanding of response functions. You are asked to identify the shapes of response functions for several different markets and marketing mixes. Also, you are asked to analyze a few response functions and decide which ones you would use in different budget situations.

Assignment

1. The marketing manager of a large consumer products firm has not yet selected a target market--and is in the process of estimating how different market segments would respond to different marketing mix variables. She is focusing on how each of four segments would respond to variations in advertising expenditures (other marketing expenditures remaining constant). Her descriptions of each segment are summarized on the next page. Study each description and then indicate which of the response functions shown in Figure 20-2 is most relevant for each segment. (Note: use all the choices.)

FIGURE 20-2

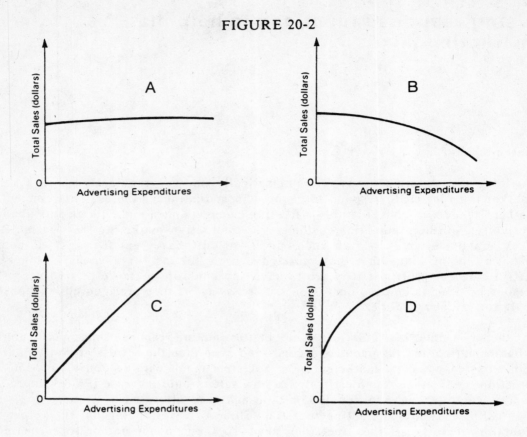

a) ____ This group relies on advertising for information about products. They are open to persuasion when the product appears to satisfy their needs reasonably well. Once they become aware of a product, they tend to make a fairly quick decision about whether to purchase--and repurchase--it.

b) ____ This group buys on "impulse" and responds well to the "power of suggestion." They have much exposure to mass media--and their buying behavior is described very well by the classical stimulus-response model.

c) ____ This group is antiestablishment, nonmaterialistic, and hostile toward "big business." They believe that producers use advertising to manipulate consumers--and are likely to boycott firms that try to "shove products down our throats." Members of this group have very strong negative feelings, for example, about children's TV shows being sponsored by cereal or toy manufacturers.

d) ____ This group behaves like "economic men." Advertising has little influence on their purchases. They watch relatively little TV--spending much of their time reading books, scientific journals, and consumer-oriented publications such as *Consumer Reports*.

2.   Use Figure 20-3 in answering the following questions:

FIGURE 20-3

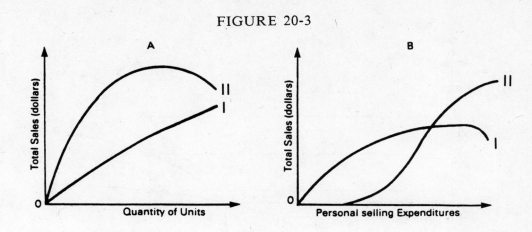

a) Graph A shows two response functions for the same target market. Each curve indicates a different price/quantity relationship--i.e., the response functions are alternative total revenue curves. Assuming that one response function suggests "skimming pricing"--while the other suggests "penetration pricing"--indicate which is which. Explain your answer.

b) Graph B shows two response functions for the same target market--one shows the use of manufacturers' agents to sell a firm's new product--and the other shows the use of the firm's own sales force to sell the new product (with all other marketing expenditures held constant). Indicate which response function reflects the use of manufacturers' agents and which shows the use of the firm's own sales force. Explain your answer.

FIGURE 20-4

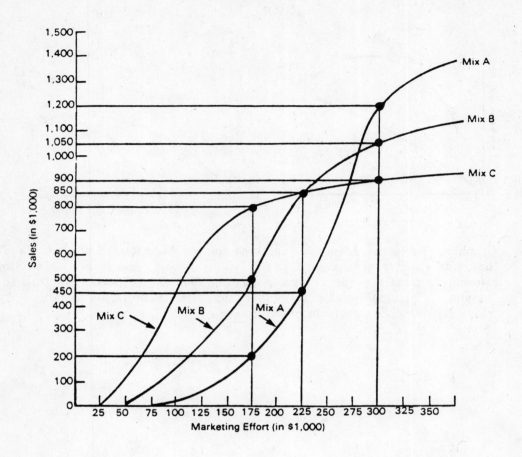

3. Figure 20-4 shows three estimated response functions which show how a firm's target market is likely to respond to each of three alternative marketing mixes. Explain which marketing mix the firm should choose and *why* if:

    a) its budget for the coming year provides $175,000 for marketing expenditures:

    b) its budget for the coming year provides $225,000 for marketing expenditures:

    c) its budget for the coming year provides $300,000 for marketing expenditures:

Question for Discussion

Do response functions *really* have any value for marketing strategy planners--given the difficulty of estimating the shape of response functions for individual marketing variables and for alternative marketing mixes?

Exercise 20-3

Adjusting marketing strategies over the product ife cycle

Introduction

A marketing manager must take a dynamic approach to marketing strategy planning. Markets are continually changing--and today's successful strategy may be tomorrow's failure. Competitive advantages are often achieved and maintained by firms who are best able to anticipate and respond positively to changes in their uncontrollable environments. Some changes may be completely unpredictable, of course--but other changes may be somewhat predictable and should be planned for in advance. Otherwise, by the time the planner realizes that some important changes have taken place, it may be too late to adjust an existing strategy or, if necessary, to plan a new strategy.

Among the changes that are more predictable--and which should be considered when developing marketing plans--are the typical changes in marketing mix variables which are often made over the course of a product life cycle. Exhibit 20-12 on page 581 of the text shows some of these typical changes.

Assignment

This exercise stresses how marketing strategies may need to be adjusted over the product life cycle. Read the following case and follow the instructions.

SERVCO, INC.

Servco, Inc. manufactures a broad line of electric equipment for industrial buyers. Its sales and profits have stopped growing in recent years--and the firm's top executives are anxious to diversify into the consumer products market. However, they do not want to enter a new market with just another "me too" product. Instead, they hope to discover a real "breakthrough opportunity"--an unsatisfied market with large profit potential.

For several years, Servco's marketing research and product planning departments have been working together in search of an innovative new product for the firm's entry into the consumer market. Now, the top executives believe that they have finally found such a product. The new product is a "freeze-dry unit" for foods. The unit makes it easy for consumers to make instant versions of just about any food--just as freeze-dried coffee makes great instant coffee. The unit can process almost any type of food (ranging from eggs to hamburger to oatmeal, rice, and fruits) which are available at any supermarket. It has the capacity to cook up to two-pound batches of a food product and convert it to freeze-dried "pellets." Whenever the consumer is ready, the freeze-dried pellets can be put in a microwave oven with water and heated to produce fresh-tasting soups, sauces, gravy, drinks--and hundreds of other items which are otherwise time consuming to cook in small quantities. With the unit, a gourmet cook would be able to make fancy sauces on an impulse, an office worker could create a favorite type of homemade soup to take to work without the mess, and busy singles could keep

FIGURE 20-5
Planned Changes in Marketing Strategy for Freeze-Dry Unit
over the Course of Its Product Life Cycle

Item	*Market Introduction Stage*
Target market dimensions	
Nature of competition	
Product	
Place	
Promotion	
Price	

Market Growth Stage	Market Maturity Stage

pellets ready for when there's no time to go to the store or cook something from scratch. At first the new product idea seemed strange--perhaps even hard to believe--but in tests with consumers it has generated a very favorable response.

Moreover, the freeze-dry unit is inexpensive and easy-to-operate, and it is expected to retail for about $100.

Servco's marketing manager believes the new product will appeal to convenience-oriented families--and also health-conscious people who want to make their own "instant" foods but with more nutritious ingredients and without the preservative typically found in packages at the store. He feels the product has almost unlimited potential--citing the rapid growth of prepared and instant foods and the wide use of microwave ovens. Further, the firm's research and development staff is sure that it will take any potential competitors at least a year to introduce a similar product.

The electric freeze-dry unit is really a revolutionary new concept--and will probably require a major promotion effort to gain consumer acceptance. Moreover, Servco has no established channels of distribution in the consumer products market--and middlemen may be reluctant to handle an unproven product which lacks a well-known brand name. Also, the firm is not sure what pricing policies to adopt, because it has no previous experience in the consumer products market.

To further complicate his strategy planning efforts, Servco's marketing manager recognizes that he will probably need to modify his marketing strategy over time--as the new product passes through the various stages of its life cycle. So that the firm will be in a position to adjust quickly to changing market conditions, he wishes to plan his future marketing strategies for the freeze-dry unit--as well as his beginning strategy.

1.   Assume the role of marketing manager for Servco, Inc. and fill in Figure 20-5 to show how your marketing strategy for the electric freeze-dry unit would vary over the stages of its product life cycle. (See Exhibit 20-12 on page 581 of the text for some general ideas about what you might include in your answers.) Be specific.

Question for Discussion

What kind of product will the "freeze-dry" unit be--that is, what product class--and what type of marketing mix would be typical for such a product? Are there any other factors that should be taken into account in planning the marketing mix for this product?

Exercise 20-4

Using case analysis to analyze and apply marketing strategy planning

Introduction

Throughout the text and the *Learning Aid*, we have stressed that marketing strategy planning consists of two basic tasks:

a.   Selecting a target market

b.   Developing an appropriate marketing mix for that target market

In most of the prior exercises, we studied each of these tasks separately. First, we looked at how to select target markets. Then, we broke down the "marketing mix" into its four basic variables--Product, Place, Promotion, and Price--working with one variable at a time.

Now, we will try to "tie all the pieces together" by doing some "case analysis." Case analysis adds a touch of realism and shows how marketing theory can be applied in practice. Two cases will be analyzed. The first case deals with consumer goods, while the second focuses on industrial goods.

After reading each case, you will be asked to answer a "checklist" of items relating to the case. This checklist will rely heavily on the important marketing terms you have learned in this course. When completed, the checklist will provide you with a detailed description of the situation in the case. When answering the checklist, *it is extremely important that your answers be consistent with each other.* For example, it would be wrong to identify a product as a "convenience good"--and then to say later that the same product has achieved "brand insistence." Thus, you may need to change some of your prior answers as you move along to different items on the checklist.

After you have completed the checklist, you will be asked to summarize and evaluate the marketing strategy of the firm described in the case. You may want to compare what the firm *is* doing with some "ideal" marketing strategy--what the firm *should* be doing. Is the firm aiming at a target market and, if so, is the target market appropriate? Will the firm's product satisfy the needs of the target market? Is the proper channel of distribution being used? And so on.

To do some parts of this exercise, it probably will be necessary for you to make some *assumptions*--because no case is complete in every detail. For example, the case may say very little, if anything, about a particular item on the checklist. Here, you will need to rely upon your background to arrive at some logical answer which is consistent with the facts presented in the case. But typically there are more facts in a case than most students realize--so be careful to identify and use all the facts before you make any assumptions. Through careful analysis--including "reading between the lines"--you should be able to pull a lot of information out of each case.

Assignment

Read the following two cases carefully and answer the questions which relate to each case.

Case A   BYRON PHARMACEUTICAL COMPANY

The Byron Pharmaceutical Company is a well-known manufacturer of high-quality cosmetics and ointments. A little over a year ago, Mr. Alcott, the president of Byron, was scanning the income statements for the last three quarters and did not like what he saw. At the next board meeting he stated that Byron should be showing a larger profit. It was generally agreed that the reason for the profit decline was that the firm had not added any new products to its line during the last two years.

Management was directed to investigate this problem--and remedy it if possible.

Mr. Alcott immediately asked for a report from the product planning group and found that it had been working on a new formula for a toothpaste that might be put into production immediately if a new product were needed. Mr. Emerson, the head of the research department, assured Mr. Alcott that the new ingredients in this toothpaste had remarkable qualities. Clinical tests had consistently shown that the new, as yet unnamed, dentifrice cleaned teeth better than the many toothpastes furiously battling for market share. Based on these tests, Mr. Alcott concluded that perhaps this product was what was needed and ordered work to proceed quickly to bring it to the market.

The marketing research department was asked to come up with a pleasing name and a tube and carton design. The results were reported back within two months. The product was to be called "Pearly" and the package would emphasize eye-catching colors.

The marketing department decided to offer Pearly along with its other "prestige" products in the drugstores which were carrying the rest of Byron's better-quality, higher-priced products. Byron's success had been built on moving quality products through these outlets, and management felt that quality-oriented customers would be willing to pay a bit more for a better toothpaste. Byron was already well established with the wholesalers selling to these retailers and had little difficulty obtaining distribution for Pearly.

It is now six months after the introduction of Pearly, and the sales results have not been good. The regular wholesalers and retailers carried the product but relatively little was purchased by final customers. And now many retailers are asking that Byron accept returns of Pearly. They feel it is obvious that it is not going to catch on with consumers--despite the extremely large (matching that of competitors) amounts of advertising which have supported Pearly.

Mr. Alcott asked the marketing research department to analyze the situation and explain the disappointing results thus far. An outside survey agency interviewed several hundred consumers and has tabulated its results. These are pretty well summarized in the following quotes:

The stuff I'm using now tastes good. Pearly tastes terrible!

I never saw that brand at the supermarket I shop at.

I like what I'm using...why change?

I'm not going to pay that much for any toothpaste...it couldn't be that much better!

What recommendation would you make to Mr. Alcott? Why?

Next, turn to pages 403-6 of this Learning Aid and answer the questions on Byron found there.

Case B   DELLER COMPANY

Jim Deller graduated in business from a large university in 1983. After a year as a car salesman, he decided to go into business for himself. In an effort to locate new opportunities, Jim placed several ads in his local newspaper--in Calgary, Alberta explaining that he was interested in becoming a sales representative in the local area. He was quite pleased to receive a number of responses. Eventually, he became the sales representative in the Calgary area for three local manufacturers: the Caldwell Drill and Press Co., which manufactured portable drills; the T. R. Rolf Co., a manufacturer of portable sanding machines; and the Bettman Lathe Co., which manufactured small lathes. All of these companies were relatively small and were represented in other areas by other sales representatives like Jim Deller.

Deller's main job was to call on industrial customers. Once he made a sale, he would send the order to the respective manufacturer, who would in turn ship the goods directly to the particular customer. The manufacturer would bill the customer, and Deller would receive a commission varying from 5 percent to 10 percent of the dollar value of the sale. Deller was expected to pay his own expenses.

Deller called on anyone in the Calgary area who might use the products he was handling. At first his job was relatively easy, and sales came quickly because there was little sales competition. There are many national companies making similar products, but at the same time they were not well represented in the Calgary area.

In 1985, Deller sold $150,000 worth of drills, earning a 10 percent commission: $100,000 worth of sanding machines, also earning a 10 percent commission; and $75,000 worth of small lathes earning a 5 percent commission. He was encouraged with his progress and was looking forward to expanding sales in the future. He was especially optimistic because he had achieved these sales volumes without overtaxing himself. In fact, he felt he was operating at about 70 percent of his capacity.

Early in 1986, however, a local manufacturer with a very good reputation--the Bonner Electrical Equipment Company--started making a line of portable drills. It had a good reputation locally, and by April 1986, Bonner had captured approximately one half of Caldwell's Calgary drill market by charging a substantially lower price. Bonner was using its own sales force locally, and it was likely that it would continue to do so.

The Caldwell Company assured Deller that Bonner couldn't afford to continue to sell at such a low price and that shortly Caldwell's price would be competitive with Bonner's. Jim Deller was not nearly as optimistic about the short-run prospects, however. He began looking for other products he could handle in the Calgary area. A manufacturer of hand trucks had recently approached him, but he wasn't too enthusiastic about this offer because the commission was only 2 percent on potential annual sales of $150,000. Now Jim Deller is faced with another decision. The Phillips Paint Company in Edmonton, Alberta, has made what looks like an attractive offer. They heard what a fine job he was doing in the Calgary area and felt that he could help them solve their present problem. Phillips is having trouble with its whole marketing effort and would like Jim to take over.

The Phillips Paint Company has been selling primarily to industrial customers in the Edmonton area and is faced with many competitors selling essentially the same product and charging the same low prices. Phillips Paint is a small manufacturer. Last year's sales were $140,000. They would like to increase this sales volume and could handle at least double this sales volume with ease. They have offered Deller a 12 percent commission on sales if he will take charge of their pricing, advertising, and sales effort in the Edmonton area. Jim was flattered by their offer, but he is a little worried because there would be a great deal more traveling than he is doing at present. For one thing, he would have to spend a couple of days each week in the Edmonton area, which is 110 miles away. Further, he realizes that he is being asked to do more than just sell. But he did have some marketing courses in college and thinks the new opportunity might be challenging.

What should Jim Deller do? Why?

Next, turn to pages 360-64 of this Learning Aid and answer the questions on the Deller Company found there.

Case A: Byron Pharmaceutical Company

1. What kind of firm is Byron Pharmaceutical?

____ a. Manufacturer
____ b. Wholesaler
____ c. Retailer

2. Byron should probably be classified as:

____ a. Production-oriented
____ b. Marketing-oriented

3. Byron's main objective is to:

____ a. Maximize profits
____ b. Expand sales volume
____ c. Diversify its marketing program
____ d. Increase market share
____ e. Increase profits

4. Which of the following best describes Byron's approach to marketing "Pearly"?

____ a. The management has not selected a target market.
____ b. The management is aiming at the "mass market."
____ c. The management has selected a target market(s).

Describe the target market(s):

5. Byron's established line of cosmetics and ointments should probably be classified mainly as:

___ a.   Convenience goods
___ b.   Homogeneous shopping goods
___ c.   Heterogeneous shopping goods
___ d.   Specialty goods
___ e.   Unsought goods

6. What degree of brand familiarity appears to exist for Byron's line of cosmetics and ointments?

___ a.   Primary nonrecognition
___ b.   Primary brand recognition
___ c.   Primary brand preference
___ d.   Primary brand insistence
___ e.   Primary brand rejection

7. What kind of competition is Byron facing for its cosmetics and ointments?

___ a.   Pure competition (or close to it)
___ b.   Monopolistic competition
___ c.   Oligopoly
___ d.   Monopoly

8. Byron sees "Pearly" toothpaste as being a:

___ a.   Convenience good
___ b.   Homogeneous shopping good
___ c.   Heterogeneous shopping good
___ d.   Specialty good
___ e.   Unsought good

9. Potential customers appear to see "Pearly" toothpaste as being a:

___ a.   Convenience good
___ b.   Homogeneous shopping good
___ c.   Heterogeneous shopping good
___ d.   Specialty good
___ e.   Unsought good

10. What degree of brand familiarity appears to exist for "Pearly"?

___ a.   Primarily nonrecognition
___ b.   Primarily brand recognition
___ c.   Primarily brand preference
___ d.   Primarily brand insistence
___ e.   Primarily brand rejection

11. What kind of competition is "Pearly" facing?

    ____ a.   Pure competition (or close to it)
    ____ b.   Monopolistic competition
    ____ c.   Oligopoly
    ____ d.   Monopoly

12. In what stage of its product life cycle is "Pearly"?

    ____ a.   Market introduction
    ____ b.   Market growth
    ____ c.   Market maturity
    ____ d.   Sales decline

13. Byron Pharmaceutical uses:

    ____ a.   A direct channel system
    ____ b.   An indirect channel system

14. What degree of market exposure is Byron seeking for "Pearly"?

    ____ a.   Exclusive distribution
    ____ b.   Selective distribution
    ____ c.   Intensive distribution

15. What degree of market exposure is *usually* sought for products such as toothpaste?

    ____ a.   Exclusive distribution
    ____ b.   Selective distribution
    ____ c.   Intensive distribution

16. Which of the following best describes Byron's promotion blend for "Pearly"?

    ____ a.   Uses only advertising
    ____ b.   Uses only personal selling
    ____ c.   Emphasis on advertising--with some personal selling
    ____ d.   Emphasis on personal selling--with some advertising

17. What kind of advertising, if any, does Byron use?

    ____ a.   Pioneering
    ____ b.   Competitive
    ____ c.   Reminder
    ____ d.   Institutional
    ____ e.   None

18. In introducing "Pearly" to the market, Byron chose to use a:

    ____ a.   Skimming price policy
    ____ b.   Penetration pricing policy
    ____ c.   Prestige pricing policy
    ____ d.   Psychological pricing policy

19. Summarize and evaluate Byron Pharmaceutical's marketing strategy for its line of cosmetics and ointments.

20. Summarize and evaluate Byron's strategy for marketing "Pearly" toothpaste. How does this marketing mix for "Pearly" compare with the marketing mixes of competitive brands of toothpaste?

21. Compare Byron's view of "Pearly" toothpaste with the way consumers see it.

22. Does "Pearly" fit in well with the rest of Byron's product line? Why or why not? *Be specific.*

23. Is "Pearly" likely to achieve the increased profits that Byron is seeking? Why or why not? What specific recommendations would you make to Byron?

Case B: Deller Company

1. What kind of businessman *is* Jim Deller?

   ___ a.   Manufacturer
   ___ b.   Wholesaler
   ___ c.   Retailer

2. Individuals who are in the same business as Jim Deller often differ in the degree to which they are marketing- or production-oriented. Based on the description given in the case, how would you describe Deller?

   ___ a.   Production-oriented
   ___ b.   Marketing-oriented

3. Deller's immediate objective is to:

___ a.   Maximize profits
___ b.   Expand sales volume
___ c.   Maintain status quo
___ d.   Expand market share
___ e.   Seek profitable growth

4. Which of the following best describes Deller's present situation?

___ a.   He has not selected a target market.
___ b.   He is aiming at the "mass market."
___ c.   He has selected a target market(s).

   Describe the target market(s): _____

   _____

   _____

5. What kind of products does Deller handle *currently*?

___ a.   Installations
___ b.   Accessory equipment
___ c.   Raw material
___ d.   Component parts and materials
___ e.   Supplies

6. What degree of brand familiarity appears to exist for the products currently handled by Deller (either because of the product itself or because of Deller's selling efforts in Calgary)?

___ a.   Primary nonrecognition
___ b.   Primary brand recognition
___ c.   Primary brand preference
___ d.   Primary brand insistence
___ e.   Primary brand rejection

7. What kind of competition does Deller face in *Calgary*?

___ a.   Pure competition (or close to it)
___ b.   Monopolistic competition
___ c.   Oligopoly
___ d.   Monopoly

8. At first, Deller's job was relatively easy and sales came quickly--but lately, selling has become increasingly difficult for him. What stage of the product life cycle do Deller's products fall into?

    ____ a.   Market introduction
    ____ b.   Market growth
    ____ c.   Market maturity
    ____ d.   Sales decline

9. What kinds(s) of products would Deller handle for the Phillips Paint Company?

    ____ a.   Installation
    ____ b.   Accessory equipment
    ____ c.   Raw materials
    ____ d.   Component parts and materials
    ____ e.   Supplies

10. What degree of brand familiarity probably exists for the products manufactured by Phillips?

    ____ a.   Primarily nonrecognition
    ____ b.   Primarily brand recognition
    ____ c.   Primarily brand preference
    ____ d.   Primarily brand insistence
    ____ e.   Primarily brand rejection

11. What kind of competition would Deller face in Edmonton?

    ____ a.   Pure competition (or close to it)
    ____ b.   Monopolistic competition
    ____ c.   Oligopoly
    ____ d.   Monopoly

12. Deller now operates as part of:

    ____ a.   direct channel system
    ____ b.   an indirect channel system

13. What kind of middleman is Jim Deller?

    ____ a.   Merchant wholesaler
             Specify type: _____
    ____ b.   Agent middleman
             Specify type: _____
    ____ c.   Retailer
             Specify type: _____

14. If Deller accepts the Phillips Paint Company's offer, what kind of businessman will he become?

    ____ a.   Marketing manager
    ____ b.   Manufacturer
    ____ c.   Merchant wholesaler
            Specify type: _____
    ____ d.   Agent middleman
    ____ e.   Retailer
            Specify type: _____

15. How does Deller determine prices in the Calgary market?

    ____ a.   Cost-plus approach
    ____ b.   Marginal analysis
    ____ c.   Meet competition
    ____ d.   None of the above

16. How would Deller probably determine prices in the Edmonton market?

    ____ a.   Cost-plus approach
    ____ b.   Marginal analysis
    ____ c.   Meet competition
    ____ d.   None of the above

17. At the present time, Deller should be classed as:

    ____ a.   An order getter
    ____ b.   An order taker
    ____ c.   A missionary salesperson
    ____ d.   A technical specialist

18. Summarize and evaluate Jim Deller's marketing strategy for portable drills, portable sanding machines, and small lathes.

19. Compare and contrast the functions or tasks Deller is currently performing with those he will be required to perform if he accepts the Phillips Paint Company's offer.

20. Are the jobs in Calgary and Edmonton compatible? That is, would Deller's present marketing strategy be suitable for the Edmonton operation also? Why or why not?

21. Do you think Jim Deller understands the nature of his present job in Calgary? Explain.

22. Should Jim Deller accept the Phillips Paint Company offer? Why or why not. *Be specific.*

   a. If your answer is "yes," state *why* this is a good marketing strategy and discuss the future implications of such a move.

   b. If your answer is "no," state what Deller *should* do (i.e., what better alternatives are there for him to consider?).

Chapter 21

Controlling marketing plans and programs

What This Chapter Is About

Chapter 21 shows that a wealth of information may be available from a firm's own records. But it will be useless unless the marketing manager knows how it can be obtained and used--and then asks for it!

Various sales and cost analysis techniques are presented in this chapter. They can be useful for evaluating and controlling the marketing activities of a firm. These techniques are not really complicated. They require only simple arithmetic, and perhaps a computer if a large volume of adding and subtracting is required.

Be sure to distinguish between straightforward sales or cost' analysis and performance analysis. Also, be sure to distinguish between the full-cost approach and the contribution-margin approach to cost analysis. Each can be useful in certain situations. But uncritical use of either method might lead to the wrong decision.

This is an important chapter. Marketing plans are not always easy to implement. The marketing manager must know how to use these control-related tools. They help keep a plan on course--and point to situations where a new plan is needed.

Important Terms

control, p. 595
sales analysis, p. 596
performance analysis, p. 597
performance index, p. 599
iceberg principle, p. 602

natural accounts, p. 604
functional accounts, p. 604
full-cost approach, p. 610
contribution-margin approach, p. 610
marketing audit, p. 616

True-False Questions

____ 1. Control is the feedback process that helps the marketing manager learn how ongoing plans are working and how to plan for the future.

____ 2. Because of the 80/20 rule--traditional accounting reports are usually of great help to marketing managers in controlling their plans and programs.

____ 3. Routine sales analyses are best done by manually reviewing data stored in sales invoice files.

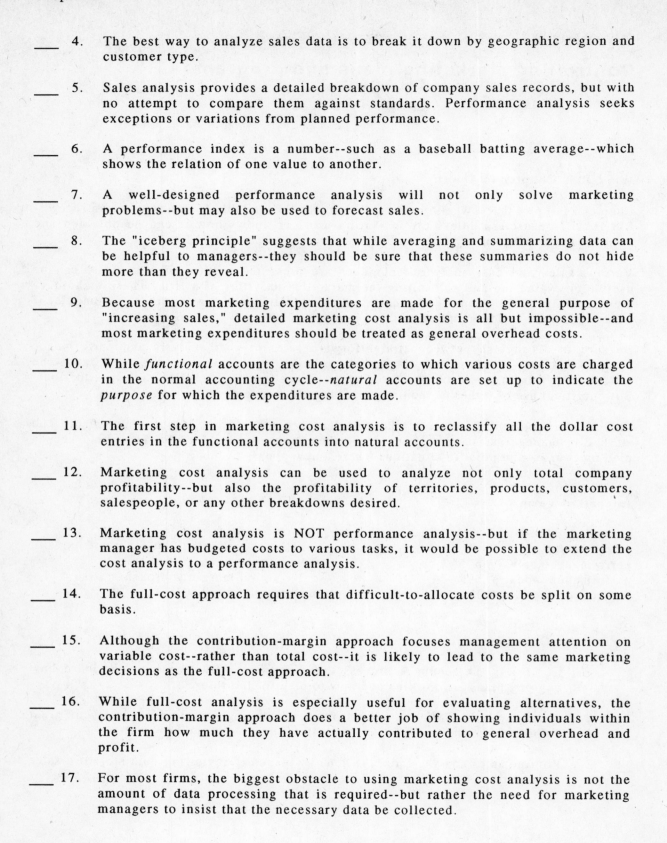

____ 4. The best way to analyze sales data is to break it down by geographic region and customer type.

____ 5. Sales analysis provides a detailed breakdown of company sales records, but with no attempt to compare them against standards. Performance analysis seeks exceptions or variations from planned performance.

____ 6. A performance index is a number--such as a baseball batting average--which shows the relation of one value to another.

____ 7. A well-designed performance analysis will not only solve marketing problems--but may also be used to forecast sales.

____ 8. The "iceberg principle" suggests that while averaging and summarizing data can be helpful to managers--they should be sure that these summaries do not hide more than they reveal.

____ 9. Because most marketing expenditures are made for the general purpose of "increasing sales," detailed marketing cost analysis is all but impossible--and most marketing expenditures should be treated as general overhead costs.

____ 10. While *functional* accounts are the categories to which various costs are charged in the normal accounting cycle--*natural* accounts are set up to indicate the *purpose* for which the expenditures are made.

____ 11. The first step in marketing cost analysis is to reclassify all the dollar cost entries in the functional accounts into natural accounts.

____ 12. Marketing cost analysis can be used to analyze not only total company profitability--but also the profitability of territories, products, customers, salespeople, or any other breakdowns desired.

____ 13. Marketing cost analysis is NOT performance analysis--but if the marketing manager has budgeted costs to various tasks, it would be possible to extend the cost analysis to a performance analysis.

____ 14. The full-cost approach requires that difficult-to-allocate costs be split on some basis.

____ 15. Although the contribution-margin approach focuses management attention on variable cost--rather than total cost--it is likely to lead to the same marketing decisions as the full-cost approach.

____ 16. While full-cost analysis is especially useful for evaluating alternatives, the contribution-margin approach does a better job of showing individuals within the firm how much they have actually contributed to general overhead and profit.

____ 17. For most firms, the biggest obstacle to using marketing cost analysis is not the amount of data processing that is required--but rather the need for marketing managers to insist that the necessary data be collected.

___18.   Ideally, a marketing audit should not be necessary because a good manager should continually evaluate the effectiveness of his operation--but, in practice, a marketing audit is probably needed because too many managers are "so close to the trees that they can't see the forest."

Answers to True-False Questions

1. T, p. 595	7. F, p. 597	13. T, p. 609
2. F, p. 596	8. T, p. 602	14. T, p. 610
3. F, p. 596	9. F, p. 603	15. F, p. 610
4. F, p. 597	10. F, p. 604	16. F, pp. 609-612
5. T, p. 596	11. F, pp. 604-605	17. T, pp. 612-614
6. T, p. 599	12. T, p. 605	18. T, pp. 615-617

Multiple-Choice Questions (Circle the correct response)

1.   According to the "80/20 rule":

   a.   marketing accounts for 80 percent of the consumer's dollar.
   b.   only 20 out of every 100 firms use formal marketing control programs.
   c.   about 20 percent of a typical firm's customers are unprofitable to serve.
   d.   even though a firm might be showing a profit, 80 percent of its business might be coming from only 20 percent of its products or customers.

2.   A marketing manager who wants to analyze his firm's sales should be aware that:

   a.   sales invoice files contain little useful information.
   b.   the best way to analyze sales data is according to geographic regions.
   c.   sales analysis involves a detailed breakdown of a company's sales forecasts.
   d.   sales analysis may not be possible unless he has made arrangements for collecting the necessary data.
   e.   a manager can never have too much data.

3.   Performance analysis differs from sales analysis in that performance analysis involves:

   a.   detailed breakdowns of a company's sales records.
   b.   analyzing only the performance of sales representatives.
   c.   comparing performance against standards--looking for exceptions or variations.
   d.   analyzing only people--not products or territories.
   e.   budgeting for marketing expenditures on the basis of contribution margins.

Chapter 21

4. If Salesperson X had a performance index of 80 and Salesperson Y had a performance index of 120, then:

   a. Salesperson X may be having some problems and his sales performance should be investigated.
   b. the two would average out to 100--and this would suggest that "all is well."
   c. Salesperson X's performance should be investigated as a guide to improving everyone's performance.
   d. Salesperson Y probably should be fired.
   e. Salesperson Y obviously had higher sales than Salesperson X.

5. Which of the following statements best describes the "iceberg principle"?

   a. Problems in one area may be offset by good performances in other areas--and thus the problems may not be visible on the surface.
   b. Ten percent of the items in inventory usually account for 80 percent of the sales.
   c. Within a company's sales force there are usually one or two sales reps who don't carry their weight.
   d. Many sales reps do not make their quotas because they ignore certain clients.
   e. Airfreight is less risky than shipping by boat.

6. Which of the following statements regarding marketing cost analysis is *false*?

   a. Functional accounts include items such as salaries, social security, taxes, raw materials, and advertising.
   b. The costs allocated to the functional accounts will be equal in total to those in the natural accounts.
   c. Functional accounts can be used to show the profitability of territories, products, customers, sales representatives, and so on.
   d. Cost analysis is not performance analysis.
   e. Traditional accounting methods do not show the purpose for which marketing expenditures are made.

7. If one were using the "full-cost" approach to marketing cost analysis, then allocating fixed costs on the basis of sales volume would:

   a. make some customers appear more profitable than they actually are.
   b. not be done--because only variable costs would be analyzed.
   c. make some products appear less profitable than they actually are.
   d. decrease the profitability of the whole business.
   e. Both a and c are true statements.

8. Which of the following statements about the contribution-margin approach is *false*?

   a. It is concerned with the amount contributed by an item or group of items toward covering fixed costs.
   b. This approach suggests that it is not necessary to consider all functional costs in all situations.
   c. It is not used by many accountants because the net profit obtained using this approach is misleading.
   d. This approach frequently leads to data which suggest a different decision than might be indicated by the full-cost approach.
   e. It focuses on controllable costs--rather than on total costs.

9. Which of the following statements about a "marketing audit" is *true*?

   a. A marketing audit should be conducted only when some crisis arises.
   b. It probably should be conducted by someone inside the marketing department who is familiar with the whole program.
   c. A marketing audit should evaluate the company's whole marketing program--not just some parts of it.
   d. A marketing audit should be handled by the specialist most familiar with each of the marketing plans in the program.
   e. All of the above are true statements.

Answers to Multiple-Choice Questions

1. d, p. 596
2. d, p. 596
3. c, p. 597

4. a, p. 599
5. a, pp. 602-603
6. a, p. 604

7. e, pp. 610-611
8. c, p. 610
9. c, pp. 615-616

Exercise 21-1
Sales and performance analysis

Introduction

This exercise shows how sales analysis and performance analysis might be used to help plan and control marketing programs. *Sales analysis* begins with a detailed breakdown of the company's sales records and can take many forms--since there is no one best way to analyze sales data. As outlined in the text, any one of several sales breakdowns may be appropriate--depending on the nature of the company, its products, and which strategies are being evaluated.

Performance analysis seeks exceptions or variations from planned performance. In contrast to simple sales analysis--where facts and figures are merely listed--performance analysis involves the use of predetermined standards against which actual results are compared. Here, the purpose is to determine where--and why--performance was better or worse than expected.

Sales analysis and performance analysis can be useful in pinpointing operating problems which may require corrective action--or in identifying areas in which the company may be performing exceptionally well. Such analyses will *not* reveal *what* is causing a given problem--nor will they provide a *solution* to the problem. This requires sound management judgment--both in interpreting the data and in developing solutions. By using sales and performance analyses, however, marketing managers can rely on factual evidence--rather than guesswork--when problems do arise--and thereby improve the quality of their decision making. Better yet, by continually auditing their marketing programs--by analysis of well-chosen data--they may be able to anticipate problems and take action *before* they become serious.

Assignment

Assume you are the marketing manager for a small manufacturer of electrical products. Your company's products are sold by five sales reps--each serving a separate territory--who earn a straight commission of 10 percent of sales. The company's accountant has just given you the data shown on the next page describing last year's sales. Actual sales were less than expected, so you decide to analyze the data further to help you decide what to do.

TABLE 21-1

Sales Territory	Sales Quota	Actual Sales	Total Calls	Total Orders	Total Customers
A	$ 960,000	$ 480,000	1,200	360	420
B	600,000	600,000	1,320	780	300
C	720,000	360,000	480	300	240
D	900,000	1,080,000	1,560	1,200	480
E	360,000	540,000	720	360	120
Total	$3,540,000	$3,060,000	5,280	3,000	1,560

1. a) Calculate a *sales performance index* for each sales territory. Show your work. One answer is provided as an example:

   Territory A:

   Territory B:

   Territory C:

   Territory D: ($1,080,000 / 900,000) X 100 = 120.0

   Territory E:

   b) What do the performance indices indicate about the relative selling performance of each salesperson? One answer is provided as an example.

   Territory A:

   Territory B:

   Territory C:

   Territory D: This salesperson's actual sales were much higher than expected for some reason. We should try to find out why.

   Territory E:

2. Some additional sales analysis would be desirable to help you decide *why* the sales reps performed as they did. Therefore, using the data in Table 21-1, make the necessary calculations to complete the following table. Some answers have been provided as a check on your work.

TABLE 21-2

Sales Territory	Order/Call Ratio	Average Sale per Order	Average Sale per Customer	Sales Commissions
A	30.0%			
B			$2000	
C				$36,000
D		$900		
E				
Average for All Territories	56.8%			

3. On the basis of your sales and performance analyses, what do you conclude about the sales performance of each salesperson? What factors would you want to investigate further before taking any corrective action?

Territory A:

Territory B:

Chapter 21

Territory C:

Territory D:

Territory E:

Question for Discussion

Does the above analysis suggest any specific management action which was not clearly indicated by a review of Table 21-1? How does this illustrate the "iceberg principle"?

374

Exercise 21-2

Controlling marketing plans and programs with marketing cost analysis

Introduction

This exercise shows the importance of marketing cost analysis in controlling marketing plans and programs. Our focus will be on analyzing the profitability of different *customers*--but marketing cost analysis could also be used to determine the profitability of different *products*. (Try it!)

The first step in marketing cost analysis is to reclassify all the dollar cost entries in the natural accounts into functional cost accounts. This has already been done for you in this exercise--to simplify your work. The next step is to reallocate the functional costs to those customers (or products) for which the expenditures were made. Here, careful judgment is required--because although no single basis of allocation is "correct," in some cases one may be better (i.e., make more sense) than others. Further, the basis of allocation selected can have a very significant effect on the profitability of a customer (or product).

Assignment

1. Using the data in Tables 21-3 and 21-4, calculate profit and loss statements for each of three customers. Show your answers in Table 21-5. Where you must make allocations of costs to products or customers, indicate under "Comments" the basis of allocation you selected and why. (See the example on pages 605-608 of the text for suggestions.)

TABLE 21-3
Sales by Product

Product	Cost/Unit	Selling Price per Unit	Number of Units Sold	Items/Unit	Items Packaged
A	$11	$22	5,000	1	5,000
B	6	12	10,000	2	30,000
C	10	17	6,000	3	12,000

TABLE 21-4
Sales by Customer

Customer	Number of Sales Calls	Number of Orders	Number of Units of Each Product Ordered		
			A	B	C
1	20	10	500	4,000	1,000
2	25	20	2,000	3,500	3,000
3	15	10	2,500	2,500	2,000
Total	60	40	5,000	10,000	6,000

Other expenses from functional cost accounts:

Sales salaries	$48,000
Clerical expenses (order and billing)	12,000
Advertising	33,000
Packaging expenses	11,750
Administrative expenses	36,000

Comments:

TABLE 21-5
Profit and Loss Statement by Customer

	Customer 1		Customer 2		Customer 3		Whole Company	
Net Sales:								
Product A								
B								
C								
Total Sales								
Cost of Sales								
Product A								
B								
C								
Total Cost of Sales								
Gross Margin								
Expenses:								
Sales Salaries								
Clerical Expenses								
Advertising								
Packaging Expenses:								
Product A								
B								
C								
Total Expenses								
Net Profit (or Loss)								

2.   What do you conclude from your analysis? Should any of the customers be dropped? Why or why not? What factors must you consider in answering this question?

Question for Discussion

Which of the two basic approaches to cost analysis--full cost or contribution margin--was used in the above exercise? Would your conclusions have been different if the other approach had been used? If so, which approach is "correct"?

Chapter 22

Marketing strategy planning for international markets

What This Chapter Is About

Chapter 22 highlights the types of opportunities that are available in international marketing. The typical evolution of corporate involvement in international marketing is explained. It is noted that some corporations become so deeply involved with international marketing that they become "multinational corporations."

Six stages of economic development are discussed--to suggest the varying marketing opportunities in different economies. The trend toward cooperation among neighboring countries is discussed--pointing up the need for marketers to think of running multinational operations.

This chapter stresses that much that has been said about marketing strategy planning throughout the text applies directly in international marketing. The major stumbling block to success in international marketing is refusal to learn about and adjust to different peoples and cultures. Try to see that making such adjustments is not impossible and that, therefore, your marketing strategy planning horizon probably should be broadened from domestic marketing to international marketing.

Important Terms

globalization, p. 634
exporting, p. 642
licensing, p. 643
contract manufacturing, p. 643
management contracting, p. 643
joint venturing, p. 644

wholly-owned subsidiary, p. 644
multinational corporations, p. 645
tariffs, p. 652
quotas, p. 652
gross national product (GNP), p. 658

True-False Questions

____ 1. The United States is the largest exporter and importer of products in the world.

____ 2. When a manufacturer moves into exporting, it usually is primarily concerned with selling some of what the firm is currently producing to foreign markets.

____ 3. Licensing is a relatively easy--but risky--way to enter foreign markets.

____ 4. Management contracting--in international marketing--means turning over production to others, while retaining the marketing process.

_____ 5. A domestic firm wishing to enter international marketing can use a joint venture--which simply involves entering into a partnership with a foreign firm.

_____ 6. If a foreign market looked really promising, multinational corporations might set up a wholly-owned subsidiary--which is a separate firm owned by a parent company.

_____ 7. A multinational company is one that earns over 30 percent of its total sales or profits by exporting domestic production to foreign markets.

_____ 8. The typical approach to becoming involved in international marketing is to start with the domestic firm's current products and the needs it knows how to satisfy.

_____ 9. Most industrial products tend to be near the "insensitive" end of the continuum of environmental sensitivity.

_____ 10. If the risks of getting into international marketing are difficult to evaluate, it usually is best to start with a joint venture.

_____ 11. Segmenting international markets is usually easy because so much good data is available.

_____ 12. Tariffs are simply quotas on imported products.

_____ 13. A nation in the first stage of economic development offers little or no market potential.

_____ 14. An excellent market for imported consumer products exists among countries or regions which are experiencing the second (preindustrial or commercial) stage of economic development.

_____ 15. When a nation reaches the primary manufacturing stage of economic development, it will begin to export a large portion of its domestic production of consumer products.

_____ 16. Once a nation reaches the fourth stage of economic development, it will usually manufacture most of its consumer durables--such as autos and televisions.

_____ 17. A nation which reaches the sixth stage of economic development normally exports manufactured products which it specializes in producing.

_____ 18. When a nation reaches the stage of capital equipment and consumer durable products manufacturing, industrialization has begun--but the economy still depends on exports of raw materials.

____ 19. A mass distribution system is desirable for any country--regardless of its present stage of economic development.

____ 20. With the exception of a few densely populated cities around the world, most of the world's population is fairly evenly distributed in rural areas.

____ 21. The best available measure of income in most countries is gross national product (GNP).

____ 22. An analysis of literacy in various countries shows that only one tenth of the world's population can read and write.

____ 23. A basic concern in organizing for international marketing is to be sure that the firm transfers its domestic know-how into international operations.

Answers to True-False Questions

1. T, p. 634	9. T, p. 648	17. T, p. 654
2. T, p. 642	10. T, p. 649	18. T, p. 654
3. F, p. 643	11. F, pp. 649-650	19. F, p. 656
4. F, p. 643	12. F, p. 652	20. F, p. 657
5. T, p. 644	13. T, p. 652	21. T, p. 658
6. T, p. 644	14. T, p. 653	22. F, p. 659
7. F, p. 645	15. F, pp. 653-654	23. T, pp. 659-660
8. T, p. 646	16. F, p. 654	

Multiple-Choice Questions (Circle the correct response)

1. When a business firm in one country sells a firm in another country the right to use some process, trademark, or patent for a fee or royalty--this practice is called:

   a. exporting.
   b. contract manufacturing.
   c. joint ventures.
   d. licensing.
   e. management contracting.

2. To minimize its own risks, the Boomtown Petroleum Corp. of Calgary, Alberta, operates a South American oil refinery which is wholly owned by residents of that country. Boomtown is engaged in an activity known as:

   a. management contracting.
   b. a joint venture.
   c. exporting.
   d. licensing.
   e. contract manufacturing.

3. A multinational corporation:

    a. is any U.S.-based corporation with direct investments in several foreign countries.
    b. is one which sells the right to use some process, trademark, patent, or other right for a fee or royalty to foreign firms.
    c. is a worldwide enterprise which makes major decisions on a global basis.
    d. is any firm which earns over 30 percent of its sales and profits in foreign markets.
    e. All of the above are true statements.

4. A Canadian firm trying to sell to customers in a foreign market should:

    a. use the same product and promotion it uses in Canada.
    b. keep its product the same--but adapt its promotion to meet local needs and attitudes.
    c. adapt both its product and its promotion to meet local needs and attitudes.
    d. develop a whole new product and a whole new promotion blend.
    e. Any of the above might be effective--depending on the opportunity.

5. According to the "continuum of environmental sensitivity":

    a. industrial products need to be adapted to foreign markets more than consumer products.
    b. faddy or high-style consumer products are easily adaptable to foreign markets and thus involve very little risk in international marketing.
    c. it is extremely risky to market basic commodities in international markets.
    d. some products are more adaptable to foreign markets than others--and thus may be less risky.
    e. All of the above are true statements.

6. International marketing:

    a. usually involves simply extending domestic marketing strategies to foreign countries.
    b. always involves a great deal of risk.
    c. requires far less attention to segmenting than domestic marketing.
    d. usually involves very complex and often unfamiliar uncontrollable variables.
    e. All of the above are true statements.

7. With the "unification of Europe" in 1992:

    a. most of the taxes and rules that have limited trade among member countries of the European Community will be eliminated.
    b. the need to adjust strategies to reach submarkets of European consumers will disappear.
    c. Europe will become the second richest market in the world.
    d. consumer prices are expected to rise.
    e. All of the above are true statements.

8. In the "primary manufacturing" stage of economic development,

    a. almost all the people are above the "subsistence" level.
    b. there is a strong demand to keep local manufacturers in business.
    c. the country no longer imports capital products and consumer durable products.
    d. the country begins to export manufactured products.
    e. there is some processing of raw materials that once were shipped out of the country in raw form.

9. What stage of economic development is a country in which small local manufacturing of products such as textiles has begun and the dependence on imports for nondurable products is declining?

    a. Capital products and consumer durable products manufacturing stage
    b. Exporting of manufactured products stage
    c. Nondurable consumer products manufacturing stage
    d. Commercial stage
    e. Primary manufacturing stage

10. A multinational manufacturer will usually find the biggest and most profitable foreign markets for its products in countries that are in which of the following stages of economic development?

    a. Primary manufacturing
    b. Capital products and consumer durable products manufacturing
    c. Preindustrial or commercial
    d. Nondurable and semidurable consumer products manufacturing
    e. Exporting manufactured products

11. Which of the following countries has the *highest* GNP per capita?

    a. United States
    b. Canada
    c. Sweden
    d. Israel
    e. Japan

12. A marketing manager should not rely too much on GNP per person in evaluating international marketing opportunities because:

    a. such data is not readily available for most foreign countries.
    b. the exchange rates fluctuate regularly.
    c. national incomes may not be distributed evenly among all consumers.
    d. foreign governments tend to inflate the data.
    e. both a and c.

Answers to Multiple-Choice Questions

1. d, p. 643	5. d, p. 648	9. c, p. 654
2. a, p. 643	6. d, pp. 649-650	10. e, pp. 654-655
3. c, pp. 645-646	7. d, pp. 651-652	11. c, p. 658
4. e, p. 646	8. b, pp. 653-654	12. c, p. 658

Exercise 22-1

Strategy planning for international markets: Consumer products

Introduction

Today, more and more firms are turning to international markets in search of new profit opportunities. Basically, marketing strategy planning is no different for international markets than for domestic markets. The firm should choose a target market and develop a marketing mix to satisfy the needs of that target market.

International marketing strategy planning can be much more difficult, however. Strategy planners must deal with unfamiliar, uncontrollable variables. And there may be big differences in language, customs, beliefs, religion and race, and even income distribution from one country to another. Even identical products may differ in terms of which needs they satisfy, the conditions under which they are used, and people's ability to buy them.

Further, reliable data for market analysis may be harder to obtain when a firm moves into international markets. The wealth of published data which American marketers tend to take for granted may not exist at all. And consumers in some countries are far less willing to take part in market research studies than most Americans.

This exercise shows how some market analysis might be done for international markets--and shows some of the common mistakes a marketer is likely to make in planning international marketing strategies.

Assignment

Read the following case and answer the questions which follow:

NATURAL BEVERAGE CORPORATION

The Natural Beverage Corporation recently developed a new beverage named "Constant Delight" which was expected to appeal to almost anyone who drinks beverages with meals. Constant Delight met with instant success when introduced for sale in Canada a year ago. Weekly sales far exceeded all previous forecasts--and at first the company had trouble producing enough of the product to satisfy demand.

Constant Delight did not appeal equally well to all Americans. According to a survey conducted by a market research firm, Constant Delight attracted about 30 percent of the tea drinkers in the country, 20 percent of the coffee drinkers, and about 25 percent of those who normally drink soft drinks. In each case, the Constant Delight buyers switched about 10 percent of their meal beverage purchases to Constant Delight. Little acceptance was achieved among wine, milk and water drinkers.

Encouraged by the success of Constant Delight, Natural Beverage Corporation decided to expand its market coverage overseas. The following four countries were being considered as potential new markets: England, France, Spain, and West Germany. However, only *one* of these countries could be chosen at the present time because of limited company resources. Therefore, the marketing manager of Natural Beverage was asked to decide which of the four countries would offer the highest dollar sales potential.

As a start, he obtained the market data shown in Table 22-1 by looking up the populations of the four countries in the *U.S. Statistical Abstract* and then asking a market research firm to estimate the average per capita expenditures in these countries for tea, coffee, and soft drinks. Next, he was able to determine the dollar sales potential for each country by estimating the percentage of tea drinkers, coffee drinkers, and soft drink users who could be expected to purchase Constant Delight. For example, if 30 percent of the tea drinkers in a country can be expected to switch 10 percent of their beverage purchases to Constant Delight, then the per capita expenditures on Constant Delight will be 3.0 percent (30 percent X 10 percent) of the per capita expenditure on tea, and so on.

TABLE 22-1
Estimated Average Annual per Capita Expenditures on
Selected Meal-Time Beverages in Four Countries

| Country | Population | Per Capita Beverage Expenditures | | |
		Tea	Coffee	Soft Drinks
United Kingdom	56,400,000	$80	$40	$10
France	55,000,000	10	20	40
Spain	38,800,000	30	10	40
West Germany	60,900,000	20	60	80

1. Using the switching rates for domestic tea, coffee and soft drink drinkers, determine the dollar sales potential for Constant Delight in France, Spain, and West Germany by completing Table 22-2. The sales potential for the United Kingdom has already been calculated for you as an example.

Name: _____   Course & Section: _____

TABLE 22-2
Per Capita Expenditures and Total Sales Potential for
Constant Delight in Four Countries

Country	Per Capita Expenditures for Applejoy by Beverage Switchers			Total per Capita Expenditures for Applejoy	Total Sales Potential in Country
	Wine	Beer	Liquor		
United Kingdom	$2.40	$0.80	$0.25	$3.45	$194,580,000
France	____	____	____	____	____
Spain	____	____	____	____	____
West Germany	____	____	____	____	____

Calculations:

2. Which one of the four countries would offer the highest dollar sales potential for Constant Delight?

3. What do the above calculations assume about the Natural Beverage Corporation's potential target markets for Constant Delight?

4. Will Natural Beverage Corporation have to change its marketing mix when it expands overseas? Why or why not?

5. What type of involvement would you recommend for Natural Beverage Corporation in its efforts to expand into international markets--exporting, licensing, contract manufacturing, management contracting, joint ventures, or a wholly-owned subsidiary? Why?

Question for Discussion

The per capita beverage expenditures shown in Table 22-1 are just imaginary--but an actual market research study would no doubt show that beverage expenditures do in fact vary considerably among these and other countries. What factors might explain such differences in per capita beverage expenditure patterns? Should a firm's marketing strategy planning be based solely on such data *and* Canadian experience--or would further study or even test marketing be desirable?

Exercise 22-2

Strategic planning for international markets: Industrial products

Introduction

In Chapter 8, we saw that industrial products marketers should consider the number, kind, size, and location of potential customers--as well as the nature of the buyer and the buying situation. These same dimensions apply both to domestic and international markets. A key difference, however, is that the international marketers must first consider in which nations the firm wishes to market its products.

The first step in segmenting international markets, therefore, is to conduct a *preliminary screening* of all prospective markets to determine in which regions or countries the firm may wish to operate.[1] Although this preliminary screening should be as comprehensive as possible--using all readily available information--it need not become an especially complex task. Some nations may be quickly ruled out as potential markets due to unfavorable climatic conditions, unfriendly political and legal environments, or any inappropriate stage of economic development.

For the remaining countries, published import-export data can be useful in selecting attractive marketing opportunities from a widely diversified array of international markets. One excellent source of such data is the United Nation's *Commodity Trade Statistics* series, which provides import-export data for most countries on a quarterly basis--broken down by commodity according to the Standard International Trade Classification (SITC).[2]

Assignment

This exercise is designed to illustrate the use of import-export data during the "preliminary screening" phase of international marketing. The exercise focuses on international markets for metalworking machinery (SITC #715). Read the following case carefully and answer the questions that follow.

TRADER MACHINERY COMPANY

The Trader Machinery Company of Windsor, Ontario, manufactures a broad line of standard and custom-made metalworking machinery. The firm has experienced a sharp decline in sales and profits in recent months due to intensive price competition in the face of an economic recession in Canada.

---

(1) Franklin R. Root, *Strategic Planning for Export Marketing* (Scranton, Pa.: International Textbook Company, 1966), pp. 20-23

(2) Standard International Trade Classification, Revised, United Nations Statistical Papers, Series M. No. 34.

In hopes of discovering new profit opportunities, Trader's marketing manager has begun to explore the possibility of marketing the firm's products to customers outside Canada. Because of the firm's limited resources, the marketing manager plans to restrict the firm's international efforts to one region of the world at first--and to only a few countries within that region. Further--to avoid the intense competition often found in developed economies--he plans to focus on developing economies which offer considerable market potential.

As a first step in determining which regions or countries might represent attractive markets for Trader's products, the marketing manager turned to the most recent issue of the United Nation's *Commodity Trade Statistics* to locate data concerning Canadian exports of metalworking machinery to foreign nations. He discovered that Canadian exports for his commodity classification (SITC #715) totaled about $88 million for the previous year. Developed economies accounted for approximately 85 percent of this total, developing economies about 11 percent, and central planned economies about 4 percent. The dollar value of Canadian machinery exports to *developing* economies was about $9,665,000--the bulk of which was distributed by region or trading group as follows:

Destination	*Value of Canadian Exports*
Africa	$ 68,000
Asia	2,750,000
Caribbean Nations	580,000
Central American Common Market	1,251,000
Latin American Free Trade Association	4,693,000
Middle East	323,000

From the above data, the marketing manager concluded that Trader should concentrate its initial international marketing efforts on the Latin American Free Trade Association (LAFTA)--since its member nations accounted for almost 50 percent of the Canadian exports to developing economies. His next task was to select those LAFTA member nations which appeared to offer the most attractive market potential for metalworking machinery--using *Commodity Trade Statistics* export data for individual nations, as shown below.

LAFTA Member Nations	*Value of Canadian Exports in U.S. $*
Argentina	$ 305,000
Brazil	2,646,000
Mexico	1 206,000
Peru	201,000
Venezuela	264,000

1. Based on the above data, which nations probably offer the most market potential for Trader's metalworking machinery? Why? (Note: For the sake of simplicity, assume that all of these nations are equally "friendly" toward Canadian firms. In an actual situation, a firm would, of course, have to give careful consideration to the political and legal environments in each country before selecting its target markets.)

2. The data used in the above analysis include only Canadian exports of metalworking machinery to various regions or individual nations. Do these data accurately reflect the market potential offered by each region or nation? What very important uncontrollable variable would Trader's marketing manager be overlooking if he based his preliminary screening on these data alone? How might he avoid making such an error?

3. In conducting his preliminary screening, should Trader's marketing manager consider only those nations whose machinery imports have been relatively *high*--or should he also consider other nations whose machinery imports have been relatively *low*? Explain your answer, emphasizing what (specifically) you would want to know about each potential market.

4. Once Trader's marketing manager has determined in which regions or countries the firm might wish to market its products, what other tasks must he perform *before* selecting the marketing strategy he will implement?

Question for Discussion

Some multinational firms reorganize themselves as worldwide operations to achieve foreign sales instead of just exploring their domestic production. Would import-export data be useful to these firms? If so, how?

Chapter 23

Marketing in a consumer-oriented society:
Appraisal and challenges

What This Chapter Is About

Chapter 23 provides an evaluation of the effectiveness of both micro- and macro-marketing. The text explains the authors' views, but their answers are far less important than their reasoning. It is extremely important to understand the arguments both pro and con--because the effectiveness of marketing is a vital issue. How well you understand this material--and how you react to it--may affect your own feelings about the value of business and the contribution you can make in the business world. Do not try to memorize the "right" answers. Rather, try to understand and evaluate the authors' reasoning. Then, develop your own answers.

When you have studied this chapter, you should be able to defend your feelings about the worth of marketing--using reasoned arguments rather than just "gut feelings." Further, you should have some suggestions about how to improve marketing--if you feel there are any weaknesses. Perhaps you yourself--as a producer and/or consumer--can help improve our market-directed system.

True-False Questions

_____ 1. Although our economic objectives may change in the future, at the present time marketing probably should be evaluated according to the basic objective of the Canadian economic system--which is to satisfy consumer needs--as *consumers see them*.

_____ 2. Since individual consumer satisfaction is a very personal concept, it probably does not provide a very good standard for evaluating macro-marketing effectiveness.

_____ 3. At the micro-level, marketing effectiveness can be measured--at least roughly--by the profitability of individual marketers.

_____ 4. According to the text, macro-marketing does not cost too much, but micro-marketing frequently does cost too much, given the present objective of the Canadian economic system--consumer satisfaction.

_____ 5. One reason why micro-marketing often costs too much is that many firms are still production-oriented and not nearly as efficient as they might be.

_____ 6. Companies should encourage dissatisfied customers to complain--and should make it easy for them to do so.

___ 7. According to the text, greater use of cost-plus pricing would result in better, more efficient, micro-marketing decisions.

___ 8. Our present knowledge of how consumers behave confirms the view that pure competition is the ideal way of maximizing consumer welfare.

___ 9. The performance of micro-marketing activities in monopolistic competition probably leads to the same allocation of resources that would be found in a pure competition economy--and no difference in consumer satisfaction.

___ 10. Despite its cost, advertising can actually *lower* prices to the consumer.

___ 11. According to the text, it is probably fair to criticize the marketplace for fulfilling consumers' "false tastes" because marketing creates most popular tastes and social values.

___ 12. A good business manager might find it useful to follow the following rule: "Do unto others as you would have others do unto you."

___ 13. Consumer advocates have placed great emphasis on the need for *consumers* to behave responsibly to make our macro-marketing system work.

___ 14. The text suggests that socially responsible marketing managers should try to limit consumers' freedom of choice for the good of society.

___ 15. Given the role that business is supposed to play in our market-directed system, it seems reasonable to conclude that a marketing manager should be expected to improve and expand the range of goods and services made available to consumers.

___ 16. Market-oriented business managers may be even more necessary in the future if the marketing system is expected to satisfy more subtle needs--such as for the "good life."

Answers to True-False Questions

1. T, p. 665	7. F, pp. 668-669	12. T, p. 678
2. T, p. 665	8. F, p. 672	13. F, p. 681
3. T, p. 667	9. F, p. 672	14. F, pp. 682-683
4. T, p. 667	10. T, p. 673	15. T, p. 683
5. T, p. 668	11. F, p. 675	16. T, p. 683
6. T, pp. 667-668		

Multiple-Choice Questions (Circle the correct response)

1. Consumer satisfaction:
   a. is the basic objective of all economic systems.
   b. is easier to measure at the macro-level than at the micro-level.
   c. depends on one's own expectations and aspirations.
   d. is hard to define.
   e. is totally unrelated to company profits.

2. Which of the following statements about marketing does the text make?

    a. Micro-marketing never costs too much.
    b. Macro-marketing does not cost too much.
    c. Marketing is not needed in all modern economies.
    d. Micro-marketing always costs too much.
    e. Macro-marketing does cost too much.

3. According to the text, micro-marketing may cost too much because:

    a. some marketers don't understand their markets.
    b. prices are frequently set on a cost-plus basis.
    c. promotion is sometimes seen as a substitute for product quality.
    d. All of the above are true statements.
    e. None of the above--marketing never costs too much!

4. Which of the following does NOT support the idea that "MICRO-marketing often DOES cost too much"?

    a. Many firms focus exclusively on their own internal problems.
    b. Distribution channels may be selected on the basis of personal preferences.
    c. Product planners frequently develop "me-too" products.
    d. Costly promotion may try to compensate for a weak marketing mix.
    e. Many firms try to maximize profits.

5. Those who criticize our MACRO-marketing system and argue for pure competition as the welfare ideal:

    a. think that we need more persuasive advertising--to encourage the economic comparisons required for a purely competitive economy.
    b. base their arguments on the fact that consumers have varied demands.
    c. would like to see more money spent on marketing activities.
    d. assume that marketing activities are unnecessary and do not create value.
    e. a and b are both true.

6. The text concludes that:

    a. pure competition should be the welfare ideal.
    b. advertising can actually lower prices to the consumer.
    c. marketing makes people buy things they don't need.
    d. marketing makes people materialistic.
    e. marketing's job is just to satisfy the consumer wants which exist at any point in time.

7. The future poses many challenges for marketing managers because:

    a. new technologies are making it easier to abuse consumers' rights to privacy.
    b. the marketing concept has become obsolete.
    c. it is marketing managers who have full responsibility to preserve our macro-marketing system.
    d. social responsibility applies only to firms--not to consumers.
    e. ultimately it is marketing managers who must determine which products are in the best interests of consumers.

Answers to Multiple-Choice Questions

1. c, p. 665
2. b, p. 667
3. d, p. 667

4. e, pp. 668-669
5. d, pp. 671-672

6. b, p. 673
7. a, p. 680

Exercise 23-1

Does micro-marketing cost too much?

Introduction

One reason that micro-marketing often *does* cost too much is that some production-oriented firms insist on clinging to their traditional ways of doing things--ignoring new marketing mixes and strategies. In a dynamic market, this can lead to higher than necessary costs--and perhaps even to the bankruptcy of the firm.

This can easily be seen in channels of distribution--where many inefficient and high-cost channels exist even today. High-cost channels are not *necessarily* evidence of inefficiency, however. If some target markets really do want some special service which is relatively expensive--then perhaps that is the best channel system for them. But this possible reason for "high-cost" channels of distribution does not explain all such systems. Some do appear to be more expensive than necessary because the established firms insist on buying from and selling to their usual sources and customers--even though other available channels would do as good a job (or maybe better), at lower cost.

This exercise shows how the use of alternative channels of distribution might lead to different--and in some cases higher--prices to final consumers. You are asked to calculate the probable retail prices which would result if a manufacturer were to use several different channels to distribute its product.

Assignment

1. A manufacturer of a new toothpaste is planning to use several different channels of distribution, as listed below. Each middleman in each of the alternative channels uses a cost-plus approach to pricing. That is, each firm takes a markup on its selling price to cover operating expenses plus profit. The manufacturer sells the toothpaste to the *next* member of each channel for $1.00 per "large" tube.

    Using the data shown on the next page for markup estimates, calculate the *retail* selling price in each channel of distribution. Show your work in the space provided. The price for the first channel is calculated for you as an example.

	Percent	
	*Operating Expenses**	*Profit Margin**
Retail		
Small drugstores	39%	2%
Supermarkets	20	1
Chain drugstores	33	3
Mass merchandisers	29	2
Wholesale		
Merchant wholesalers	13	2
Rack jobbers	18	2

*Note: operating expenses and profit margin are given as a percentage of sales

a) Manufacturer to merchant wholesalers who sell to small drugstores:

13% + 2% = 15%   = Merchant wholesalers' markup on selling price

$\dfrac{\$1.00}{100\% - 15\%} = \$1.18$ = Price to retailers

39% + 2% = 41%   = Retailers' markup on selling price

$\dfrac{\$1.18}{100\% - 41\%} = \$2.00$ = Retail price

b) Manufacturer directly to a national chain of drugstores:

c) Manufacturer to merchant wholesalers who sell to supermarkets:

    d)   Manufacturer directly to a regional chain of mass merchandisers:

    e)   Manufacturer to rack jobbers who sell to supermarkets:

2.   Consider the different retail prices that you calculated for Question 1. Assuming that it wanted to maximize profit, which channel(s) should the manufacturer choose to develop an effective marketing strategy or strategies? Why?

3.   Assume that each of the five channels in Question 1 were to survive in the marketplace. From a *macro* viewpoint, should the "high-cost" channels be made illegal to "protect" consumers--and develop a fair and efficient marketing system? Why or why not?

Question for Discussion

What other reasons besides "tradition" help explain why micro-marketing often *does* cost too much? What can (should) be done to make sure that micro-marketing does *not* cost too much in the future?